Pam Allyn's impressive book, *Be Core Ready,* provides practical, useful, and insightful advice on how to implement the Common Core State Standards. Her conversational tone, passion for literacy, and, above all else, her unwavering commitment to doing what is best for all learners will help educators build core strengths in every student. Multiple copies belong in every school's professional development collection.

—John Schumacher, Teacher-Librarian and *Library Journal* Mover and Shaker

As expected, Pam is here to inspire us again! Her take on the CCSS [Common Core State Standards] is positive and practical. Pam extracts the shifts needed in teaching and learning, provides us with entry points to meet those, and submerges us in her expertise. Voilá!

—Emma Suárez-Báez, Literacy Coach

[T]his is a great way to teach ELA . . . a group of teachers could use this to change their core reading program. . . . I see this as a way to truly become a reader and writer for today's world.

—Edward Karl Schultz, Midwestern State University (Wichita Falls, TX)

This book is so inspiring! I hope many districts adopt your program! It will change the lives of many students for the better!

—Elizabeth Smith, Madison Elementary School (VA)

I own *Your Child's Writing Life* and *Best Books for Boys* and just downloaded *What to Read When* on my iPad last night. Your suggestions have helped turn my 7 year old son into a super reader and I am now tackling reading aloud with my 16-month-old son. I can't wait to *Be Core Ready*!

—Meredith Momoda, Mother and Television Marketing Executive

Be Core Ready

Powerful, Effective Steps to Implementing and Achieving the Common Core State Standards

Pam Allyn

Executive Director of LitLife and LitWorld

CABRINI COLLEGE LIBRARY
610 KING OF PRUSSIA ROAD
RADNOR. PA 1908

PEARSON

Boston • Columbus • Indianapolis • New York • San Francisco • Upper Saddle River
Amsterdam • Cape Town • Dubai • London • Madrid • Milan • Munich • Paris • Montreal • Toronto
Delhi • Mexico City • São Paulo • Sydney • Hong Kong • Seoul • Singapore • Taipei • Tokyo

#79436O994

Vice President, Editor in Chief: Aurora Martínez Ramos
Editor: Erin K. L. Grelak
Associate Sponsoring Editor: Barbara Strickland
Editorial Assistant: Katherine Wiley
Senior Marketing Manager: Christine Gatchell
Production Editor: Karen Mason
Production Coordination: Electronic Publishing Services Inc.
Electronic Composition: Jouve
Text Design and Illustrations: Electronic Publishing Services Inc.
Cover Illustration: Steve Morrison
Cover Designers: Diane Lorenzo and Jenny Hart

Photo Credits: p. v, author's photo courtesy of Leah Joseph; p. 1, © Alx/Fotolia LLC; p. 2, © Monkey Business/Fotolia LLC; p. 5, © Monkey Business/Fotolia LLC; p. 6, photo courtesy of the author; p. 9, © hxdbzxy/Shutterstock; p. 10, © oxilixo/Fotolia LLC; p. 14, © Igor Nikolayev/Fotolia LLC; p. 18, © goodluz/Fotolia LLC; p. 21, © Marzanna Syncerz, Fotolia LLC; p. 28, photo courtesy of the author; p. 32, © pressmaster/Fotolia LLC; p. 39, photo courtesy of the author; p. 41, © Jacek Chabraszewski/Fotolia LLC; p. 50, © Monkey Business/Fotolia LLC; p. 53, © Michael Chamberlin/Fotolia LLC; p. 55, © Prod. Numéaccentrik/Fotolia LLC; p. 59, © Monkey Business/Fotolia LLC; p. 61, © nami66/Fotolia LLC; p. 63, © pressmaster/Fotolia LLC; p. 67, © sculder 1909/Fotolia LLC; p. 72, © Isaiah Love/Fotolia LLC; p. 77, © szefei/Shutterstock; p. 78, © Marcel Mooij/Fotolia LLC; p. 81, © Isaiah Love/Fotolia LLC; p. 83, © mozZz/Fotolia LLC; p. 84, © Nmedia/Fotolia LLC; p. 87, © Jacek Chabraszewski/Fotolia LLC; p. 89, © Rob/Fotolia LLC; p. 91, © Andresr/Shutterstock; p. 94, © Woodapple/Fotolia LLC; p. 101, © Giuseppe Porzani/Fotolia LLC; p. 108, © pressmaster/Fotolia LLC; p. 113, photo courtesy of the author; p. 115, © Zurijeta/Shutterstock; p. 116, © Darrin Henry/Fotolia LLC; p. 118, © Barbara Reddoch/Fotolia LLC; p. 124, Dawn Shearer-Simonetti/Dorling Kindersley; p. 127, © Pixelbliss/Fotolia LLC; p. 132, © Lisa F. Young/Fotolia LLC; p. 134, © Monkey Business/Fotolia LLC; p. 137, © Rob Marmion/Shutterstock; p. 140, © Andy Dean/Fotolia LLC; p. 143, © micromonkey/Fotolia LLC; p. 144, © AVAVA/Fotolia LLC; p. 157, © mangostock/Fotolia LLC; p. 158, © Jacek Chabraszewski/Fotolia LLC; p. 163, © Monkey Business/Fotolia LLC; p. 166, © Alexander Raths/Fotolia LLC

Text Credits: The Common Core State Standards for the English Language Arts are © Copyright 2010. National Governors Association Center for Best Practices and Council of Chief State School Officers. All rights reserved.
Page 111, "In the Garden," from *Poems by Emily Dickinson, Series Two*, Section III, Nature, Poem XXIII. Edited by T. W. Higginson and Mabel Loomis Todd, Boston: Roberts Brothers 1892.

Copyright © 2013 by Pearson Education, Inc. All rights reserved. Manufactured in the United States of America. This publication is protected by Copyright, and permission should be obtained from the publisher prior to any prohibited reproduction, storage in a retrieval system, or transmission in any form or by any means, electronic, mechanical, photocopying, recording, or likewise. To obtain permission(s) to use material from this work, please submit a written request to Pearson Education, Inc., Permissions Department, One Lake Street, Upper Saddle River, New Jersey 07458, or you may fax your request to 201-236-3290.

Library of Congress Cataloging-in-Publication Data
Allyn, Pam.
  Be core ready: Powerful, effective steps to implementing and achieving the Common Core State Standards / Pam Allyn.
    p. cm. —
  Includes bibliographical references and index.
  ISBN-13: 978-0-13-290746-0
  ISBN-10: 0-13-290746-1
  1. Language arts (Elementary)—Standards—United States. I. Title.
  LB1576.A6147 2013
  372.6—dc23

2012024833

10 9 8 7 6 5 4 3 2

ISBN 10: 0-13-290746-1
ISBN 13: 978-0-13-290746-0

About the Author

Pam Allyn is an authority in the field of literacy education and a world-renowned expert in home and school literacy connections. As a motivational speaker, expert consultant, author, teacher, and humanitarian advocating for children, she is transforming the way we think about literacy as a tool for communication and knowledge building.

Pam currently serves as the executive director of LitLife, a national literacy development organization providing research-based professional development for K–12 educators. She founded and leads LitWorld, a groundbreaking global literacy initiative that reaches children across the United States and in more than 60 countries. Her methods for helping all students achieve success as readers and writers have brought her acclaim both in the United States and internationally. Pam is also recognized for founding the highly acclaimed initiative Books for Boys for the nation's most struggling readers.

Pam is the author of 11 books for educators and parents, including the award-winning *What to Read When: The Books and Stories to Read with Your Child—And All the Best Times to Read Them* (Penguin Avery), *Pam Allyn's Best Books for Boys* (Scholastic), and *Your Child's Writing Life: How to Inspire Confidence, Creativity, and Skill at Every Age* (Penguin Avery). Her work has been featured on *Good Morning America, The Today Show,* Oprah Radio, *The Huffington Post, The New York Times,* and across the blogosphere.

Contents

Chapter 12
Making Assessment Matter 137

Chapter 13
Engaging Core Ready Families and Communities 157

Be Core Ready and the Core Ready Program

All students can meet and exceed the hopes, dreams, and goals we have for them as readers, writers, speakers, and listeners. I have written this book and created the Core Ready program to answer the call of the Common Core State Standards to create a new vision for what teaching and learning will look like in the 21st century. Core Ready students will master texts of all kinds; connect with fellow readers and writers from around the world; and see the value of reading, writing, speaking, and listening as powerful tools for communication, collaboration, creativity, and community. This book sets forth a brand-new framework in which literacy is no longer flat on the page, but is instead the multidimensional key to opening doors and entering new worlds. This framework is called the Four Doors to the Common Core.

Sign Language, School Reform, and the Dusty Roads from Home to School

I began my career as a teacher of the deaf. Many of my students not only did not learn English until middle school, but they first learned sign language then too. This was when I began to formulate ideas about the teaching of reading and writing specific to linguistically diverse students and special needs students—ideas that turned out to be applicable to all students. In my decade at the Teachers College Columbia University Reading and Writing Project, I led school reform work in New York City in hundreds of schools, building capacity among administrators for literacy leadership and training teachers. I built an understanding of the connections between reading and writing and studied children's own reactions and responses to independent choice in reading and writing instruction. In 2002 I founded LitLife, a professional development organization designed to coach teachers to become effective literacy leaders. With the input of families and community leaders, I developed the idea of "wraparound" support for schools, best practice strategies for coming together as a true team to create a Core Ready community, ensuring all students can learn to read and write fluently, dynamically, and purposefully.

The Common Core State Standards have so much to offer: they put everyone on the same page in a common conversation for perhaps the first time ever, and in this way help us build a common vision for what we want for our children. In my travels, I have watched students walking many long miles along hot and dusty roads just to get to school. They are that hungry for an education that they will go hungry to get one. It is in this work that I have discovered there is nothing more fundamental than the right to read and write. It is the source of one's own power and one's own ability to protect one's self and make oneself strong, healthy, economically empowered, and happy.

An Egg, a Soda Bottle, and a Plastic Bag

Question: What do an egg, a soda bottle, and a plastic bag all have in common? **Answer:** They are all amazing innovations when used by children who are thinking like entrepreneurs. In rural Kenya, girls are raising their own chickens to create a "Chicken Initiative," selling their eggs to the local markets. They have just learned to read and write, and with those skills they are building a business. A young man in the slums of the Philippines figures out that if he cuts a hole in the roof of his tin home covering and inserts a soda bottle full of water into it, he can bring sunlight in where there used to be darkness, thereby enabling him to do his homework and win a spot at a secondary school. In southern California, a group of schoolchildren collect all the plastic bags left on the ground and turn them into "bricks," building furniture for playgrounds.

The world is changing, and everyone—young and old, near and far—can be innovators. You, my friends, can reach out and communicate with all of them. And they can communicate with you. And, surely, literacy and the language arts are all about communication.

Because of this changing world, we need a changed curriculum. We need to reframe the way we teach and how we as adults learn to learn in a brand-new world. We need a shared vision to take us into the new era. The Common Core State Standards (CCSS) have come along at just the right time.

Recently, I asked a group of kindergarteners to describe for me the "perfect school." Earnestly, they told me many wonderful and magical ideas, most of which involved fantastic uses of the dress-up box, many hours of recess, as well as glorious and dreamy snacks in their lunchboxes. But then one little boy who was standing shyly by, listening intently, said to me, "Mrs. Allyn, I know what I'd have in the perfect school." His eyes shining, he turned to his friends, opened his hands like the pages of a book and said, "Stories. I'd have stories all day and all night."

Children are so wise. Invention, imagination, play, sustenance, and . . . stories. The reason I love the Common Core State Standards is that they give us a way to, at long last, tell a new story about ourselves in education. They also value stories in their reverence for literature and in their emphasis on argumentative writing, showing us that the value of literacy is having the power to tell your story the way you want it to be told. Yes, the stories might be those we find in journalism, those called "information," or those stories might be the ones we find in folktales, those we tell on the streets to our neighbors, or those we tell in hushed whispers to the baby falling asleep. They are the stories that sustain us and lift us up. They get us walking down those dusty roads to school. They get us hungry to connect with each other.

You Belong to Core Ready

This book is for teachers, prospective teachers, administrative leaders, media specialists, ELL and special needs educators, and literacy coaches. But this book is also for families and community leaders so they become part of the Core Ready initiative too. Maria, the mother of third grader Stella, approached me recently at a school her daughter attends. "I never really know what to do to help my daughter at home to improve as a reader," she shared with me. "I want to be on the team." The CCSS provide the destination, what each child must achieve and by when in order to become "college and career ready." This book and the ones to follow provide you with a way to create a team for Stella. By getting together and sharing a common vision, and effecting the changes that must come, we are all *for* Stella. Enrolling Stella's teacher, Stella's principal, Stella's student teacher, Stella's after-school program leader, Stella's ELL coach, Stella's media specialist, and Stella's mother in the work of achieving standards, Stella has a transformational opportunity to achieve and to excel.

The Four Doors to the Core

The Core Ready program launched by *Be Core Ready* is a series of books that share reading, writing, speaking, listening, and language lessons created for use in a Core Ready classroom—where the CCSS can come to life.

These lesson sets are organized around the Four Doors to Core Ready, my easy-to-use framework purposefully designed to make life simpler for you and with the language drawn right from the CCSS:

- The Journey to Meaning: Comprehension and Critique
- The Shape of Story: Yesterday and Today
- The Road to Knowledge: Information and Research
- The Power to Persuade: Opinion and Argument

This book's coverage of close reading, text complexity, assessment, and the role of new media in literacy learning is guided by the concept that the Common Core State Standards are a *new academic Bill of Rights for children*. Teachers, leaders, and prospective educators will gain concrete knowledge and best practices for creating a Core Ready classroom—one that focuses on helping students achieve and exceed standards in literacy.

This book can be read on its own to get your community genuinely excited to make some changes in the spirit of the Common Core State Standards and it can also be read as the launch book for the detailed grade-level books that follow—12 of them for grade levels K–8. You will find these books chock-full of lesson plans and specific daily activities that you can use right away.

All students can become Core Ready. With this book and this series, we can make it happen for each and every one. Let your power come from your core and from the Core. And then let us build core strengths in every reader, every writer for this, the 21st century.

Acknowledgments

I thank the team at Pearson for inviting me to create the vision for this book and series to follow. Aurora Martínez is a passionate and radiant leader who makes all things possible. Thanks to Erin Grelak for getting it all started. Thanks to Bill Triant for making it all happen. Thanks to Karen Mason and all the Pearson team, and Karla Walsh and the team at Electronic Publishing Services Inc., for such wonderful support.

Thanks to my colleagues at LitLife. Gratitude to Debbie Lera for her superlative wisdom, skill, grace, and friendship. Thanks to the dream team on this project of Carolyn Greenberg, Jen Scoggin, and Katie Cunningham, who create lessons and craft teaching and learning opportunities that change lives. To Carolyn, abundant gratitude for her wisdom and leadership at every step of the way and for her calm and beautiful heart for the work. Thanks to LitLife colleagues Patty Vitale-Reilly, Laurie Pastore, Jenny Koons, and Jaime Margolies, all of whom provided clear and thoughtful counsel. Thanks to Dorothy Lee, Madison Graboyes, Yaya Yuan, Brooke Stone, Jeff and Ken Okoth, Rose Mureka, and Sofia Mukatia for compassionate work on behalf of the children of LitWorld. Thanks beyond measure to the extraordinary Sue Atkins, chair of the LitWorld board, for her invaluable leadership, to our board members for their wisdom and grace, and to team leaders, volunteers, and interns at LitWorld for their dedication to children.

Thanks to Flynn Berry and Megan Karges for exquisite support. Thanks to Shannon Bishop, Rebekah Coleman, and Erin Harding for glorious input at every step. Thanks to Danny Miller, who is my rock star in the world of words.

Thanks to Michael Lavington, who said: "Let's get these ideas out into the world." His humor and brilliance make it all a joy.

Gratitude to Jud Whidden, and Cheri Mosley, who contribute their unique talents to the work we do together. Thanks to the team of experts in many areas of education who contributed their valuable insights to this book: Nancy Barlow for the texture and magic of her classroom life; wise and wonderful leader Lou Cuglietto and the extraordinary teachers and students of the JFK Magnet School in Port Chester, New York, with a special thanks to Kristin Pascuzzi; Maria Della Raggione and Ingrid O'Brien for their important teachings in the nuances of ELL education; Deb Brennan, Christa Begley, and Marie Miller for their many contributions; Lauren Wells for wisdom about the power of community; and Elizabeth Fernandez for technology love, the beautiful words of Donald Hall, and other treasures.

Thanks to Mark Nieker, who said, "My goal is to help people who are genuinely trying to do what is right for kids. And I like for it to be fun." His tireless work on behalf of children and their right to read and write is deeply inspirational and life changing.

Thanks to Jim, Katie, and Charlotte, and to Anne, Bill, Cindy, Lou, Teddy, Liz, Julie, and many others for a blessed family life outside the book.

Thanks to the educators who touch the lives of so, so many, and my greatest gratitude to the students we all serve, who make it certain I will not ever forget that it is all about them, from start to finish.

CourseSmart eBook and Other eBook Options Available

CourseSmart is an exciting new choice for purchasing this book. As an alternative to purchasing the printed book, you may purchase an electronic version of the same content via CourseSmart for reading on PC or Mac, as well as on Android devices, iPad, iPhone, and iPod Touch with CourseSmart Apps. With a CourseSmart ebook, readers can search the text, make notes online, and bookmark important passages for later review. For more information or to purchase access to the CourseSmart ebook, visit **www.coursesmart.com**. Also look for availability of this book on a number of other ebook devices and platforms.

PD  TOOLKIT™

Accompanying *Be Core Ready*, there is an online resource site with media tools that, together with the text, provides you with the tools you need to implement the lesson sets.

To purchase a 12-month subscription to the PDToolkit for Pam Allyn's *Be Core Ready* series, please visit http://pdtoolkit.pearson.com. Be sure to explore and download the resources available at the website. Currently the following resources are available:

- Pearson Children's and Young Adult Literature Database
- Videos
- PowerPoint Presentations
- Student Artifacts
- Photos and Visual Media
- Handouts, Forms, and Posters
- Lessons and Homework Assignments
- Assessments

In the future, we will continue to add other resources. To learn more, please visit **http://pdtoolkit.pearson.com.**

The Core Ready Student

New Commitments for a New Century

"Learning is not attained by chance, it must be sought for with ardor and diligence."

—Abigail Adams

The student of the 21st century participates in the most astonishing developments in human communication since the invention of language. Spoken words can be communicated effortlessly and inexpensively anywhere in the world. Translation software improves on a daily basis, rendering the chaos of different languages into a minor bump in the road of understanding between different peoples. Stories can be told visually, through videos seamlessly uploaded and transmitted to anyone with an Internet connection. The filters that have always existed between the storyteller and the mass audience fall like dominoes. The future holds amazing promise for our children to find one another across previously insurmountable barriers of access, geography, and language (Kist, 2009). The entire world is their audience.

And while the future beckons with vast potential, the child of the 21st century also enjoys unparalleled access to the richness of the past, to the creations of cultures that have come before. Emily Dickinson's poems are available online. Plato's philosophy can be found readily, with a quick browser search leading to more information about Greek life in his time, political infighting, or the history of philosophy from Socrates to Sartre. Charlotte weaves her web, the ducklings still need to find their way, and Charlie's eyes widen with delight at the golden ticket in his hand.

Into this future have come the Common Core State Standards (CCSS), which provide us with common language to describe what it is we are all striving to do as educators. And to help you make sense of the standards and to be empowered to use them to help all your students achieve and succeed beyond your greatest hopes, I have created Core Ready: steps to standards success.

Students as Co-Creators of Content

The myth about the 21st century is that students are "victims" of technology—that the information and images they absorb are overwhelming and will preclude them from learning. I disagree. We now have the opportunity to teach our children in a brand new way, to give them the agency to be co-creators of new content that will change all our lives. The child who uses an app to make art on a digital device can then upload his creation onto a collaborative sharing site and add text to explain his process. The child who loves music can post a link

to her composition and invite others to create music in response. A teacher can share a short video on life in a village on the other side of the world, inviting students to respond and even send messages to the children in that video.

The world is on fire. And the students are fired up too. Their ideas matter, really and truly. Their ideas can actually intersect with ideas already in the world. Students can communicate in an instant with other students across the world. At the age of 8, they can change people's minds—and ultimately change the world.

Students as Communicators and Collaborators

The Internet makes it possible for students to communicate with many people—whether friends in Kenya posting on a blog, two students in different classrooms emailing each other, or entire schools joining via Skype to celebrate World Read Aloud Day. Students can be heard by peer audiences everywhere and connect to new friends thousands of miles away. The Common Core State Standards

charge us to use technology "strategically and capably." They are a clarion call for us not to miss this moment, but rather to embrace the potential these tools have to make more people literate than ever before. In this book, I frame the use of technology as a central feature of standards-based literacy instruction. In the books to follow in the series, the Core Ready Program, I offer both high-tech and low-tech options in the lessons, for I know all too well there are students who are still not receiving equal access to technology. Either way, communication is going to be the name of the game in literacy. Writing a five-paragraph essay that only the teacher will see is becoming a task of the past. The entire purpose for literacy through the lens of the Common Core State Standards will be to truly communicate with others.

Students as Global Citizens

Students can participate in the world as global citizens. In an instant, they can register opinions that can be seen worldwide and influence legislatures. Students can mobilize for change by starting a group that connects to thousands of other groups. Years ago, Maya Lin shocked the world when she won the competition to design the Vietnam War Memorial at the age of 21. Now this is not so strange. We understand that young people can create valuable new ideas. The Internet gives them a platform from which to spread these ideas quickly, but students need to be efficient, effective, intuitive, and collaborative readers, writers, speakers, and listeners to do this well.

Students as Creators of Great Questions

Consider the student who is given a problem and believes the teacher must have the answer. So he makes a good best guess, trying to formulate the response the teacher expects. There is far less need for this scenario today. The student in the 21st century must instead be prepared to seek problems and find solutions on his own. The child must be able to construct and craft an effective question

independently, using tools like Google, the most brilliant website in the history of the Internet because it is a clean and elegant platform for our inquiries. Crafting questions and finding solutions are part of the student's evolving roles as a learner, a thinker, and a citizen. Learning how to ask questions that lead to new knowledge is one of most important activities for the student in the 21st century classroom.

Our students are growing up in a world where questions are valued; they drive the marketplace. Students may aspire to become engineers or electricians, attorneys or artists, computer programmers or doctors. In any of these cases, a learner growing toward passion and knowledge stokes the fires for active problem solving and clear, creative thinking, rather than learning to fill in the blanks on rote questions. Writing and reading change when their purpose is not just about regurgitating old ideas. Instead, we must formulate our own questions and know how to ask them so that the questions lead us toward what we really want and need to know. This kind of learning requires new curricula and new modes of teaching that are far more interactive and include deep and significant connections to and between content areas. The students themselves can help us envision a new era for education if we invite them to help us co-create these connections and to ask the big questions. One of the primary functions of literacy education is to teach our students how to ask questions, research answers, and innovate new ideas.

The Standards as a Document for Change

The Common Core State Standards were designed to ensure that all students, no matter where they live or what obstacles they face, receive a consistent, high-quality education from school to school and state to state, and upon graduation are prepared for success in their continuing education and their entry into the workforce. The standards were also designed to improve our ability to best serve the needs of our students. They help us figure out the knowledge and skills our students should have from year to year so we can build the best lessons and environments for them.

The Common Core State Standards have come along at exactly the right time. As the world changes, we have in our hands a new document for change that we can use to find our way forward to teach, lead, and inspire. The Core Ready student will enter the workplace having had a classical yet modern education. She will know classic literature and be able to identify themes across texts, ideas, and cultures. She will see that there are common themes across the globe and across history, and that writers throughout time have been pondering and writing about those themes. She will become adept at identifying when an idea is fresh and new, when it is archetypal, and how it can be either abandoned or modified by her own innovative thinking.

The Standards as the Students' Bill of Rights

· ·

Where, after all, do human rights begin? They begin right here in your classroom and in classrooms across the United States. That is where our children become global citizens, where they learn what it means to advocate for themselves and for others. That is where they get their first taste of equal justice, equal opportunity, and equal dignity without discrimination. That is where they get their first experiences with classical and modern texts. Words on the page—or on the screen—are what connect us to one another and allow us to find common ground, shared interests, shared joy. Expressing ourselves is what makes us human, and that is why literacy rights are human rights—and why the Common Core State Standards are so much more than standards for learning. They are a Students' Bill of Rights, delineating specific educational benchmarks *every* student has the right to achieve.

The CCSS are also a Bill of Rights for teachers and educational leaders. We all have the right to clear and consistent expectations about what we teach and what our students need to know. We have the right to be supported by a solid body of knowledge and by a network of other teachers all working together to ensure that our students and our nation succeed and are working toward common goals. But we have to mean it. We have to put our muscle behind the task. We cannot just sit by the sidelines and say yes to standards. We have to

> *Where, after all, do universal human rights begin? In small places, close to home—so close and so small that they cannot be seen on any maps of the world. Yet they are the world of the individual person: the neighborhoods he lives in; the school or college he attends; the factory, farm, or office where he works.*
>
> —Eleanor Roosevelt

stand up for them. The goal for every student should be *mastery*. Nothing can stop us in reaching that goal. But if we are going to say that, we have to be willing to change our stance too. We have to change the paradigm from teacher as leader to teacher as co-traveler. We have to learn how to be coaches and mentors, champions of individualized instruction, and diagnosticians who know every student's literacy level and can quickly and efficiently take each one up the staircase of learning.

Let Your Power Come from the Core

· ·

The word *core* is a homonym: *core* and *corps*. I like that. Because it is at once about the *core* of why you teach and how you can enhance every aspect of your work to bring out your voice, your heart, and your soul. In realizing we are raising children, not making widgets, we must keep our children's destinations at the core of our teaching.

This book is also about building a true *corps* of teachers, parents, and communities working together to ensure that *every* child has the certainty of gaining college- and career-ready outcomes. Poverty has devastated the chances of many children to succeed and achieve, and we need to keep the American dream alive and give these kids a real chance to thrive and become the leaders of tomorrow. Paul Krugman in the *New York Times* (2012) writes of how children from poorer families lack adequate nutrition and health care. And upon reaching school age, "they encounter a system in which the affluent send their kids to good, well-financed public schools or, if they choose, to private schools, while less-advantaged children get a far worse education." Let us give all our children a great education.

Recent data show that despite everything we know about the critical importance of literacy and all the different models and techniques that have been developed to increase literacy outcomes, the reading competencies of American students in the past two decades are still lagging (National Governors Association Center for Best Practices & Council of Chief State School Officers, 2010). Research shows that focusing on college readiness is profoundly related to the number of students who ultimately complete college: "Unfortunately, of the 1.5 million 2010 high school graduates who took the ACT test, only 24 percent met all four College Readiness Benchmarks in English, Mathematics, Reading, and Science—indicating that fewer than 1 in 4 graduates were academically ready for college coursework in all four subject areas without needing remediation" (ACT, 2011a, p. 3). Today, we can use the Common Core State Standards as the way forward to build muscles (another meaning of the word *core*) to create a bright future for all students. By identifying common outcomes and delineating what those are at each grade level, no matter where that student moves or lives, we can guarantee that students will be given every chance to succeed. This is a big idea.

It Is Time for a New Story about Teaching and Learning

This book, along with the Core Ready Lesson Set series that follows it, will make the standards fully accessible to you and ensure that you are supported in helping every child reach and even exceed the goals the standards have set forth. The series is grouped by grade levels—kindergarten through grade 2, grades 3 through 5, and grades 6 through 8—which closely follows the framework of the Common Core State Standards. It will provide you with targeted lessons and study units in reading, writing, speaking, and listening. Each set of lessons moves upward on the staircase, so teams can see how the child ascends in his or her learning and be assured that students will not fall through the gaps.

When one initiative comes in and the previous goes out, teachers and administrators are often left on their own to figure it all out. But we have a new opportunity, here and now, to reframe what we want to achieve and what we want literacy to do for our students. Let us tell a new story about ourselves as educators and about students as learners—not as passive reactors to the forces that conspire against us, but as champions for the hope and promise every student deserves. Let us make this the moment in which we advocate for the rights of students by using the standards to improve the quality of our teaching and student learning and to transform classrooms into places of discovery, independence, achievement, and plain and simple fun. We have to tell a new story about what the purpose of education is, because if it is just the old story, the old way of providing information, our students will say, "I can get that off the Internet." Instead, the classroom of the new century needs to be dynamic, stimulating, and encouraging of the kind of learning that emphasizes critical thinking, absorption of new knowledge, mastery of the power of stories, and deep understanding of meaning. The CCSS will help us collaborate with our students to get them to a new level of mastery that we could only have dreamed of before. After all, we are the co-creators and coaches alongside our students.

The classroom hums with the work of solving problems, uncovering meaning, supporting with evidence, and mastering arguments that will solve the puzzles and the challenges of the new world. Mastering the language arts will further students' discoveries in science, math, and history; help those who wish to pursue vocational training; and enlighten students' understanding of literature, past and present. This is the new story we can tell.

What to Teach?

What exactly must we teach to achieve the goals the standards have set forth for us? This is always the burning question, but the standards do not answer this question for us. Rather, they establish a foundation and lay out the dream. Much like the Bill of Rights offers us the promise of rights that we then must strive for in order to uphold, so, too, the Common Core State Standards give us the promise of success that we then must strive for so all children will graduate to become what they dream of being. The task of determining what to teach is certainly formidable work. We are given a treasure trove of important information telling us what our students should be able to achieve by the end of each grade level, yet this information can push us in many confusing directions, with the real possibility of not reaching the goals the standards have outlined for us. The Core Ready program answers this crucial question of **what** to teach, and sets us forth on a course of action with attainable results.

Our students are growing up in a very different world outside the classroom. As educational leaders, we need not only to match what is happening out there, but also to be the advance team for what our students will be encountering as readers, writers, speakers, and listeners when they enter the world of work and scholarly or vocational studies. I have organized the goals the standards set forth within what I have identified as the Four Doors to Core Ready: The Journey to Meaning, The Shape of Story, The Road to Knowledge, and The Power to Persuade. You will find specific Core Ready lesson sets grouped inside these four doors in the books that follow this one. Each book outlines a series of lesson sets organized around the standards and arranges key literacy skills sequentially so that the lessons are not static. They are carefully calibrated to match the goals for each grade level. The Core Ready program moves our students upward, helping them become more deeply literate year by year, until the literacies they use become transformational literacies they will be able to use every day of their lives, no matter what path they choose.

Here and now, in the pages of this book, let us travel together to meet the goals of standards-rich literacy for all students. To begin, let us look at the ultimate goal of the standards: college and career readiness, and what that really means.

chapter 1

Ensuring College and Career Readiness Right from the Start

"A capacity, and taste, for reading, gives access to whatever has already been discovered by others. It is the key, or one of the keys, to the already solved problems. And not only so. It gives a relish, and facility, for successfully pursuing the [yet] unsolved ones."
—Abraham Lincoln

". . . all serious daring starts from within."
—Eudora Welty

I often think kindergarteners are more ready for college and careers than 12th graders. It is not because I do not trust a 12th grader; it is more because I worry that all that good stuff kindergarteners bring to the table gets a little lost over the course of many years of education! The Common Core State Standards do two wonderful things to counteract this: (1) they value many of those same qualities we treasure in younger students and remind us in no uncertain terms to encourage them as the child grows; and (2) they start at the end goal: college and careers, and work backward so that every grade level lines up in sync like never before. The reading, writing, speaking, listening, and language use goals are carefully outlined. But it is never forgotten what the young child brings to the table: a natural sense of independence, strong critical thinking skills, close reading capacities, and more. Right from the start, your work is to cultivate a child who is going to have a bright future.

When I ask college students about the skills and strengths they need to write powerfully in the classes they take, this is what they say their professors want from them:

- Creative, original ideas
- Support for these ideas from primary and secondary sources
- A structure that supports the claims and makes good sense for the reader
- A strong introduction
- An interesting concluding paragraph that expands on the thesis

Many students have told me they did not learn these skills until they arrived at college. Their professors say the same. Why are we waiting so long to teach these critical thinking and execution skills? If we started in kindergarten, our students would have a much better chance of achieving at far higher levels when they enter college—and a much better chance of entering college in the first place. The emphasis in the primary and middle school grades on rote responses, fill-in-the-blank answers, and regurgitating the answers the teacher expects is not moving our students forward (Darling-Hammond, 2010).

Colleges are consistently reporting that incoming students have weaker reading and writing skills than the freshman classes before them (National Governors Association Center for Best Practices & Council of Chief State School Officers, 2010), and findings also show that our children are not demonstrating writing skills that will allow them eventually to perform well in the workplace (Alliance for Excellent Education, 2006). These findings demand *immediate action*. Improving literacy performance is the key to improving students' overall success—literacy success has an impact on every subject area in school, as well as every aspect of our students' lives. Future success both in higher education and in the workplace depends on giving every student a solid literacy foundation today (Olson, 2006).

Being college and career ready means becoming a creative problem solver. Research has shown that college professors believe key cognitive strategies such as analysis, interpretation, accuracy, problem solving, and reasoning are as important as specific content knowledge (Conley, 2007). Literacy is more relevant to more people in more ways than ever before in human history. From the farmer who wants to record crop prices to the traveler on the subway looking out for his next stop to the young woman who logs on to a search engine seeking answers to a question she has, it is a radiant new world where literacy can make so many different kinds of outcomes possible, tailor-made for the hopes and dreams of each local community. High-level literacy skills also lead to a more educated citizenry—people who know what and whom they are voting for and what constitute the rules of their society. Literacy skills are crucial in the formation of a civic society that creates common goals and makes commitments to shared dreams. And creative problem solving is something kindergarteners are really, really good at, but we often do not give them nearly enough time for it. The kinds of literacy I will discuss in the forthcoming chapters all involve problem solving, and all are natural habitats for even the youngest child (especially the youngest child!).

Reading, writing, speaking, and listening are the four components of what I call the *literacy loop* (see Figure 1.1). With the advent of the Internet, the four components are now intrinsically entwined. (Although viewing images in non-print form is not in most formal definitions of literacy yet, I believe it soon will be and should be.) A person may read something, record his ideas about it, send a message out to the world, and then respond to what someone else has said in return. Reading and writing well, and speaking and listening well, are essential in the 21st century.

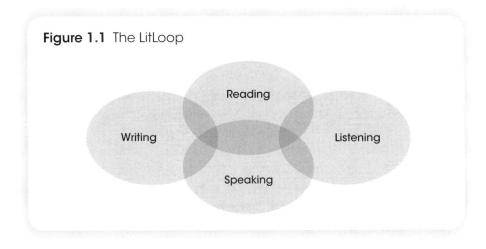

Figure 1.1 The LitLoop

Throughout this chapter, I weave in observations from college students and people in diverse fields about the importance of these skills. Take a moment with your colleagues (or parents at a back-to-school night) to use some of these reflections to discuss what kinds of skills are most necessary for college and the contemporary workplace. You may find the results of this discussion surprising. Ask your colleagues to compare the results to how they currently teach literacy in the classroom. Do they match? The Common Core State Standards set forth goals to ensure that students can do everything from speaking clearly and confidently about classic and contemporary literature to reading informational texts, to building an argument and then providing evidence for that claim in their writing. Now is the time to enact a curriculum and teaching practices that will truly meet these goals. The CCSS is subtitled "College and Career Ready." Let's take a moment to consider what that really means.

What Is College Ready?

Being college ready today means reading widely, writing powerfully, and speaking and listening dynamically. A report from ACT called *The Condition of College & Career Readiness 2011* states that "sixty-six percent of all ACT-tested high school graduates met the English College Readiness Benchmark in 2011.

Just 1 in 4 (25%) met all four College Readiness Benchmarks" (ACT, 2011b, p. 1). College ready literacy skills are complex and go across every subject area. These skills are not just about retelling or summarizing anymore. College ready is about navigating challenging texts and building one's own hypotheses from the information found within them. Essentially, literacy is the ability to apply what one knows to new problems (Darling-Hammond, 2010). College ready is the stepping stone to having a career, a vocation, but it is also a unique use of the skills and capacities for reading and writing, speaking and listening: communicating with others in a way that shows our strengths and highlights our goals. As one college graduate said, "As writers in college, our audience was primarily our professors. We had to prove to them that we had done the reading and paid attention to their lectures. We had to show our ability to take their ideas and build off of them with our own research."

---

college ready **English Major**

I believe that the skills of imagination and creativity are often overlooked as essential reading and writing tools. My most inspiring professors have emphasized those skills to me and have pushed me, in their comments on my own writing and in our discussions as readers, to locate and build on those skills.

I do think that a good grasp of grammar, organization, and clarity is a necessary tool to have as well. I feel, however, that many of those elements can be learned through the process of creating and imagining. Throughout my college career, I have learned to craft essays that move beyond thesis statements and supporting evidence. I now, instead, approach my writing as a space in which to explore my ideas, to assert my voice, and to represent the evolution of my thinking.

So the skill that has become most valuable to me is abstract, but I think that it is something that can, and should be, practiced at all points in the learning process: to know your voice, value your creativity, and treasure reading and writing as a means to representing your own individual wonderings.

college ready **Math Major**

I find I need to be able to write a succinct concluding sentence. I also need to be able to deconstruct a question into individual, usable pieces of information. Reading a math textbook can be very challenging and requires a great deal of concentration as well as the ability to break down a paragraph into smaller, more manageable pieces of information.

What Is Career Ready?

A career-ready student in the 21st century will need to be even better equipped to purposefully engage with the world. The career-ready scholar is curious, compassionate, and creative, ready for models of work that have begun to change (Oakes & Saunders, 2008). The virtual office, the conference call, Skype, and cloud computing already enable fully functional offices to exist without coworkers even being on the same continent. The corporation as a lifetime employer is a thing of the past. Students today may have many jobs over the course of their lifetimes (Ciletti, 2010). They will collaborate with peers around the world. They will bring their skills together with others to solve discrete problems and then disband, looking for other work groups. The pace of technological innovation will accelerate as each new discovery leads rapidly to others. In fact, due to advancements in information services, the amount of information that can be generated in a few years nearly equals the amount of information previously produced in the entire history of the world (Darling-Hammond, 2010). Our students' challenge will be to forge new connections in this constantly expanding world.

Emily Nussbaum, the television critic for *The New Yorker,* has remarked how "we often have a cultural fantasy about individuals. But collaboration is just as frequently the source of great things, and it's less rarely recognized. Change doesn't always happen because of one person, but that's what makes for great biographies" (Hepola, 2012). Collaboration is becoming highly valued. To work productively together, our children—from the first minute they are in school—must not merely sit at desks that resemble collaborative environments, but learn to work together to create and share new ideas, as well as listen to others' ideas and synthesize them into something new.

Your students may never meet their future colleagues face to face when they enter the workplace. What once seemed magical and nearly unimaginable is now entirely possible. Their colleagues could be as far away as India or as close as a train stop away; the need to be together in person has diminished. Now more than ever the workplace synergizes ideas across time and space. What it requires is a workforce of people with strong literacy skills who can not only manage that kind of environment but also master it.

career ready **International Business**

I help key executives make more confident decisions by connecting them with experts in various fields. We make as many as 1,000 connections per day, often between a client sitting in one country and an expert in another. As a people-based business, communication is our glue, the essential ingredient in every connection that helps us win client loyalty and provide an amazing experience for our experts.

Having overseen thousands of correspondences to make those connections possible, I can testify that reading skills are critical in helping us better understand our clients' needs. We're often relying on interpreting quick emails or complicated RFPs. Without that understanding, exceeding the clients' expectations is difficult.

During a project, reading and listening are also essential for ensuring that the expert is really knowledgeable on a topic and appropriate for the consultation. We often identify red flag statements that give us cause for concern. And without sharp writing skills and the ability to cut to the chase and "so what" of an issue, we'd be lost communicating with the most senior executives and investors on one side of our marketplace and the experts they need to engage on the other.

For my particular career, I'm extremely thankful for the crystal clear comma rules I learned in eighth grade and the intense reading I was subjected to throughout my academic career, with exposure to business, academic, and pleasure reading—all important in a field where we have to tailor our communications to various personality types.

The Era of the New Reader

The era we live in now is charged with the energy and power of diverse genres, of constant information sizzling its way back and forth between people. These transactions are potentially life changing. We are reading across multiple genres in a matter of one hour. Everything from economic updates to personal information is flying across the airwaves in a microsecond. Even many very young children can operate portable technology.

Today's reader might be reading several perspectives and genres at once: proverbs, poems, nonfiction articles, ecothrillers, political cartoons. Tracking a reader's daily journey is fascinating. If you think about what you've read even today, you will be astonished to see how many genres you traverse and how many times your passions, your wonderings, and your concerns intersect.

Students today are reading more actual print than ever before. Mobile phones make it possible for them to write and receive short bursts of texts nearly continuously. If we harness this power in school alongside the vast and deep power of literature itself, we will create a winning combination. But we must move quickly, because school as we know it is becoming outdated even as you read this. We have to change our own paradigms and get set for this new era.

---

colleague conversation   **Be the Student!**

Track your reading life briefly with your colleagues. Sketch out a timeline of your reading history from the last 24 hours. Now count how many genres you read, why you were reading, and how much time you spent on each genre.

What I Read

The Genre

The Purpose

Time Spent

Ask yourselves: How can we mirror the real-life reading we all do in the work we do with our students?

The Era of the New Writer

Students today are writing in myriad ways. They write long, formal essays, but also thousands of text messages, brief bursts of thought that flow immediately out into the world. They compose questions, seeking answers from teachers and community members as well as on social media and other online venues. Today's writer needs to write short, sharp, and strong, but also be able to research many topics and take thorough notes, combining concepts to create new ideas. The writer must synthesize and create. He must craft a message to communicate with someone about an idea that is profound to him, and he must also be able to write for a particular audience: a professor, a friend, a team leader. He must have evidence to support his claim. And he must have a distinct voice—he must not look and sound like everyone else.

---

colleague conversation   **Be the Student!**

Track your writing life briefly with your colleagues. Sketch out a timeline of your writing history from the last 24 hours. Now discuss what your purpose was, how long it took you, and who your audience was.

What I Wrote

Why I Wrote It

Whom I Wrote It For

Time Spent on It

Ask yourselves: How can we mirror the real-life writing we all do in the work we do with our students?

---

career ready **Researcher**

Even though I'm a researcher, sometimes it seems like I'm really a writer. Writing is how I develop my ideas for a study as I design the outlines of a project. Writing is how I figure out what questions to ask. Writing grant proposals is how I get funding to do my work! But most important, writing is how the quality of my work is judged, and how my findings get used. I write up the results of a study in a variety of ways—short reports for policymakers and educators, and longer reports for other researchers. I often write op-eds. If I can't present my findings effectively through writing, my work won't be seen as useful. It probably won't be seen at all.

Since my job requires all sorts of different writing-based tasks, I rely on a range of writing skills. Obviously, I need to write a coherent sentence. But I also need to understand different audiences and what type of language to use to communicate effectively with each. I need to be able to craft arguments in my writing and to use evidence to back up my points. I need to be persuasive. I need to write good questions.

Speaking and Listening Skills Really Count

Speaking and listening skills are integral parts of becoming college and career ready in the 21st century. Practice is key. The more we allow our students to practice making their arguments orally, articulating their thoughts on a particular topic, and voicing their opinions, the more adept and comfortable they will become with doing this on a daily basis. Likewise, the more we allow our students to use their deep listening skills, especially with their fellow classmates, the easier it will become for them to use that skill as they move through college and the workplace. Just as our students will be required to sift through large amounts of written information, they will also have to interact with many different types of people, in many different environments, with many different kinds of distractions, and still be able to extract the heart of what is being communicated to them. Being able to speak and listen well is crucial for our students to succeed. Does this mean all students have to be chatterboxes in class all day? Not at all! In fact, one of the essential texts for my work is a book by Susan Cain called *Quiet: The Power of Introverts in a World That Can't Stop Talking*. In Chapter 11 I talk about differentiating instruction for every learner, and this is one type of learner often underestimated and undervalued. So-called introverts may actually be great listeners, a skill that will benefit them enormously in the workplace later on.

The social, intellectual, and business world of the 21st century is one in which exchange is highly valued. We are trading ideas, selling ideas, promoting ideas, and giving ideas away. We are also idea consumers. We do this by being attentive listeners to radio, television, social media, and one another. There is certainly a cacophony of information, but it is not unmanageable if we teach our students how to identify ideas that have strong value for them and are supported by strong evidence to prove their worth. Knowing how to sift through information is a prized quality for today's speaker and listener.

Knowing how to modulate what we share is also prized, and will become more so in the future. Effective communication and healthy discourse on varieties of topics will be highly optimized in our society, and the time is now to teach our students how to read, write, speak, and listen in ways that promote the dynamic sharing of new ideas.

---

colleague conversation   **Be the Student!**

Track your speaking and listening life briefly with your colleagues. Sketch out a timeline of what has been meaningful to you first as a speaker and then as a listener from the last 24 hours. Now discuss what your purpose was, how you felt, and who your audience was.

What I Said

How I Listened

What Were the Outcomes

Ask yourselves: How can we mirror the real-life speaking and listening we all do in the work we do with our students?

---

career ready   **Lawyer**

My career has required extensive reading and writing skills. The main types of writing are persuasive texts and analytical texts:

- Briefs and motions (which are also highly analytical) for courts
- Letters and submissions to administrative agencies
- Letters to adversaries and people with whom clients had an issue

Legal writing is different from most types of writing because it is somewhat formulaic and formal, and also because you are strictly forbidden from knowingly writing anything that you do not believe to be true. It contains elements of logic and a lot of research, but the key to victory is always tapping into the emotions of the judge or jury, or at least making palatable to their emotions what is logically irrefutable.

Legal reading can be very mind numbing at times. Cases have their own style. But there is also a lot of reading about various businesses and industries. You learn an amazing amount of information about different areas of life as a lawyer. It is almost exclusively nonfiction— though it is often true that fact is stranger than fiction.

Close reading is absolutely essential. But the more prior knowledge you bring to the text, the more you can maximize the ways you can synthesize it with other texts and experiences to make your argument as strong as possible. Speaking and listening are also incredibly important skills for a lawyer, both in presenting and defending the case, as well as trying to figure out what is preoccupying the judge or your adversary. Trying to gain an understanding of the issues in the case from your own client often involves a lot of high level speaking and listening.

Speaking and listening are also about storytelling and empathy. Life is about transaction and interaction. Teaching children to speak and listen well is to teach them to communicate. Learning how people interact, sometimes virtually and sometimes face to face, sometimes in front of large groups and sometimes one to one or in small groups, is a vitally important skill. With the advent of video as a powerful communication tool, our students will need these skills in order to live the most purposeful, connected lives possible. Learning how to tell one's story includes the same skills one needs as a writer, but in speaking and listening the audience is an even more powerful force, and the response becomes extremely important. The reader, writer, speaker, and listener must not only create new ideas but also be able to adapt ideas to the needs of the audience or to what he or she is trying to accomplish, as seen here from the viewpoint of an experienced doctor.

career ready   **Cardiologist**

For the practice of medicine, the real art is learning how to translate complex medical concepts to the level that the patient can understand, recognizing that there are tremendous differences in literacy among patients. The obvious mistake that occurs over and over is when the doctor walks into a patient's room speaking in medical jargon and the patient doesn't understand a word being said. This also includes written informed consent, where patients read a poorly written legal form that makes no sense to them and must sign that they understand the risks of the procedure. There is a lot of interest now in specific "health care literacy," which reflects the ability to read and understand drug labels, medical instructions, and the like. It turns out that fewer than half of patients take the medications their doctor thinks they are taking (the way they are supposed to be taking them) and, among many factors, poor health literacy clearly contributes.

The artful parts of good medicine—some of which are innate, but many of which can be learned, modeled, and taught explicitly—include the ability to assess the knowledge and literacy of the patient, tailor the verbal and written communication accordingly, and actively listen to make sure that the communication was successful. The other part of course is the ability to convey empathy and caring, which is another skill that is partly innate but can also be improved upon with practice and feedback.

Core Learners, Core Texts, and Core Capacities

To succeed in college and the workplace, the learner in the 21st century must be a curious and collaborative critical thinker, reader, writer, speaker, and listener. Students must strengthen their capacities to read and write both independently and collaboratively, building content knowledge, thinking critically, and identifying key ideas to support their thinking. Students need to make connections that reach across genres, texts, and sources of information to build and defend their ideas and arguments. Their reading skills will flourish because they read regularly and widely across genres. Their skills are challenged by reading a variety of texts in a variety of modalities and reading both for stamina and to push their higher-order thinking skills. They will be active participants in an interconnected world, seeking information and opportunities to engage in discourse with other learners.

Students will read core texts that reflect various periods, cultures, and worldviews to enable them to talk deeply and intelligently about history, science, ethics, and human nature. The student who reads folktales and myths is the student who understands the nuances of favorite texts in which allegories appear (e.g., *The Chronicles of Narnia*) and even recognizes when the auto industry has tapped into such references (*The Odyssey*). The Core Ready learner manages the popular culture and the library of classic texts, able to talk across the modern and the classical, the ancient and the contemporary. The child who makes the connection between *The Lightning Thief* and *The Odyssey* is a child who sees paradigms and metaphors and is able to think at much higher levels than simply filling in a few random questions on a test.

career ready   **Journalist**

Journalists read everything, all of the time. Moving, for me, is always extremely time-consuming: wrapping the wine glasses in newspaper takes so long because I have to stop to read the many fascinating articles I previously missed. Of course, these days, it's much harder to read everything because there is so much written and it's available on so many different devices. (I refuse to read books on my iPhone, but I see people doing it on the subway all the time.)

The proliferation of words makes it ever more important to be a discerning reader and carefully evaluate your sources. So much of the verbiage on the Internet is just people commenting on the original work done by others. As often as possible, go to the original sources.

I find reading articles on the Internet or on a mobile device is very effective for scanning but, overall, I think the Internet is bad for reading comprehension. It teaches you to absorb large volumes of information quickly and superficially.

I still find it extremely valuable and important to sit down with actual books or newspapers to absorb information in a meaningful and lasting fashion.

For aspiring writers, the most important thing is to be a voracious reader. Reading teaches you how to write. Emulate the writers and publications that you admire. One of my girlfriends had a job delivering *The Wall Street Journal,* and she got me started reading it. I instantly fell in love with the paper's crisp, understated style. I got my job at *The Wall Street Journal* by reading the paper very closely and copying its style.

We demand so much of young writers! They must be in command of their material. Having good facts is very important for journalists. There is also a big intangible element involved: You can't teach someone to gravitate to the most surprising, enticing tidbits. Writing with clarity is essential. Reporters need to be good interviewers, good researchers, and good writers, and they have to equally enjoy each aspect of the process (although there is nothing quite so exhilarating as sitting down at the keyboard with a notebook filled with good material).

Core Ready learners are critical thinkers. They effectively identify evidence in texts to support their big ideas. They competently make connections that inspire their thinking, connecting ideas across multiple disciplines and multiple genres, from science to history, from poetry to blog posts, from the contemporary text to the classic, and they build hunches and hypotheses that are supported by facts to bolster their theories.

---

career ready **Teacher**

As a teacher I need to be able to read quickly and skim text when necessary to pull out key information, determine if it is appropriate, and summarize/synthesize large amounts of information. I also need to be able to apply what I've learned from reading to demonstrate understanding.

In the context of writing, I need to be able to effectively communicate through email (formal and informal). I also need to be able to write clearly scripted lesson plans that have step-by-step actions and detailed criteria for

---

success. Someone else should be able to use my lessons in the event that I'm unable to teach my students. My writing therefore must be clear and provide explicit directions.

The Core Ready series that follows this book stresses the use of a diverse range of texts, imparting to your students important ideas about their history and their cultural connectedness to one another, to their communities, and to the global society. Core texts are chosen based on their complexity, quality range, and purpose (National Governors Association Center for Best Practices & Council of Chief State School Officers, 2010). They are examples but by no means a final list. The Common Core State Standards are really emphasizing independence. In this way, our role is to model lifelong reading and give our students tools to do so, not restrict their reading lives with a small set of "approved" books. The widely diverse range of recommended genres includes everything from folktales, which express our human longings to make moral sense of a fractured world, to graphic novels, whose visual elements can help readers of all levels gain a deeper understanding of the material, to poetry, with its use of highly personal and intimate language, to informational texts, which use much more methodical and cerebral terminology. These, and many more, are the core texts that compose the "new" classical education every student deserves, right from the start.

By reading widely, writing regularly, and engaging in meaningful dialogue with peers and authentic audiences, our students will gain and strengthen what I refer to as the *core capacities.* These are key points identified by the Common Core State Standards. I believe they should be displayed in every classroom and known by every educator, forming the basis for a solid contract of commitment to the outcomes of our students. Students who master the core capacities will be able to

- Demonstrate independence
- Build strong content knowledge
- Respond to the varying demands of audience, task, purpose, and discipline
- Comprehend as well as critique
- Value evidence
- Use technology and digital media strategically and capably
- Come to understand other perspectives and cultures

Every lesson in the Core Ready series is designed to achieve these seven core capacities. Keep these capacities as a checklist on your portable device and somewhere visible to you, your students, and your colleagues. Use them as "check-in prompts" for yourself and for your team. Does your teaching or leadership angle students toward these capacities? They can and should be the heartbeat of our teaching and leadership.

The Core Ready learner is not merely a writer who can master the five-paragraph essay or the research paper; he or she must be able to write in a wide variety of circumstances and, perhaps most important, use economy of language to build a case, explain an idea, or ask a question. Consider this:

- The Ten Commandments are 297 words.
- The Bill of Rights is 463 words.
- The Gettysburg Address is 266 words.

To captivate their audience and to get their point across quickly, students must learn to be concise but pack a punch. Length is not how we evaluate quality of writing in this 21st century. A superb Facebook status message or tweet can stop us in our tracks, make us cry, change our minds, or even change lives.

Clarity of writing, supportive details, and crystal clear point of view are all extraordinarily important because they hone our message for the reader. These skills must be taught and practiced, however. Your students must have the opportunity to write for real audiences (across time and space, virtually and in person) and to write in ways that match what they will actually do in the real world.

---

career ready ## Executive Vice President, Investment Banking

In my workplace, we generally are required to produce persuasive written documents. In this setting, the most important writing skill is to be able to express what is often a very complex issue in a concise manner (one or two sentences at most) and then, equally concisely, set forth your recommendation for how to address that issue. All of this should be done within one short paragraph.

The balance of the written document should be devoted to supporting your recommendation. All substantive information should be conveyed in no more than a single page.

As is well known, à la Mark Twain, it is much more difficult to write a concise document than a long rambling one. This requires clarity of thought, strong sentence structure, and a broad vocabulary.

---

career ready ## Graphic Designer and Graphic Production Editor

Having excellent writing skills is a definite requirement for a graphic designer. I often find myself rewriting ad copy when the language is awkward or incomprehensible. One also has to have a sharp reading eye, since it is necessary to catch mistakes as well as tighten up the writing so it is more concise and succinct.

The same new approach is essential for the teaching of reading. We used to teach reading in a lockstep approach, with everyone reading the same book at the same time. That proved ineffective because students were not able to deepen comprehension skills at their independent reading levels, and we saw no significant improvement in reading outcomes. We introduced the idea of leveling text, or matching individual readers to books at their own levels. Children need to read material that they can understand (Allington & Gabriel, 2012). Research has shown that interventions that focus on reading comprehension significantly improve overall reading ability (Keller & Just, 2009). Matching students to leveled text at their independent reading levels has been groundbreaking because students gain comprehension and stamina when they read texts that are comfortable for them. But this, too, has some limitations. In the real world, readers must be able to navigate information and literature at many different levels—including those well beyond any ideally matched levels. They also need strategies for going far outside their comfort zones as they read across genres, media, and disciplines. In the world, all students have to synthesize and organize large amounts of information in order to innovate new ideas and communicate those ideas to others. So how to resolve this apparent conundrum? In order to learn to read at higher levels, students need to read at their independent levels. But all students also need to grapple comfortably with challenging text. Here's what I recommend.

Support readers with a solid range of resources at different levels up and down so they can reach up and dip down when necessary, depending on the purpose of their reading. In general, students should spend approximately half their time engaged with text at their level (determined using formative assessments) in order to build comprehension and stamina. One-third of their reading time should be spent engaging—both with support and independently—with more challenging text above their level to develop better reading skills. The balance of reading time (about 15%) can be spent engaging at text below level to further promote stamina and fluency. This mixture of text levels promotes comprehension while developing the skills and techniques to successfully engage with more difficult texts. Consider having an individualized book box, bag, or e-reader containing a collection that reflects not only what students can read at their levels, but also a selection of more difficult books in subject matter that is of interest to them as well as a few light reads that help them build both stamina and interest. The students can in this way curate their own reading lives, with teacher support and guidance.

---

career ready **Scientist**

The most common form of science reading is scientific abstracts and manuscripts. Scientific papers have strict word limits imposed by the publishers and, therefore, are often packed full of detailed information. A well-written abstract should provide all the important points from the paper in a short digestible form. To be efficient and effective in gleaning the important information from manuscripts, scientists must be familiar with the format of a scientific paper, know where in the paper to look for the information they are seeking, and then be able to scan the material for important points. Once the scientist has identified the important material in a paper, an in-depth reading of those sections will help provide the detailed information they seek. A few key papers closely related to the reader's project might merit an in-depth reading; however, most papers will provide just one or two elements, such as a particular result or a specific method employed, that will benefit the current project. In this case, a targeted reading approach is a crucial time saver.

The forms of writing in which the scientist most often engages are manuscript and grant writing. In writing manuscripts, scientists must be able to summarize their results succinctly and word their conclusions so as not to overstate their findings while emphasizing the importance of their work. In grant writing, the most important aspect is to persuade the reader to be interested in and excited about the proposed project. The scientist must also write in a way that clearly lays out the foundations for proposed experiments and supports the expectations of success. Without these writing skills, papers cannot get published and grants will not get funded. The welfare of the scientist depends on effective communication of his or her data and ideas.

The Core Ready reader needs to understand not only what an archetype stands for in literature, but also the position a reporter is taking in a news article or op-ed or a blog post, the directions in an online course, or even a how-to article on fixing a website's HTML. The reader needs resources to read multiple texts all at once. The old way was that every child turned the pages at the same time. Then the idea arose for different children to turn different pages at the same time. What I propose is that we teach our children to do both: read from a canonical text that defines a big idea about literary elements *and* read in a varied and purpose-driven manner to retrieve vital information and to sift through perspectives. In this book, I explain ways we can prepare our students to meet this century's demands for new reading skills. The rigor we inspire in our students must come from the *work* they do with texts, not just the *difficulty* level of texts.

A Rich Definition of Literacy

What literacy is all about, really, is the classic E. M. Forster plea to "Only connect." The authors of *Literacy as Social Practice* write of literacy as sets of social practices "rooted in life experiences. Since different people have different life experiences it follows that social practices are differentially available to various individuals and groups of people. This differential availability means that not everyone has equitable or equal access to literacy" (Vasquez, Egawa, Harste, & Thompson, 2004, p. xi).

It is therefore critically important that we make sure literacy instruction is rich and full, with access to resources that include both print and visual images. Reading texts, reading images, and reading the nonverbal ways people communicate every day add up to a rich definition of what literacy means in the 21st century and how much it means to everyone.

I work with a team of teachers from a school for the deaf. As we flash our signs to one another, I am reminded once again of what it means to "read" as my eyes catch their hands making meaning in the air. With the power of 21st century communication tools, the act of reading can feel like we are seeking meaning in the air. From the youngest ages, all our students must be equipped with the skills necessary to read, write, speak and listen, and master language skills in every possible modality.

A Cup of Coffee and a Bottle of Water

The business world has many effective strategies for selling ideas. Businesses have convinced people to pay five dollars for a simple cup of coffee. They have convinced people to buy something we can get almost for free at home (water). But somehow we educators have not been able to convince the public that we can educate children. And all the assessments in the world are not going to solve that problem. The way we convince them is to actually teach children effectively and meaningfully, and tell the story of U.S. education in a fresh, innovative way. The Common Core State Standards give us the opportunity to do just that.

Let's not now sigh, "Oh, yet another initiative." Let's instead say to parents, "We will make it possible for your child to be ready for college and a career." The CCSS are a game changer. This is the time to change the game. With the standards wrapping around us as educators and families, we now have a common language to create a shared vision. All children deserve the right to be functionally and transformationally literate.

At every workplace, in every college classroom, in every vocational setting, many forms of literacy are required—and beyond required, they will open the gateway to opportunity, personal and professional growth, and happiness. We cannot underestimate literacy as a tool that gives all people the right to the maximum levels of human happiness. Literacy alleviates loneliness, inspires independence, and cultivates understanding. In order to reach what I call transformational literacy, every student must learn the building blocks of literacy: the functional literacy skills for a lifetime. The next chapter will introduce you to the key to the Core Ready solution—the Four Doors to the Core, a way of organizing and managing the content in the CCSS and making it really easy to implement the CCSS tomorrow morning in all classrooms, everywhere.

Entering the Four Doors to the Common Core

"If you want to build a ship, don't drum up people to collect wood and don't assign them tasks and work, but rather teach them to long for the endless immensity of the sea."

—Antoine de Saint-Exupéry

This chapter introduces you to the Four Doors to Core Ready, an effective and simple solution to managing the CCSS by organizing the content into a manageable teaching framework. This chapter will also give you a quick overview of the CCSS you can use in faculty meetings and with families, to bring everyone into the discussion of what the Common Core State Standards mean and how best to use them.

The Four Doors to the Common Core State Standards: The Core Ready Approach

I was really excited when the Common Core State Standards were published. I had worked with many different sets of state standards and consulted with groups of teachers, principals, curriculum authors, college administrators, and even government officials. I had a pretty good idea of what was needed, and I felt hopeful that these would be the catalyst to the right kind of change. So when I finally got my hands on them, I dug in, hopeful that this would at last provide the support everyone needed and depart from the false hopes and dreams promised by prior initiatives. I hoped they would be the start of something real and fresh and true and focused on kids. I believe this to be so. But I saw right away they were going to overwhelm teachers and administrators and children if we did not open doors to lead the standards into the classroom. So I got to work.

I worked closely with my team at LitLife, a nationally recognized professional development organization serving teachers and students in schools across the country, to look for patterns. I developed a picture of what these standards specifically look like in real, working classrooms—the classrooms we visit regularly in our work. I thought about the children and talked with these children who populate the anthology of my own career. Real kids with attitudes, personalities, struggles, gifts. Children who have said to me in all seriousness, "I just want to learn."

And I thought about the teachers, the principals, and all of my clients who would perhaps feel concerned by these vast changes. I knew that schools would be asking me to interpret these standards. I thought about what I might recommend to schools—the best possible ways to help them understand this work and how best to apply it to their own teaching.

Then, stunningly, four major patterns began to appear that helped me make sense of the standards—and how to put them to use to create curriculum with lessons that would fulfill the goals of the standards. I realized that the entire expanse of the Common Core State Standards document honors four essential categories for learning: The Journey to Meaning, The Shape of Story, The Road to Knowledge, and The Power to Persuade. These four categories reflect the most important teaching for the 21st century—skills and knowledge every student needs, right now. With these four doors to the Core, I have created lesson sets in reading, writing, speaking, listening, and language use, constructing a user-friendly curriculum using the CCSS as our beacon, to level the playing field and at the same time raise the bar for expectations for all students.

Figure 2.1 The Four Doors to Core Ready

The Journey to Meaning

This Core Ready category—The Journey to Meaning—encompasses the strategies and skills our students need to comprehend, critique, and compose literary text as outlined in the Common Core State Standards. Today's students must be able to think deeply about the meaning of what they read and carefully select skills and strategies for doing so with purpose and flexibility. They must be able to search for key ideas and details, ask and answer questions, and make connections and draw inferences using details and examples from text. They need to be able to explore the elements of fiction and cite evidence to support their thinking about character, setting, plot, mood, and theme, and they need to develop the ability to express their critical and strategic thinking about literature orally and in writing.

Quality literature must also be used as inspiration for students to create their own fiction stories and vignettes in a variety of literary genres with attention to detail and sequence. Students must be given continuous opportunity to experiment with writing strategies, including character development, dialogue, and word choice. They will need authentic opportunities for sharing their writing and thinking with others orally, in written text, and via technology.

The Journey to Meaning allows students to experience literature the way it is intended—as art. They can independently surrender to deep meaning in a way that enables them to actively comprehend, critique, write about, and become transformed by it.

The Shape of Story

The Shape of Story encompasses exploration of a variety of genres with the corresponding craft, structures, and strategies one needs to be a successful consumer and producer of literature as required by the Common Core State Standards.

Students need to be able to approach all types of reading with the experience and skill that will help them know what to expect in a wide variety of genres, structures, and forms, all relating to the power and structure of stories. They must be able to apply appropriate strategies to each with purpose and flexibility. They must be given the opportunity to slowly and carefully explore the differences between various types of writing and learn the terminology and structures that will enable them to read and speak proficiently with others about them. They should be taught to notice purposeful choices that authors make and examine how various authors treat similar themes and topics across genres and generations.

Quality literature is key. Students should be invited to use it as a model for their own writing. They need to be able to explore the techniques and purposes of various literary text types and compose their own original text. Students should be asked to create short literary responses to many kinds of writing, to compare texts analytically, and to share their beliefs and thinking with others orally, in writing, and via technology. The child who recognizes, appreciates, and writes in a variety of genres is truly entering a lifelong journey of deep literacy. The understanding of genres, from myths to folktales to narrative to informational stories, gives the child an anchor and a field guide for understanding how to "read the world." Stories are the pulse of humanity. They forge our connections to one another. They help us explain the inexplicable. They bind cultures and communities. It is important to know how to read stories, both of our past and of our present, and to tell the stories of our future. Stories past and present link all the grade levels of the Common Core State Standards.

The Road to Knowledge

The third Core Ready category, The Road to Knowledge, encompasses research and information and the skills and strategies students need to build strong content knowledge and compose informational text as suggested by the Common Core State Standards. Every child in this generation needs to navigate informational texts and to be able to cite evidence from the time they are in elementary school. Much of reading and writing instruction has focused on fiction and the whole-class novel, yet the world demands command of informational texts.

Every student needs the opportunity to read and listen carefully to informational text to glean key ideas and details and to notice patterns of events, ideas, and concepts in a variety of text types. Students need to learn to use text features and structure with purpose to access information efficiently and effectively.

They should be encouraged to become thoughtful researchers who integrate information from multiple sources in preparation for writing, speaking, and visual presentations. They should learn to take notes, summarize, paraphrase, and cite resources.

The Road to Knowledge helps students to arrange their ideas and research in clear, well-organized informative and explanatory writing pieces and presentations as well. Students must share ideas logically and support them with details, graphics, and multimedia. They should also study content vocabulary and employ domain-specific language and transitional phrases to effectively convey and link information, and they should enjoy many chances to share their writing and thinking with others orally as well as using appropriate tools and technologies.

The Power to Persuade

The fourth Core Ready category, The Power to Persuade, encompasses instruction that explores the purposes, techniques, and strategies of effective readers and writers of various types of opinion text as delineated in the Common Core State Standards.

Core Ready students must develop an awareness of purpose and point of view as they explore text and listen to speech that persuades, argues, and presents opinions. They should identify key points in text and visual images and describe how an author or artist presents and supports ideas, and they should be allowed time to analyze multiple accounts with an eye toward differences in perspective and opinion.

Students need to be able to read thoughtfully and do research to inspire their individual point of view, and these opinions should be expressed through speech and various types of writing. They should develop a fluent ability to cite facts and details as evidence to support their ideas. They must be able to consider the power of word choice and employ appropriate vocabulary and transitional phrases to express and link ideas effectively. They should be given ample opportunities to study and practice how to express their ideas clearly, cohesively, and concisely in a manner that is appropriate to their audience, and they will need many chances to share their writing and thinking with others orally, in writing, and via technology.

The Power to Persuade takes into account the world in which we live now and the importance of writing and presenting research that uses evidence to corroborate our ideas. To do so, we must give students abundant opportunities to really say what they are thinking, and to respond to texts, ideas, and discourse in ways that are not only intuitive but also informed. We can tap into this natural tendency when kindergartners plead for extra recess time or when third graders want to get a new class pet, or when middle schoolers are campaigning for a social justice cause close to their young hearts. This generation is already well-versed in having opinions, but they need explicit teaching to help refine these skills. Students can take a far more active role in their own reading and reveal their own unique perspectives through writing. They can create new and exciting ideas and practice for the day when they have to invent or defend an idea in the college classroom or workplace.

These standards can feel overwhelming when so much change is required, but our brains seek patterns to make sense of the complex, and they help us organize our thinking. The patterns I observed became the Four Doors, and from them I built the Core Ready program (see Chapter 8), which will answer the question, "What do I teach?" Core Ready represents the dreamed-for end goal—that our students can and will meet and exceed standards through step-by-step lessons.

The Common Core State Standards at a Glance

It is important to have a familiarity with the Common Core State Standards. You should know how they are organized and what they expect across all grade levels in order to understand our students' journey as they ascend the staircase of learning. This section of this chapter gives you the streamlined version of these expectations. The CCSS ask us all to make some paradigm shifts in the classroom and school, discussed in Chapter 3. Therefore, it is crucial you know the components of the standards and be able to speak confidently about them with students, colleagues, and families.

Common Core State Standards for Reading

The Common Core State Standards for Reading stand on three pillars: Literature, Informational Text, and Foundational Skills. The inclusion of specific standards for informational text will change the educational landscape of the English language arts classroom, for it acknowledges that an enormous percentage of printed material is not purely literature.

Reading is a priceless gift for our children, and the comprehensive standards for reading will lead to well-rounded, deeply analytical readers who see the written word as living, breathing information and who fall in love with the characters they meet in the pages of a book, graphic novel, or short story. They will not just read text, but examine it, test it to see whether it stands up to their inquisition. They will struggle to find a satisfying answer for a character's motivations, dig deep to see the character's humanity, fall through the words on the page and into the deeper meanings. They will engage with the profound and deeply important power of literature and find out what they want to know from the wide world of information.

---

colleague conversation **Be the Student!**

Take a moment to reflect about the first time you were truly captivated, enthralled, and inspired by the written word. Share this experience, out loud or in a reflective journal. What was it about this particular experience that moved you? Discuss as a group. Write together the commonalities in all of these experiences: mentorship, safety, enjoyment. Then together list what kinds of conditions would be required for your students to replicate the feeling of the experience you had.

Reading Literature

Key Ideas and Details Students must be able to summarize a story and recount major plot points, but they must also analyze, ruminate on, and make inferences from what is explicitly written on the page to deduce the central theme and ideas the author attempts to convey. Core Ready learners must substantiate their claims with well-selected evidence—quotes, examples, and references to key events and plot points.

As students move through each year, they will add layers of understanding, and the details will feel richer and deeper as they go. From kindergarten to grade 2, they will ask and answer questions about the "who, what, where, why, and how" of a story. They will be able to recount stories with some understanding of the central theme and will talk descriptively about characters, setting, and plot.

Building on this, in grades 3 to 5 students will be asking their own questions about reading material, quoting from the text to substantiate their answers. When recounting plot points of a story, they will give insights into the characters as people, including their feelings, thoughts, and actions. Students will compare and contrast characters, settings, and events, drawing evidence from the text to justify their conclusions.

In grades 6 to 8, students will identify the central theme of a text and understand the many different vehicles an author uses to develop and shape this main idea, such as dialogue, setting, and character traits. At this stage in their academic careers, students will be meticulous in selecting the evidence they pull from a text to support their ideas. They will choose the most relevant examples to build a strong case to support their analysis of the text. Additionally, students will be able to give a neutral account of the main events of a text, filtering out their personal opinion.

Craft and Structure

This section of the standards is about discovering and uncovering, quantifying the intangible aspects of literature—the beauty and nuances of the English language. Children begin this journey by identifying unknown words and investigating them by seeking out their literal definitions. As their vocabulary deepens, Core Ready learners use context, rhythm, structure, and figurative language to go beyond the dictionary definitions of words to discover the emotion and meaning an author can build into a text.

As the Common Core State Standards specify, children will closely read a diverse selection of genres. In doing so, they will be able to identify the structural elements that distinguish one genre from another—a folktale from fantasy, an essay from a short story. They will understand how the paragraphs of a novel, the stanzas of a poem, or the verses of a sonnet weave together to form a cohesive plot line and communicate the overall theme of a piece of writing. When discussing each category of literature, Core Ready students can reference appropriate terminology and structural elements and comment on their use—the rhythm and meter of a poem, the dialogue of characters, the stage directions in a play.

For example, from kindergarten to grade 2, students progress from identifying unknown words and asking questions about them to understanding how the phrasing of words (rhyming, alliteration, or repeated lines) adds meaning and flavor to a story, song, or poem. They move from being able to identify common texts (storybooks and poems) to an awareness of the overall structure built into a story—an introduction to begin and an ending to conclude the action.

By grade 3, students use context to distinguish literal from nonliteral language. They also begin to use appropriate terms when referring to structural elements of a text and can separate their own point of view from that of the narrator and other characters. By grade 5, students can pick out figurative language such as metaphors and similes to uncover the full meaning of the phrases they read. They are able to evaluate a text holistically with a sense of how the chapters, scenes, or stanzas interlock to create the overall structure of a novel, play, or poem.

In the middle grades, 6 through 8, students take close stock of an author's word choice and use of figurative language. They question why a particular word or literary device was chosen, what images the author creates, and what feelings he or she provokes. At this stage, it is understood that the structure of a written piece is significant. Students will investigate how the structure of a stanza, scene, or chapter contributes to the overall meaning, tone, and style of a written piece.

Familiarity with story structure helps us enjoy stories more, making the experience of reading "like the playing of a game. And therein resides the fun of a text; only after understanding the rules, principles and fundamentals of the game can we access its pleasures" (Lockett, 2010, p. 404). By helping students understand this, we invite them into this world of rich fiction.

colleague conversation   **Be the Student!**

Select one short classic poem. (Try "Life for Me Ain't No Crystal Stair" by Langston Hughes or "The Road Not Taken" by Robert Frost; both are very accessible to all reading levels but have so much in them to discuss.) Have one member read the poem aloud. Make a graphic organizer with Key Ideas and Details on the left side and Craft and Structure on the right side. Everyone should brainstorm details for each column.

Integration of Knowledge and Ideas   Core Ready learners are critical thinkers, learning from a young age to distinguish between the reading material they do and do not like. Yet they remain open to the world, taking in stories, collecting experiences through the lives of the characters they read about, and using these to compare and contrast how different texts broach the same topic or how characters might react differently to overcome a similar obstacle. They can also analyze how visual effects and multimedia can flavor a text and how this can be done subtly or overtly depending on the genre.

Range of Reading and Level of Text Complexity   The abilities described previously develop from exposure to a wide and rich array of literature. Students will become proficient readers, steadily adding to their repertoire of literature. The standards advocate for a curriculum of stories—adventure stories, folktales, legends, fantasy, realistic fiction, myth, dramas, and poetry—from many different sources and eras. Ultimately, children should read texts of appropriate complexity for their grade level. They will be exposed to literature from diverse cultures and time periods and will read proficiently and, above all, with comprehension, for deeper meaning.

What exactly does it mean that children are being asked to read literature of appropriate complexity for their grade level? The standards have pushed for a staircase of text complexity after concluding that many students who reach college are not reading on a college level of difficulty. In fact, one statistic I found in researching text complexity was that there is a 350L (Lexile) gap between the difficulty of end-of-high-school and college texts—a gap equivalent to 1.5 standard deviations and more than the Lexile difference between grade 4 and grade 8 texts on the National Assessment of Educational Progress (NAEP) (Williamson, 2008). This essentially means that students are not on grade level as readers when they get to college.

Assuming this to be true, and assuming elementary and secondary schools strive to get their readers to meet (or exceed) grade-level expectations, then our expectations aren't high enough, so either colleges have to recalibrate and lower the complexity of their reading material, or we have to raise the complexity of ours. But we cannot raise our expectations cruelly, punishing children who are struggling to read and making unrealistic demands that are simply impossible for any human being to achieve. We want all children to learn to read at grade level, but this goal must be achieved humanely and justly.

I am able to find productive ground when I think more organically about the standards' take on text complexity—in my own work I am concerned when I see teaching points that lack rigor and developmental sophistication. I am concerned when I see materials that require more "go find the answer in the text" thinking and not materials that inspire synthesis and inference. I am concerned when I see language instruction that does not work toward an expanded and creative understanding of word meaning and usage. So I agree that many, and perhaps most, schools need to raise the rigor of instruction to make students more college and career ready. Implementing the articulated curriculum of reading, writing, speaking, and listening instruction shared in the Core Ready series will do a great deal to raise the bar and result in an ability to read more sophisticated texts.

But let's take a look at the three-point criteria the Common Core State Standards use to explain text complexity. (I discuss this issue in greater depth in Chapter 5.) Standard 10 explains that a text is complex as a result of a formula of quantitative factors (word length or frequency, vocabulary, syntax, text cohesion, etc.), qualitative factors (levels of meaning or purpose or knowledge demands in the text), and reader and task considerations. I agree with these criteria and believe that a strong teacher considers all three of these variables when designing lessons or selecting a text to teach. I also agree with the overall notion that we need to reconsider the material we ask our students to read, as I find in my work that most teachers teach their familiar texts rather than selecting a text that optimally illuminates their teaching point.

There is frequently a tendency to give too much weight to the quantitative element in determining appropriate text complexity for our students. Most of the dialogue around text bands and grade-level recommended text has to do with the quantitative criteria, so we need to be careful to remember that the determination of appropriate text complexity for our children at different grade levels is a combination of variables that includes meaning, theme, irony, subtlety, and all of the other qualitative elements that cannot be measured.

We can easily find many texts that appear extremely simple in language and yet place many demands on the reader. For example, let's take a look at a haiku by Basho:

Clouds come every now and then
To give us pause
From gazing moonward.

The vocabulary is deceptively simple, but the haiku reverberates with complexity of image, of metaphor, of mystery.

Or I can easily find a linguistically complex text that presents a relatively simple idea, such as "In mathematical operations, two addends combine to equal one sum." In this case, the vocabulary may look daunting, but the actual idea within the text is straightforward.

Both types of texts can be experienced by readers as complex reading, yet they require different kinds of processes for uncovering meaning. Teaching students to encode and decode are two different tasks in elementary school, and to some degree in middle school. These strands are unlikely to come together seamlessly for most students until high school, and by then, most texts read at that level are simultaneously complex: dense in composition and structure as well as dense and sophisticated in meaning.

But with younger readers we must teach these parts while keeping in mind the overall impact of the whole. If we want students to learn how to think while they read and draw bold conclusions or innovative connections to the text, the difficulty of the text must not overwhelm them. We need to use texts that allow us to illuminate a particular type of complexity. And I believe our instruction needs to be a balanced yet comprehensive approach. Remember, our students are learning to decode, comprehend, read smoothly (fluency), and build stamina all at the same time. There are times for teaching each of these and all of these skills, and until our students are adult readers, they are still working on all of them. Sometimes reading an "easier" book is really helpful because it helps readers to build stamina, reading for more minutes, longer and stronger. Sometimes reading an "easier" text in terms of vocabulary helps our students to dig more deeply into metaphor in that very same text. Failing to keep all of the elements of text complexity at the forefront of our thinking and planning could lead us to use the quantitative level of text complexity as the sole determiner of what we teach at each grade level—and more important, what we teach to each student.

The problem becomes evident when recommendations on text complexity refer only to grade-level reading bands and adjusted Lexile levels by grade. Here they are not considering both complexity of idea and complexity of text construction. An imbalance develops when the determination of text complexity focuses exclusively on changes in the quantitative level of text difficulty (vocabulary, sentence complexity, text cohesion) rather than on equal changes in the qualitative criteria (the opportunities inherent in the text for critical thinking).

In a 2006 report titled *Reading between the Lines: What the ACT Reveals about College Readiness in Reading,* ACT identifies this inability to understand complex ideas as the decisive gap between college-ready and college-unready students: "The clearest differentiator in reading between students who are college ready and students who are not is the ability to comprehend complex texts" (p. 2).

My experience in schools is that both skill sets—understanding of textual elements and comprehension of complex texts—are sorely lacking in college-unready students, who lag behind in competence in the basic skills of reading and writing. So our critical work in differentiating instruction for students through the work of standards 1 through 9 must continue. Any belief that the work of teaching our students the skills set forth in the standards must be done exclusively with complex informational texts matching the conditions of standard 10 is completely incorrect. We must always strive to enable children to read and write so they *can* engage in critical thinking about a text. A disastrous outcome of the Common Core State Standards would be to implement them solely through a list of wonderful but deeply challenging texts at each grade level and to teach solely and exclusively to those texts without giving our students the necessary foundational skills to successfully do so. We must use those texts and other less complex texts to teach the skills that will enable students to comprehend the complex texts on their own. Critical thinking skills, independence, and meaningful collaboration should be our goals for our children, enabling them to competently engage independently with complex texts. Our implementation of the standards in our classrooms must be designed to differentiate among our students so that *all* of them can meet the standards, engage with texts at the highest levels of complexity and critical thinking, and be career and college ready when they graduate from high school.

The solution to this challenge, for me, lies in implementation and methodology. No one who speaks about the Common Core State Standards is demanding that students abandon reading independent texts at their level. And nowhere in the standards is "frustration-level" reading quantified in terms of the percentage of reading experiences in the classroom. No one is saying 20% of a student's reading should be done at frustration level, or 40% or 60%. And no one is saying that those frustration reads should be without scaffolding. We must keep in mind that there should always be a balance of healthy struggle with stamina-building activities. A lack of that balance will throw students off and disrupt their learning.

Of course, an essential part of learning is to have rigorous conversation around and experiences with complex text. We all recognize the value of close reading and rereading of text. At the same time, students build their muscles for successfully engaging with complex text by reading at comfort levels and reading independently. (See Chapter 9 for more on close reading.) With this in mind, I am able to recommend the following pedagogy to provide students with instructional reading experiences in challenging texts: read-alouds, shared reading, and small-group reading instruction. In these three ways, I can address my students' needs and tackle text complexity of different kinds.

The read-aloud provides an opportunity for us to demonstrate and model close reading of complex text and to purposefully interact with grade-level texts and even above-grade-level texts. Shared reading allows us to use the text instructionally through close reading and to follow up that work with continued practice or rereading of that text, collaborative discussion of the shared text, or parallel practice in a related text during independent practice. Students will still have many opportunities to read at their independent level, which provides recursive practice and builds fluency and stamina.

Small-group work has always been and will continue to be a powerful venue for using instructional-level text with students. A regular, systematic schedule of small-group work allows teachers to differentiate instruction for their students while creating a more accountable, intimate learning environment in which the focus can be on the quantitative (as well as qualitative) challenges in texts.

The use of these teaching methods will allow us to provide students with experience in challenge-level texts and also allow us to align teaching with standard 10 while moving our students forward as independent readers.

Reading Informational Text

Think about the different places you encounter words in your day-to-day routine. Reading informational text is how you know to microwave your popcorn for a reasonable amount of time. It is how you navigate your way to a new restaurant, or make a visit to the museum truly meaningful. It is where you meet your beloved heroes like Eleanor Roosevelt, Albert Einstein, or Martin Luther King, Jr.

Key Ideas and Details By reading texts in history, social studies, science, and other disciplines, students build a foundation of knowledge in these fields that will also give them the background to be better readers in all content areas. Though they may be confronted with technical terms or unfamiliar topics, Core Ready learners confidently tackle unknown territory, understanding that even in nonfiction texts there are main ideas, events, and concepts an author is trying to convey, and that just as in literature, they must collect facts and evidence to support their theories. They will develop a familiarity and comfort with the structural elements that are unique to informational texts, understanding the connection between the procedural steps of a science experiment or the directions for building a bookshelf.

In many ways, the objectives and outcomes for informational text mirror those of literature. For example, students in kindergarten through grade 2 will dissect the "who, what, where, why, and how" of a text. Initially they will need prompting and support, but by grade 2 they will progress to pulling out key details and main ideas independently. A grade 2 student will understand the main topic of a multi-paragraph text and state the focus of an individual paragraph. This is also a time when students start to understand the idea of cause and effect. What is the connection between this event and that event? Why did one step in a procedure have to be done before the next?

Climbing the staircase of text complexity, students in grades 3 to 5 will begin to quote from the text and identify the main ideas using evidence to justify their conclusions. This is also a time to deepen the analysis of the relationship between a series of historical events, scientific concepts, or steps in technical procedures. Students examine the context of scientific or historical events, uncovering how they might have been shaped by human interaction or how one event might directly affect or instigate another event.

In grades 6 to 8, as we saw in the standards for literature, students extract the central theme of a text and track how an author uses supporting points, facts, and evidence to develop this idea over the course of the text. In turn, when writing or discussing their analysis of an informational text, students can provide an objective summary and are able to cite relevant evidence from the text, using the facts that most profoundly support their arguments.

Craft and Structure Certainly informational texts contain more jargon or technical terms than are present in literature. However, with practice and experience students will be at ease when confronted with new terms, steadily collecting new definitions and incorporating them into their vocabulary.

There is also a noticeably different tone and structure between, say, *Charlotte's Web* and a text about the digestive system. As they move through the Common Core State Standards year after year, students will capably read a particular text and categorize its overall structure—cause/effect, chronology, problem/solution—and be able to make comparisons between two or more texts written about the same subject.

Students in kindergarten to grade 2 will steadily build their comfort with informational text. At first they will simply identify certain features—front and back cover, table of contents, headings, glossaries, menus, and icons. They will ask and answer questions about unknown words to clarify meaning and understand how the words and illustrations convey information in different ways.

Students in grades 3 to 5 will expand their arsenal of language, learning the meaning of technical words as they pertain to a certain subject. As they are exposed to more and more types of text, they will have the opportunity and ability to compare and contrast different structures. They can comment on why the author chose a particular style (cause/effect, chronology, problem/solution) to convey his or her message and when it is most appropriate to use a particular style. In addition, they will read multiple accounts of the same event and analyze the similarities and differences that arise from different perspectives.

At the grade 6 to 8 level, students' comfort and familiarity with technical terms will allow them to move past literal definitions to analyze word choice, which is equally important in informational text as in literature. Moreover, they will examine the structure of sentences and paragraphs to understand how each is used to explain, fortify, and refine key concepts. Students will also be reading informational texts to identify the author's viewpoint or argument. They will examine how an author has included or omitted opposing viewpoints.

Integration of Knowledge and Ideas Informational texts often present new information in unfamiliar subjects or new topics. We know that students begin "reading" picture books by relying heavily on the illustrations and using them to interpret the text. Informational texts use increasingly more complex visuals to clarify meaning. Students begin with concrete depictions, illustrations, or pictures of people, places, and things in kindergarten. With support, students can identify how these visuals connect with the text, and over the primary division, progress to more abstract diagrams—for example, to explain an image depicting how a machine works in grade 2, and to infer details and context from photographs and maps in grade 3. By grades 4 and 5, students are using information presented orally, visually, and quantitatively—such as in charts, graphs, digitally, and online—to solve problems or arrive at answers quickly and efficiently. At the grade 6, 7, and 8 levels, students are analyzing how the method of presenting information might alter the interpretation of the message or portrayal of a subject. For example, they might discuss the advantages and disadvantages of using photos, illustrations, print, or audio to communicate an idea, or they may discuss how the delivery of a speech changes the impact of the words.

Informational texts are written with the author's bias and with evidence that can be limited by the research available at the time of printing or by the author's analysis and interpretation of facts. It is essential that students are able to deconstruct the points and proof given in a text, evaluate the argument and validity of the reasoning, and analyze whether there is sufficient relevant evidence presented. This skill is developed, with help, in kindergarten by identifying the reasons an author gives to support points in an informational text. By the end of grade 3, students are expected to be able to follow the logical connection between sentences and paragraphs—for example, cause and effect and sequences of points being made. In grades 4 and 5, students look for the reasons and evidence the author is presenting to support points in the text and then further understand how the proof is connected to each particular point. Students in grades 6, 7, and 8 will be critical of the evidence presented by an author. They will decide whether he or she has built a strong enough case using evidence that is relevant to the central theme or whether there are gaps in the analysis or weak supporting points.

Because many texts are written about the same topic or theme, it is important for students to be able to analyze two or more of these texts, not only to build knowledge but also to compare the different approaches taken by each author. Beginning in kindergarten, students are prompted and supported to identify basic similarities and differences in two texts on the same topic; for example, books that describe the signs of winter or directions for making cinnamon toast. By the end of grade 3, students can compare and contrast the important points and key details of two texts on the same topic independently. In grades 4 and 5, they are able to apply the information they have extracted from similar texts and integrate it to speak or write about the topic knowledgeably themselves. Through grades 6, 7, and 8 our students are thinking critically about the differences between two texts written on the same subject. They are analyzing the different treatment of facts on many levels. How do the authors differ in their interpretation of facts? In the case of conflicting information, do the authors disagree on matters of fact, or in their interpretation?

---

colleague conversation **Be the Student!**

Choose a current events topic and bring three different sources on it to the table. For each source, create a graphic organizer with these headings: Source, Author Bias, My Response, Discuss. Does it change the way you read to be aware of bias and perspective in informational text from the start?

---

career ready **Nurse Practitioner**

The field of medicine requires a tremendous amount of reading to keep current, so the ability to read quickly, absorbing the most pertinent information and filtering out what is not useful, is important. You also have to "translate" complicated medical information into language that patients can understand, which takes some creativity and use of metaphors.

Range of Reading and Text Complexity   Genres of informational text to be included in the curriculum include history/social science texts, scientific readings, and technical documents. The Common Core State Standards always come back to the staircase approach to learning. For students to build knowledge systematically, the material they read should have an obvious connection. For example, students might learn about the human body, beginning with the five senses in kindergarten. In grade 1, they may learn about germs and their effect on the body, and by grade 5 they will have reached the circulatory system.

The Core Ready lesson sets provide all students with opportunities to work with texts deemed appropriate for their grade level as well as texts at their specific instructional level. Through shared experiences and focused instruction, all students engage with and comprehend a wide range of texts within their grade-level complexity band. We suggest a variety of high-quality complex text to use within the whole-group lessons and recommend a variety of additional titles under Choosing Core Texts to extend and enrich instruction. Research strongly suggests, however, that during independent practice and in small-group collaborations all students need to work with texts they can read with a high level of accuracy and comprehension (i.e., at their appropriate instructional level) in order to significantly improve their reading (Allington, 2012; Ehri, Dreyer, Flugman, & Gross, 2007). Depending on individual needs and skills, a student's instructional level may be above, within, or below his grade-level band.

---

colleague conversation **Be the Student!**

Type a topic of interest into a search engine like Google on your phone, tablet, or computer. Together, discuss the results of the search. Make a T-chart. On the left side of the chart, write the heading "Text Types" and list three nonfiction text types that appear in the search results (e.g., website, magazine article, blog). On the right side of the chart, write the heading "Skills Needed" and list the specific skills students need to negotiate those text types (e.g., skimming, questioning the source).

Foundational Skills

As with anything else in life, foundational skills are necessary for success. Reading foundations range from the directionality of text to the sounds of the language, from written letters and words to complex vocabulary—the raw materials used to craft fictional and informational texts.

Print Concepts   A very young child notices when one of her board books is upside down. She carefully opens the cover and flips through each page, beginning to end. Eventually she notices that the text flows from left to right, top to bottom. She begins to name the letters of the alphabet and to point to groupings of letters, noticing that they constitute words. These are the earliest print concepts.

Phonological Awareness   When you watch a toddler proudly singing the ABCs, did you ever stop to think that this is one of the first steps on the way to independent reading? Though often confused with phonics, phonological awareness concerns only the sounds of language. When a kindergartner makes up a jump rope rhyme or a first grader rolls on the floor in fits of laughter while replacing the first letter of his friends' names with other letters, phonological awareness is at work.

Phonics and Word Recognition   "Mommy, that says 'stop,'" says the toddler from the backseat of the car. Students acquire high-frequency sight words from seeing them consistently in their environment and in print, beginning well before kindergarten. They begin to decode words and develop strategies to attack words in order to become good readers. In kindergarten, one-to-one letter–sound correspondence is stressed, along with the sounds of the five vowels. As students progress through the primary grades, they focus on multiple letter combinations for consonants and vowels, syllables, and prefixes and suffixes. Because the English language has many irregularly spelled words that do not fit the patterns, they must be explicitly taught as appropriate for each grade level. By junior high, students are using word analysis skills to decode multi-syllabic words both in and out of context.

The *Oxford English Dictionary* contains entries for more than 100,000 words currently used in the English language. Dictionary.com registers 3.6 billion

searches annually, with the goal of turning vocabulary expansion into an interactive word discovery experience in which people explore words in useful and creative ways that meaningfully enhance language command. With so many words at their fingertips, students need strong building blocks for decoding unknown words. Like a painter mixing colors together to achieve the effect of the sun sparkling on the ocean at dusk, children can set moods, portray emotion, and paint pictures with words. Students will have a rich palette of words to express themselves to the fullest extent.

Fluency   There is nothing more frustrating than sitting down to read and having to struggle over every other word, reaching for a dictionary and searching for the correct meaning and pronunciation. Avoiding this disjointed reading experience across all grades, Core Ready students will develop the skills and stamina for reading on-level and even above-level texts with accuracy, purpose, and understanding. This fluency is the true gateway to a lifelong relationship with the written word. It also means that we do a much better job of matching text to readers, because building fluency muscle depends largely on readers practicing with text that is just right for them. However, if the text is high interest—if, for example, your student loves, absolutely loves soccer—then his fluency rate will increase by reading even a higher-level text about soccer. The key to building fluency? Eyes on text, every day, until the work of reading becomes smoother and smoother. Eyes on text, with that text either at the student's independent reading level or so high interest that the student seeks breakthroughs and reads smoothly through even the hardest parts. And let us not ignore lower-level texts as a tool to build fluency in our most struggling readers. Familiar, beloved texts reread by our students build their capacity for smoothness that they then can apply to higher-level reads.

---

colleague conversation **Be the Student!**

Recall a time in your life when reading fluency was problematic for you. (When you were new to this country? While reading a college textbook? In fifth grade, when your teacher made you read aloud from a text that was not comfortable for you?) Share this experience and your feelings about it with your colleagues or in a reflection journal.

Common Core State Standards for Writing

Technology makes it possible for many of us to go an entire day (or many days) without holding a pen, and yet it has dramatically increased the amount of writing and correspondence that occurs in a single day—take a moment to consider the number of unread messages that greet you on a Monday morning after a work-free weekend. Let us prepare children to write in this fast-paced environment, crafting pieces of text that are clear, concise, convincing, and elegant. Writing is not about spelling alone. Writing is about having the ability to put forth opinions, hopes, arguments, stories, and expertise in writing in both formal and informal settings.

Text Types and Purposes

To build a foundation for college and career readiness, the Common Core State Standards establish criteria for three distinct strands of writing: argument and opinion, informational and explanatory, and narrative and storytelling.

Argument and Opinion   The art of articulating an opinion through writing to persuade and educate an audience is a powerful weapon. This will ring true for any of us who have engaged in a friendly debate, intense meeting, or challenging negotiation and thought of a perfectly worded, exceptionally intelligent, and irrefutable argument . . . on the drive home, half an hour too late. But no longer! Our students will use writing as a vehicle to capture their point of view from every angle. They will present the reader of their work with a logical progression of arguments fully supported with facts, textual evidence, and relevant details. The piece itself will have a clear structure—an introduction, paragraphs of supporting arguments, and a summarizing conclusion that aptly conveys the main idea and theme.

In kindergarten, children use words and pictures to state an opinion on a certain topic (e.g., "The giraffe is the most interesting animal"). By grade 2, children begin to elaborate on their opinions, providing reasons for their statement as well as an introduction and concluding sentence. From grades 3 to 5, students progressively flesh out their point of view, using a cohesive structure with an introduction, a clear statement of opinion, a logical grouping of arguments bolstered with relevant evidence, and a concluding paragraph. Grades 6 to 8 are a time for students to strengthen the structure of their argument, and to be mindful of organizing their carefully collected evidence logically and cohesively. In addition to being concise and thorough with the treatment of their own argument, they must take time to outline other opinions on a topic, distinguishing their point of view from existing discourse.

Informational and Explanatory   When attempting to educate an audience, students must learn to communicate information clearly. The writing must be organized to make their document user-friendly and avoid technical jargon and wordiness. They should take full advantage of multimedia as a teaching tool, understanding that when used appropriately, visuals are a wonderful way to illustrate hard-to-explain concepts.

Students are challenged to demonstrate understanding of subjects they are exploring from the earliest age. Students in kindergarten through grade 2 use a combination of words and pictures to introduce a topic. They provide some information, facts, or a definition to accompany the main idea and finish with a conclusion. Students in grades 3 to 5 use greater clarity and specificity to convey information. As in opinion pieces, students will need to create a solid structure, taking advantage of features unique to informational text, such as headings and diagrams. The topic they are writing about should inform the vocabulary within the piece, and students should provide concrete details about their topic using technical and domain-specific words as required. As students progress through grades 6 to 8, the topics they write about are more complex. To properly explain these subjects to their audience, Core Ready learners must be deliberate when organizing their written pieces, categorizing information and using formatting and visuals such as headings, charts, graphs, or diagrams to clarify concepts for their audience. In addition to the overall organization of a piece, it is essential that the language used throughout is precise and maintains a formal style and that vocabulary is appropriately technical when necessary.

Narrative and Storytelling   Writing about real or imagined stories is a creative and joyful experience when students are free to express themselves. We want our children to relish the ability to create a world of their own making, to take their audience on a journey from whatever perspective resonates with them. This requires providing their readers with adequate background details, character development, and a well-presented plot line.

Students in kindergarten through grade 2 begin creating stories by dictating or drawing a single event and work toward narrating a sequence of related events. At first the narrative will simply recount the plot, but by grade 2 it will include characters' thoughts, emotions, and reactions to the main events in a story.

In grades 3 to 5, students start to use narrative techniques more thoughtfully, using dialogue to recount a story and capture characters' reactions and viewpoints. Descriptive details and clear event sequences will allow readers to immerse themselves in the story without having to stop to connect any dots or ponder extraneous details.

Grades 6, 7, and 8 are a time for students to get even more creative when telling stories and to experiment with narrative techniques (e.g., dialogue, pacing, description, reflection) to create unique stories while establishing a clear context and point of view and developing the plot through a logical unfolding of events. We want to encourage students to use the vocabulary they have acquired to play with language, using description and sensory language to evoke images and feelings in their audience and to create characters that feel authentic.

Production and Distribution of Writing

Writing is a process. Often children have a linear view of this process, beginning with an introduction and persevering until the conclusion that signifies completion. Certainly this is a valid method for capturing an initial draft; however, the standards also insist that students spend adequate time reflecting on what they have written, revising, editing and reworking paragraphs when necessary, and testing different approaches for communicating their overarching message. Consideration for the intended audience should shape this process as well. Students will tailor the tone and language of their writing to suit the eventual audience: coworkers, employers or potential employers, professors, family members, or government officials. In truth, writing is messy business. A very wise editor once advised me, "It will never feel done, just eventually massaged enough to share with others."

Once students have organized all the ingredients of a writing piece into a clear, coherent, and polished piece of writing, it is time to release it into the wild for others to enjoy, discuss, and respond to. This can mean posting a simple comment, publishing to an Internet blog, or printing and binding it into a true book for circulation. At all grade levels, this is done under the guidance and support of adults and peers.

Research to Build and Present Knowledge

While of course our children have incredible tacit knowledge, they develop the capacity to build knowledge on a subject through research projects. Research is how they will fortify their opinions and written work, making them unshakable in the face of scrutiny. With the overwhelming amount of information available on the Internet and in libraries, students will assess digital and printed resources with a critical eye and a sensitive nose, ensuring that the content they read passes the "smell test" of credibility. An equally important skill they will hone is the art of paraphrasing instead of plagiarizing and the proper way to include the source of the information they collect—a special challenge in the information age, when we do not habitually record the source of everything that we take into our repertoire.

Students must have a clear understanding of what they are trying to prove, explain, or argue in order to guide their quest for facts and evidence, and they must also develop the ability to carefully distinguish credible sources from those that do not carry as much weight.

Range of Writing

Writing is a process, and writing is a *practice*. Not surprisingly, children build their writing stamina by sitting down to write every day. This does not mean hours upon uninterrupted hours; rather, the Common Core State Standards dictate projects of varying lengths. Short stints that can be completed in a single sitting can be combined with longer, more involved projects that span a week or two and allow time for research, reflection, and revision. Also keep in mind that some writing work does not involve the act of writing, but may instead involve gathering, organizing, considering, collaborating, revising, and editing. All of this is key to building stamina in this art form.

Common Core State Standards for Listening and Speaking

Before the advent of text, humans communicated almost exclusively through listening and speaking. The invention of text enabled us to communicate with one another across distance and time. Ideas written in a book in Germany in 1500 can be translated into English and read by us in our homes in the 21st century. But the need to speak and listen—critical to our interpersonal relationships at home, in school, and in the workplace—has remained vital. With technology now providing the means for us to see and speak directly with colleagues in different lands through technologies like Skype, the importance of true competence and excellence in these communication skills has never been greater.

Comprehension and Collaboration

One of the most desirable traits in the working world is the ability to communicate clearly and to work effectively in a team. Certainly group work looks much different in the 21st century, different now than it did even five years ago. The power to connect through the Internet expands our network of peers geographically while at the same time making the world feel smaller—or perhaps *closer* is a more accurate term. Now we can have meetings using Skype with colleagues in Kenya and it feels as though they are sitting in the next room. The Common Core State Standards have students practicing and preparing for this landscape. Core Ready learners participate in well-structured group discussions of varying sizes (whole class, small groups, or partners). It is imperative for students to present their own thoughts and opinions succinctly, with logical arguments to sway their audience. Following agreed-upon behavior and protocol when engaging in discussion, students will balance sharing their own ideas with listening, asking questions to clarify points, and seeking follow-up information. They will weigh the input of their peers and integrate information that bolsters their own viewpoint while staying confident and true to their own voice.

---

colleague conversation   **Be the Student!**

When has collaboration felt successful for you? Take a moment to describe the experience, listing where you were, what you were doing, and what felt good about it. Now share with your colleagues. What are the commonalities in your experiences? What makes collaboration rich? What conditions must be right for collaboration to work really well? (For the facilitator: Possible common conditions might include a feeling of trust, solid structures, or clear outcomes and goals.)

Presentation of Knowledge

If you have ever sat through a monotone lecture, a keynote speaker who believed in making a short story long, or a meeting illustrated by a PowerPoint with slide after boring slide, you'll understand the importance of this particular section of the standards. This is an opportunity to help develop a whole generation of engaging, multi-tonal, dynamic presenters. This generation of presenters will use multimedia strategically and creatively to enhance and elevate a presentation. They will revise their speaking notes and talking points to include only essential information that will captivate an audience. Core Ready learners will make presentations for a variety of purposes, tailoring their language and mannerisms appropriately. When the time comes for children to enter the working world, they will comfortably address any audience—peers, clients, heads of state—in formal or informal settings.

Students in kindergarten through grade 2 describe people, places, and things that are familiar to them and progress to recounting a story or experience with feeling and emotion. Initially they will make drawings to illustrate their main points; later the multimedia component of their presentation might evolve to include audio recordings or more advanced visual displays. Students will become comfortable speaking audibly with proper enunciation and develop their vocabulary to include grade-appropriate words.

During grades 3 to 5, students are presenting more complex subjects, including facts and key points. Their multimedia components are more advanced and truly enhance their overall presentation. Comfortable talking in complete sentences, these students are now thinking about their audience, adapting their tone and language for formal and informal settings.

In grades 6, 7, and 8, we look for signs that students are becoming more confident and comfortable in front of an audience: making eye contact with their peers, projecting their voices to ensure they are heard at the back of the room, and enunciating their words. At this stage, students should organize their speaking points in a logical manner and not waver from the topic at hand. The multimedia that accompanies an oral presentation must add value and meaning, clarifying subject matter or substantiating point of view. More important, these visual or interactive components must add interest and feel like an extension of the presentation, not a disjointed afterthought.

colleague conversation   **Be the Student!**

When did a presentation make you stop to think? What were its qualities? Think in terms of content, visuals, and reflection (what you learned, what you saw, and what you took away with you). Turn and talk with your colleagues about when this was and why it stayed with you.

Common Core State Standards for Language

Be honest; how long did it take before you made proper use of *it's* versus *its*? How many times have you debated whether climate change has a negative affect or effect on polar bears' habitat? This section of the standards ensures our children will make these important distinctions and also rid their vocabulary of nonwords, and ain't that exciting?

Make no mistake, assigning a strand of standards to conventions, effective language use, and vocabulary in its own right is not an implication that such skills are cultivated in isolation from all other strands of the Common Core State Standards. In fact, this is an acknowledgment that such skills need to be intentionally developed and prioritized precisely *because* they are intrinsic in the quest to build reading, writing, listening, and speaking capacities.

Conventions of Standard English

When we read an article or novel, we expect that certain writing conventions will be in place. In fact, when there are typos in a newspaper, readers often complain or write critical letters to the editor. These conventions of English are almost a kind of politeness or social "nicety" that we, as readers and listeners, expect. But even beyond that purpose, conventions are markers that convey emotion, assertiveness, doubt, and joy. Strunk and White's classic *Elements of Style* is a must-have for your classroom collection, for both teacher and student.

And if you encourage your students to take a closer look at *Charlotte's Web* by E. B. White, that classic of children's literature, they will see how White took his own advice to heart to create not only a story that makes hearts soar but also a story with perfectly constructed sentences, one after the next.

It is important that students systematically begin their understanding and proper use of written and spoken conventions beginning with basic concepts in kindergarten. In writing, correct use of capitals, punctuation, and spelling follows a progressive plan that expands to include more complex verb tenses and the proper use of quotation marks and commas by grade 5. Grade 6 students thoroughly examine and dissect pronouns, using the proper case and correcting vague pronouns and inappropriate shifts in pronoun number and person. Students continue to wade deeper into the conventions of English so that by the end of grade 8 they can use verbs in both active and passive voice and correctly identify and form verbs in the appropriate mood (indicative, imperative, interrogative, and subjunctive).

Knowledge of Language

Authors use language to create different effects depending on their audience and the voice they want to convey. Being able to understand how this is done and to use language to make effective choices for meaning or style are fairly challenging accomplishments. Students do not begin to look at formal and informal uses of English until grade 2. By grade 5, they look at refining sentences to make them more interesting and meaningful and examine different English dialects found in literature. As students master the conventions of English, we see this incorporated into their sentence development. By grade 8, they are writing sentences that manipulate verbs to express feelings and emphasize action. At this stage, we see students turning a critical, creative eye toward sentence structure. Editing to eliminate redundancy and playing with sentence length will entertain and delight their readers.

Vocabulary Acquisition and Use

The English language contains many words that have multiple meanings (a *duck* flew overhead; you need to *duck* quickly) or even dual pronunciations (a *live* wire, *live* a healthy life). We also use figurative language regularly, for exam-

ple, "I'm as hungry as a horse!" which can be confusing to an English language learner. In addition, the English language has borrowed phrases, affixes, and root words from other languages. These varied uses of vocabulary must be acquired and then used accurately in reading, writing, speaking, and listening.

Students begin in kindergarten to identify new meanings for familiar words, sort words by category, find opposites, act out a variety of words for a similar action, and so on. By grade 5, the complexity of understanding and application has increased to looking at Greek and Latin affixes and words and using a variety of reference materials, including digital resources, to find the pronunciation and meaning of words and phrases. Students also understand similes and metaphors as part of figurative language. In grade 8, students use context, reference materials, and knowledge of Greek and Latin root words to investigate the meaning of unknown words. This confidence extends to decoding figurative language (verbal irony, literary allusions) and distinguishing the connotation of words with similar definitions (e.g., *energetic* or *lively* versus *rowdy* or *unruly*).

---

career ready **International Business Leader**

I need to be a good communicator. I must have the ability to get my message across (written or oral) in a succinct, understandable, and credible way. Because time is money, it is often necessary to produce written work as a one-page summary (always an excellent discipline). Less is more. I need to listen and interpret what is being said into actionable initiatives.

Sentence structure and spelling are also important. Any report that is poorly written or contains numerous spelling mistakes will not be well received, even if the content is spot on.

I need to be a good presenter. The ability to engage an audience and keep them engaged throughout the presentation is important. Less is always more.

Voice training is also important. I've learned to use different tones for emphasis and theatrical pauses for dramatic effect. Nobody wants to listen to a monotonous speaker.

After this reading and exploration of the Common Core State Standards, you may recognize that your curriculum needs to be updated, refreshed, or redeveloped. This is where the Core Ready program can help you. I have organized the standards for you, grouping the major components of all standards into the Four Doors with lesson sets for all of them. Your needs in developing instruction for reading, writing, speaking, and listening for all students will be met. If you already have a curriculum, you can pull from Core Ready the lesson sets that most fill any gaps and be on your way to having all your students meet and exceed the CCSS's guidelines.

chapter 3

Preparing the Classroom and the Community for the Common Core State Standards

"Literacy is a bridge from misery to hope. It is a tool for daily life in modern society. It is a bulwark against poverty, and a building block of development, an essential complement to investments in roads, dams, clinics and factories. Literacy is a platform for democratization, and a vehicle for the promotion of cultural and national identity. Especially for girls and women, it is an agent of family health and nutrition. For everyone, everywhere, literacy is, along with education in general, a basic human right. Literacy is, finally, the road to human progress and the means through which every man, woman and child can realize his or her full potential."

—Kofi Annan

So what do the CCSS mean for you, for your school, for your community? What key changes must you make in your own practice or leadership to align with the Common Core State Standards? There are eight core paradigm shifts that will move you toward the dynamic classroom that reflects literacy for the 21st century Core Ready learner. The EngageNY website (www.engageny.org) has set forth six key shifts, to which I have added two more.

Shift 1: Balancing Literary and Informational Text

The Common Core State Standards suggest that it is now everyone's responsibility in schools to teach reading in every subject area. But it is now also the English language arts teacher's responsibility to teach how to read widely in all genres. Here is the shift: The goal is not merely for students to complete texts, to finish novels, to understand them; the goal is for students to become lifelong readers, and to read and write in multiple genres. This responsibility does not belong just to the English teacher. It belongs to all of us, in every subject area, at every grade level.

The excitement of these standards is that we can intermingle genres too. If we are studying heroes in a middle school unit of study, we can indeed read about archetypal heroes and dig deeply into the rich and great literature in this tradition. But at the same time, we can weave in readings about heroes in the real world: stories about Carnegie Award winners or courageous people in the news.

Tradition, Tradition: The Best of Literature

The standards ask us to return classical literature to its rightful place in the primary grades and all throughout our students' education. By closely reading quality literature from day one, students build the academic vocabulary necessary to comfortably analyze, discuss, and apply the critical themes in these stories to their own lives.

From folktales and myths, to fairy tales and tall tales, to memoirs and biographies, we are inviting students to study archetypes—the standards on which so many other points of meaning are based. If we begin early by introducing our students to archetypes, from the trickster to the mentor, from the sidekick to the hero, they will recognize them in contemporary literature too. They will understand the cornerstones of modern thought. They will recognize the allusions politicians, poets, academics, and the greatest thinkers of our time make to archetypes. If they are introduced early to these classic references, they will be far more prepared to study Shakespeare at higher levels later. Let us give our students a staircase approach to understanding, recognizing, and utilizing the archetypes, structures, and themes that bring great literature to life—and that help us understand life itself.

Purposeful Study of Informational Text

The Common Core State Standards also call for a more systematic focus on informational text. Think for a minute about everything you read yesterday. How much of that reading was literary text? Informational text? My guess is that, unless you were lucky enough to spend a day at the beach with a novel, most of your reading yesterday was in the form of informational or explanatory text. The standards suggest that prekindergarten through eighth-grade students' reading consists of far more informational text than ever before. This shift aims to honor the traditions already in place for fiction but to also better prepare students for the demands of real-world reading beyond school. With more of a focus on informational text, students in these grades will also have increased opportunities to explore their natural interests in science and history through the windows of books.

There has historically been an intense emphasis on narrative fiction in the English language arts classroom, from the earliest grades through high school. Our middle and high schools are loaded with book lists that have not changed much in 50 years. Hemingway and Fitzgerald are still predominant. Ask any high schooler what his image of the English classroom is and he will relate that journey from the first page of the novel to the last, with all the class in a lockstep. What has been missing from this equation is a more nuanced and balanced study of the genre of nonfiction, both informational and persuasive, in the classroom. As adults, most people in the workplace are reading and writing approximately 90% nonfiction texts every day, whether we are seeking to learn something new or communicate information to someone else.

of students and teachers. The collections of classroom text used for language arts and content area lessons will require more variety and will need to include more media-based and purposeful, modern informational sources. We will need to restructure our planning around a great number of in-depth studies throughout the year, and we will need to adopt an important philosophy of engaging our students in deeper, more authentic sets of lessons that better enable us to combine various genres of text at once. And we need to consider carefully the ways we assess our students within these tasks, improving on the archaic "right and wrong" deficiency models by welcoming more performance-based, authentic assessment. Chapter 12 helps you better understand assessment in the new era.

Shift 2: Building Knowledge in the Content Areas

We are all teachers of reading and writing, and this shift reminds us that everyone has an active responsibility to support students' ascent up the Common Core State Standards staircase. Primarily targeting teachers of grades 6 to 12, this shift requires content area teachers to become teachers of reading and writing. Content area teachers outside of the English language arts classroom must emphasize literacy skill in their planning and instruction more than ever before.

Primary source documents are of key importance in the content areas, and though students have been introduced to them, to date little instruction has been included that explicitly teaches students how to access the meaning in these very important texts. Primary source documents tend to be extraordinarily complex in nature. They require knowledge of historical context, an understanding of the authors, and a familiarity with the intended audience. These texts require a great deal of inference and analysis of the key themes within them and the impact they had on society. To fully access all these documents offer, much more English language arts instruction is needed before the documents are introduced.

The standards make a strong case for incorporating informational text into every aspect of our curriculum, starting in kindergarten. "A variety of studies suggest young children can interact successfully with informational text when given the opportunity to do so" (Duke, 2003, p. 1). Duke (2003) continues to argue that informational text is not only appropriate for young children, but in some cases, it is also actually preferable, because it builds on young children's inherent curiosity, supports their vocabulary development and word knowledge in natural ways, and works to develop their growing concepts of reading and writing.

No more leaving it to the history or science teacher to teach our students how to read and write nonfiction. Like fictional text, informational text requires focused study. How does informational text work? What types of informational text exist? What are the prominent features of the different types of informational text? What are the various purposes of informational text? Where once informational text was simply assigned to students, now it is time to pull this type of text into the objectives of our lessons and to explicitly teach students how to interact with it at all grade levels.

The implications of this shift are vast. The very texture of the classroom reading collection will take on a fresh look and a new purpose in the daily lives

Content area texts are also important in the later grades, as older students are expected to learn a great deal of information from textbooks. Science, social studies, foreign language, art, and even math books follow unique formats and structures and contain complex academic vocabulary that make them very difficult to read. And yet, at some point in most U.S. children's education, it seems that we stop teaching strategies that can actually help students negotiate these types of texts—they are simply given reading assignments and expected to know what to do.

Additionally, students in the content areas are routinely asked to write. They are assigned summaries, responses to informational articles, lab reports, letters, persuasive essays, and a host of other genres. Yet they are not always taught the strategies for writing these genres well.

All content area teachers need to shift toward teaching reading and writing in order to continue the work of the elementary teachers and English language arts teachers and to support students as they engage in these tasks with real texts. Content area teachers need permission to slow down with their content and to spend more time teaching not only the content, but also the skills and behaviors needed to access that content in text. Teachers need to pull students into the art of analyzing complex texts, formulating opinions about them, and speaking and writing in ways that draw evidence directly from those texts. Students also need permission to slow down with these texts; they need to practice new strategies for reading them, and for talking and writing about them in ways that rely on the text for evidence to support their opinions and assertions.

According to literacy researcher Elizabeth Birr Moje (2011), a true call for change that includes reconceptualizing the way literacy is taught in the secondary grades requires attention to "three central aspects of disciplinary learning: discourses and practices, identities and identifications, and knowledge" (p. 100).

Discourses and Practices

The type of reading and writing in subject area content and the strategies for those skills vary greatly depending on the discipline. In science, for example, problems are identified and precise forms of data are required before claims can be made. History plays by different rules, still incorporating investigative processes but requiring a more elaborate dependence on time. Math follows the same investigative processes as science and history, but the ways in which information is conveyed diverge radically. Drawing attention to these discourses and practices should be part of the literacy instruction in the disciplines because students' awareness of them helps make them better readers and writers while engaging in these studies (Moje, 2011).

Identities and Identifications

Another important consideration is the various roles students slip into throughout the secondary school day as apprentice scientists, historians, artists, mathematicians, and more. Each of these roles has different expectations that predicate the types of reading, writing, listening, and speaking that should accompany them. Students need explicit teaching in these expectations and the tools and opportunities for practicing them. What behaviors would a scientist demonstrate when she sets out to answer a question? How would a historian communicate his theories about the effects of a historical time on its people? What tools might a mathematician use when she demonstrates how she solved a complex problem? These identities and identifications must also be part of the explicit teaching of literacy within the disciplines and not simply expected during class time activities, as these skills help lay the foundations for the unique types of reading and writing required within the content areas (Moje, 2011).

Knowledge

Content area teachers must also give some consideration to the role that prior knowledge plays in the success students have with text in the disciplines. Some background knowledge of a particular subject supports the continued learning of new concepts within that subject. The fact that new knowledge is best built collaboratively should also be recognized. Content area teachers can and should give students plenty of time with content area text so students can build background knowledge, negotiating and constructing new understandings about each discipline. This means offering more time with all types of texts, including those most familiar to this generation of students—e-text (Moje, 2008).

A New Way of Thinking about Content Area Teaching and Learning

In the past, the content areas have been heavily dependent on traditional models for teaching and learning. Direct instruction, memorization, and multiple-choice tests have dominated the terrain of the disciplines. But if we are going to shift toward a deeper focus on teaching the specific domain-based literacy skills that are necessary for moving thoughtfully and successfully within the disciplines, then the ways we teach will also have to be examined. The literacy loop, as it relates to the disciplines—reading, writing, listening, and speaking—has to be explicitly taught and practiced.

Shift 3: The Staircase of Complexity

This shift is a critical paradigm change for many teachers. The Common Core State Standards make use of a model that enables every child to climb gracefully and systematically up with each grade level, eventually arriving at the top, where he will be prepared for the complexities of college or professional texts. These standards call for greater emphasis on carefully chosen literary and informational texts and for the necessary time to linger over, savor, and deeply study these texts. Students must be able to read them, understand them, apply them to their lives, discuss them, and write about them using the academic vocabulary necessary to do so thoughtfully. In essence, students achieve success when they are reading thoughtfully selected core and independent texts and when reading to make meaning is the primary task. The Common Core State Standards call for us to give children the gifts of time and appropriate scaffolding for these text-based skills to develop, and for us to make a collaborative effort to keep the child moving up that staircase, gently guiding the ascent.

All students have the fundamental right to access quality text in the form it was intended to be consumed. To deny students this right is to deny them not only the chance to fall deeply and madly in love with these texts and to have fun and lose themselves in the world of a story, but also the opportunity to think deeply about the meanings behind them and to apply them to their lives. Offering students only a bland diet of texts that are too simplified or too complex is unrealistic and doesn't reflect the real world of a reader. We all struggle as readers, and sometimes that feels great—the way a great athlete loves to play a hard game. That is what we want for our students: that they build stamina and endurance and then can get out into the thick of it, wrestling with text. I love the feeling of not always knowing, but that is because I am an expert reader. Students have to both practice building their muscles on texts they can master and be given opportunities to wrestle with text, confidently and with support.

More Complex Texts

Millions of U.S. children are graduating from high school ill-equipped for the complexity of reading material they will encounter in college or the workforce. To close this gap, the authors of the Common Core State Standards worked backward from college and professional texts to write the standards for every grade level K–12. The result is that the texts and skills required at each grade level are now more complex. These standards upped the ante on the texts we should be using in our lessons. We must examine texts for classroom instruction carefully, through an analytical lens, to decide whether they are of high enough quality and sophistication.

Core Ready identifies specific texts for you in the lesson sets, but the program also encourages you to know how to choose appropriately complex texts for your lessons. Think about the classroom text collection you have used in the past and consider reexamining these texts for the increased text complexity now required by the Common Core State Standards. But I urge you not to abandon the variety of text levels in your classroom; your readers need to practice their stamina and other aspects of their reading development on both lower- and higher-level texts, depending on the purpose. Daily minutes spent reading is key for the developing reader, and for this to happen the children must have choices in what they read. (See Chapter 5 for more information about text complexity.)

Access

These standards make the case that all students must be given entry points into more complex texts. They do not outline how to accomplish this. Core Ready does. Every classroom will be inhabited by a vast array of learners, so the pathways into these more complex texts must vary too. Chapter 9 details specific strategies for supporting students to gain full and complete access to the texts they should be able to master at their grade-level step on the staircase. Although the routes taken by English language learners (ELLs) (see Chapter 10), special needs students (see Chapter 11), and even typical learners may diverge, the ultimate objective remains the same—that all students experience powerful connections with text.

Time

Time is an important theme in the 21st century classroom. Everywhere I go, I hear teachers worrying about time. The chief concern is that there never seems to be enough of it. This is true if we think of the standards as a linear checklist. Yet the staircase of complexity requires us to rethink how we organize our time—to plan in such a way that we group standards into deeper studies around specifically selected texts. We can no longer teach isolated lessons in lockstep, checking off boxes as we complete each one. Instead, we need to view our year as a series of in-depth journeys through more relevant investigations. We need to view the year as a series of rich lesson sets.

By layering multiple standards into sets of lessons, we can create more opportunities for the optimal combination of direct instruction, scaffolding, and guided practice that students need to be able to access these complex grade-level texts. Core Ready recognizes the necessity for each of these elements of reading instruction and offers opportunities for teachers to apply them to their own classrooms in a way that helps them best differentiate and scaffold for the various needs of all students. Additionally, by grouping standards into lesson sets, you will enjoy more time to go deeper into your study of these rich texts.

Whole-Staff Collaboration

It has never been more important for teachers at various grade levels to plan together. The Common Core State Standards have created specific roles for teachers to play in the coaching of students' ascent up the staircase, but the climb will not happen automatically without purposeful collaboration between members of the team. We simply cannot close our doors and teach in isolation, figuring that our only responsibility is to meet our grade-level obligations. The Common Core State Standards are not linear, so this model simply will not work anymore. The standards require more collaborative planning across grade levels. In the other books in this set, you will note that lesson sets are grouped across grade levels so you can see the progression of thinking and the staircase of complexity in thought and choices of texts. Grade levels cannot exist in isolation. We must collaborate to best serve our students.

Teachers, administrators, and curriculum organizers must take into account the bigger picture—the student's pathway through the entire system. By articulating the skills needed to access college- and career-ready texts, we can then more fully understand our individual roles in that overall goal. The well oiled machine enables the students to have the skill set they need at each grade level.

put it to use

By eighth grade, students in a typical middle school school must be able to "[a]nalyze how particular lines of dialogue or incidents in a story or drama propel the action, reveal aspects of a character, or provoke a decision" (CCSS RL.8.3) in appropriately complex eighth-grade literature (National Governors Association Center for Best Practices & Council of Chief State School Officers, 2010). The staff recognizes that a lot of teaching is required for an eighth grader to master this standard—more than can be provided in one grade. They collectively rally to ensure that the foundation is in place by the time students arrive in eighth grade, identifying common core skills and vocabulary and carefully selecting exemplar texts to use at each grade level. The kindergarten teacher sets forth to introduce characters, setting, and events in literature. She uses these terms as she discusses literature and expects that her students will do the same. The second-grade teacher teaches his students to not only identify characters but also describe them. During this year, the students are given plenty of time to practice these new skills and terms—drawing connections, comparing, discussing, and writing about characters in the stories they read. The students learn the word *dialogue* and use it as they discuss stories with their classmates. By grade 3, the teacher builds on these concepts by teaching the skills to describe characters by using words like *motivation* and by considering how the words and actions of characters influence stories. In fifth grade, the students spend time comparing and contrasting characters, using these terms in their writing and discussions. The sixth-grade teacher continues this study and adds key words to the students' academic vocabulary: *plot, rising action, trait.* Here, the students analyze the plot in stories by focusing on how episodes within the plot might change or affect the characters. By eighth grade, the students are finally ready to focus on this standard. They now have the academic vocabulary and experience to learn the concepts slated for this grade level. The eighth-grade teacher counts on this as she designs her lessons for deep study of how dialogue works to reveal key details about characters.

Shift 4: Depending on the Text for Answers

This next shift urges teachers to make subtle changes to instruction that veer students toward text rather than away from it when they engage in reading work. A recent trend in modern classrooms is to use text to jump-start conversations, projects, or response writing, but in a way that pulls the work away from the original text and into another nucleus of thought. This shift reminds us that the conversations, projects, and analysis should be about the text itself in order to dive deeply enough into it to fully understand it.

This shift also requires thoughtful study so that the work is directed into the text and so that time is allotted to developing the habits of mind that enable students to turn to the text when they search for answers. This requires explicit instruction in how to find the answers in the text and how to support arguments and opinions with text-based evidence in both writing and discussion. Understanding this nuance requires a careful plan and a pointed commitment on the part of the teacher. This shift isn't just about teaching skills, but about helping readers build habits and behaviors that make them stronger readers.

Many of us are well-versed in extension activities. Many curricular programs even set up text study this way: A story is read together as a class, and then students answer comprehension questions, do a brief book report or a project, and then move on to the next one. This shift asks us to shelve those cursory practices and instead adopt a richer method of experiencing text together as a community. It asks us to look at text as art and to invite our students to give themselves over to the art wholly in order to experience all that it has to give.

Another recent trend is the focus on connections. We ask students to connect the text they have read to another text, to themselves or to the world in general. But by focusing our study of text on these connections, we first assume a level of understanding of the particular text that may not exist, and we also pull the thinking away from the text so that soon the text is not even the focus of the conversation anymore. Here, we are being invited to give the text itself joyful consideration (and let's keep it joyful). The great poet Billy Collins wrote "Introduction to Poetry," a poem in which he despaired that teachers are beating down the essential, ephemeral beauty of poetry when they overanalyze it to the point that its essence is lost, and to the point where no other viewpoints can be considered. I don't want to return to those days. Instead, I want to use the call to action of the standards to relish text and savor it in an appropriate manner. I discuss close reading in further detail in Chapter 9.

Questioning

This shift requires the teacher to become versed in the art of questioning in a way that steers students back to the text to find the answers. "What," "why," and "how" questions can be subtly changed to fit this bill. "What is this author saying? What do these words mean? Why does this sentence sound like this? Why is this organized in this manner? How did you feel when you read this part? Listen to this sentence. Listen to it again. Now read it yourself. Now read it to a partner. What is the significance of that one single sentence?" All of these questions depend on the original text for answers. We must move beyond the transparent ("What color was the woman's dress?") and focus more on the inferential ("What is going on in this paragraph?").

In addition to the "what," "why," and "how" questions, teachers should commit the "how do you know" question to their repertoire. These powerful questions guide the student to understand that the art of reading does not stop at finding a fact or developing an opinion. Successful readers—readers who truly have command of their craft—can also support these facts and opinions with evidence pulled directly from the text. If a student says, "The author is trying to slow down the action with those words," the teacher should answer with, "How do you know that? Show me evidence from the text that made you come to that thought," urging the student to bring specific textual evidence into the conversation. Teachers at all levels need to build in plenty of opportunities for students to back up their knowledge gleaned from text with evidence from that same text, and to do so both in conversation and in writing. Over time, teachers should gradually release the responsibility for asking these questions to the students so this deeper, richer way of reading becomes more natural.

Shift 5: Writing from Sources

Shift 5, writing from sources, uses evidence to inform or make an argument. While the narrative still has an important role in the English language arts classroom, students develop skills through written arguments that respond to the ideas, events, facts, and arguments presented in the texts they read.

This shift may be a bit painful for some who feel a deep sense of attachment to narrative prose, but it asks you to take an honest look at your writing instruction and decide whether it truly prepares students for the types of writing and thinking that will be asked of them in college and career settings. While there is still room to help students develop a deep sense of voice and purpose in narrative writing, informational and explanatory writing might be more in line with what they will be asked to do in the real world. This shift asks that you ensure your students go further with the type of academic work they are doing in their reading and develop the skills necessary to place that work in their own written text.

To be college and career ready, students need the ability to report information, synthesize information, and persuade others to their line of thinking, and they must be able to do so in writing while making use of source materials.

Synthesize

More and more, we are called on to take in information from various sources and synthesize it into a single, new thought. This skill is required in college when students are asked to write papers on just about everything. It is required in the workforce when an employee is asked to write a report. This skill is required outside of these settings too—when we are asked to vote or when we consume news from various sources, we are bringing facts together to formulate our understanding of it all.

Report

To be college and career ready, students also need to develop the ability to report facts with precision and accuracy. Most careers, from the arts to the sciences, from technology to education, require this skill. A museum curator must write a report on her budget. A NASA scientist must write a lab report on the results of his most recent experiment. A software engineer must write a summary on her latest code changes. A teacher must write a report on his students' assessment data. These tasks, in these careers, in college, and now beginning in the earliest grades, require the ability to extract facts from text, interactions, and data and communicate those facts in writing in a variety of formats.

Here, accuracy is key. This shift asks you to accept the "right and wrong" philosophy when working with your students. There is a time and place for more creative thinking and writing, but the ability to report researched facts relies on accuracy.

Reflect

Another key skill when writing from sources is the ability to reflect on the facts and skills that have been summarized and reported. To be college and career ready, students must develop the ability not only to gather and report, but also to summarize this information and reflect on it to develop their own interpretations. What does it all mean? What new understanding does this all point to? This is part of this shift toward writing from sources as well.

Again, in college and career, this ability is critical. Consider an example: As a teacher, you are worried that one of your students is performing below grade level. You ask the student study team at your site for help. You then gather and compile the student's most recent assessment data, summarize the data, and report on the results. But your report is not complete until you reflect on the data and explain what it means for your student. This part of the report should include your thoughts about *why* your student struggles and about *how* you think those struggles should be addressed. This final step is what makes you a professional . . . the ability to use data and information to make a new determination about your subject.

Persuade

Students must also use their writing to persuade audiences to their ways of thinking. Authors will be much more likely to persuade their readers to accept their points of view by relying on multiple sources and presenting reports and arguments in ways that are fully supported with evidence. In this way, a student is called on not only to formulate and present an opinion, but also to tell the world about that opinion in a way that is much more conclusive and valid. Students need to be given the permission not just to present facts or opinions in isolation, but to combine them to lend more credence to the content of their writing.

Again, these are the skills that are required in college, in careers, and in 21st century life in general. We are more powerful citizens when we can gather information from many different sources, formulate our own informed opinions, and present those opinions to the world in ways that sway other people. This requires us to look closely at the type of writing we are asking our students to do. Are you too heavily focused on narrative writing? Are you scaffolding your students as they synthesize facts to create their own understandings? Are you giving them enough time and opportunity to write their understandings for real audiences? These are the skills they will need in order to be ready for the world beyond school. Our youngest writers can begin doing this right from the start. Fiona, in first grade, wrote about nursing homes because her grandpa was in one. She interviewed him as a primary source. Based on her interviews

with him, she concluded that nursing homes can be a good alternative for an aging relative. The topic meant a great deal to her and she was very proud of her evidence-based reporting. Persuasive writing is discussed further in Chapter 6.

Shift 6: Emphasizing Academic Vocabulary

The sixth paradigm shift prescribed by the Common Core State Standards suggests that we be more mindful of giving our students the language they must know to engage successfully in school and in the workplace. Students need the tools to move gracefully within academic and professional settings, and these tools are vastly different from those needed in more informal settings. A strong command of academic language ensures success at school and at work. A strong command of academic language empowers.

What Is Academic Language?

Social language is informal. It is texting between friends, an email from Mom, a chat with a sister. Academic language is more formal. It is the language of the classic novel, a news article, a debate, a presentation, a professional letter, a report. Academic language is more cognitively demanding, more structured, and more nuanced than the language that is needed for a simple social exchange. To be truly college and career ready, students need to develop deeper understandings of phonology, better command of spelling, more sophisticated comprehension of grammar, and much larger vocabularies as they progress through school.

Academic language has more rules than informal language, and students need to understand these demands. The differences can be confusing. The language of an informational report might make use of passive voice—a technique you wouldn't generally want to encourage in your students' social language. A formal letter demands more sophisticated transitions than an informal email. A debate demands a more layered vocabulary than a conversation between friends. So we have to teach academic language explicitly from the earliest ages and with a greater sophistication, and we have to be mindful to encourage academic language use naturally throughout our lessons.

Setting Expectations High

The Common Core State Standards emphasize the teaching of academic language throughout all the grades. We can encourage our students to begin using the term *narrative* rather than *story* in fourth grade. We can encourage our students to move beyond problem and solution in the study of narrative and help them see rising action. We can study closely the nuances of grammar in persuasive essays. We can deeply analyze the language of poetry and the techniques poets use to make great impact.

Consider an example. Elementary students love fantasy novels, and good fantasy follows the format of classical texts. Using academic language that highlights the complexities of fantasy fiction, even elementary-age children can begin to engage in rich discussions that will become the foundation on which richer discussions are based later on. The hero in the fantasy novel faces trials and the supreme ordeal. In alignment with academic language, students can learn such terms and also learn how to talk deeply about the novel, using complex sentences and transitional words to help understand big ideas about the text.

Our expectations of academic language use must be high at all grade levels. Very young children will not discern which new words they learn. So go ahead and teach the academic versions of the simpler terms you might have once used. Your students will surprise you.

Academic Language in Action

A first-grade classroom is immersed in writing informational text. The teacher is sitting at the back table interacting with three students, while the rest of the class is gathered in little clumps around the room. The conversations are rich and peppered with the words of literacy.

"I think my page layout needs to look better," says Max, age 6.

"Maybe you could put more color in your illustrations and then put in some captions to explain them more," says Brendan, also 6.

"Oh, that's a good idea. That dinosaur book has those," muses Max.

"Mrs. S. told us about those, too, remember? Captions explain about the pictures, and labels just tell the name of something, like one word," recalls Brendan.

"Yup, the chart is right there on the wall," says Max, pointing.

"There are labels in the back of that book *Dog*. They tell the dogs' names. I love that one. I'll get it. You can use it as your mentor text," suggests Brendan.

Age 6? Really? "Captions," "labels," "page layout"? Yes! These terms have been taught and modeled, and there is now both an expectation and an opportunity for these students to use them.

"I'm writing about cats in the first person," says Emily, age 7.

"Oh, I love doing that! You can pretend to be the animal. It's fun," says her friend Kyle, age 6.

"But I'm stuck on this part. I need to tell about what food cats eat, and cat food is gross so I can't figure out what to write in first person," Emily says.

"Maybe you could close your eyes and pretend you are a cat and think about the food," suggests Kyle.

"My favorite food is chicken, but I like any kind of meat, even liver," says Emily, smiling.

"Ewwwwww."

"Hahaha. That's good, I'll write that."

First grade? Really? "First person"? Yes! Again, these terms have been explicitly taught and modeled, and the tools for acquisition of these terms are within easy reach. There is an expectation and an opportunity for these students to try out the terms they learn. The best part is that the classroom is a playful and safe environment within which to practice.

Honoring the Natural Process of Vocabulary Acquisition

Children are in the word business from the day they are born. As babies, they are fascinated with the sounds their parents make—joyfully parroting and experimenting with the tones of the language. They begin pointing to and begging for the names of everything in their environment. Words eventually become sentences that narrate play. Toddler vocabularies explode as they interact with their families and the world around them. Their lexicons swell monthly, weekly, daily, even.

This process is collaborative and interactive. Instinctively, mothers of babies sing, chant, rhyme, and repeat words all day long. We narrate even the most mundane actions while our babies laugh and coo, mimic and produce sounds, all the while picking up the subtleties of the language. Soon toddlers are interacting with the world by using full sentences, surprising us by the minute with words they have acquired and are now using correctly.

These are the primary ways in which children learn language in the first five years of their lives—the ways in which their vocabularies begin. Children learn words as they are spoken to them: used in context. Children learn words when they have the opportunities to try them. Children learn words in collaborative, interactive, social, and authentic interactions. They learn words when their environments support vocabulary acquisition.

Yet somehow, between school and home, vocabulary acquisition transforms from this natural process into something more rote. Students come to school with the rich vocabularies of their home lives, acquired through warm social interactions, ready for more of the same, and then someone hands them a list and asks them to sit quietly and write the words three times each.

We need to be mindful of the ways students' vocabularies optimally are created in the first five years of their lives and set up our curriculum for more of the same. This means that we need to be sure to provide our students with plenty of opportunities for authentic reading, writing, listening, and speaking during which they can both acquire and use academic language.

put it to use

Identify a list of academic vocabulary words for a lesson set you plan to teach. Keep this list near you throughout the course of the study. Create a chart called "Words We Are Using as We Study _____." Add to this chart gradually throughout the study. Incorporate these words into your lessons, your conversations, your one-on-one coaching time, and your small-group time. Encourage students to incorporate these words into their collaborative conversations.

Collaboration

As we plan lessons that encourage the acquisition and use of academic language, collaboration plays a critical role because it is during interactions that students negotiate meaning. Small groups of students can collaborate around complex texts to deeply analyze the author's craft. Partners can collaborate to create written texts of their own, such as blogs or other informational websites. A whole class can negotiate the deep intentions of a poem. With adequate modeling from you, the teacher, through these interactions students will begin to take on the academic vocabulary you teach.

put it to use

During close reading of texts, build in time to "Turn and Talk," when students turn to a partner and engage in a brief discussion. Give students a text-dependent topic to discuss that relates to the purpose of the close reading, such as "Together with your partner, find three words or phrases that describe the main character."

Systematic Planning

Academic language skill is not just incidental. The Common Core State Standards help us approach it systematically via the staircase. Because we can easily see how specific skills such as grammar conventions, knowledge of language, and vocabulary build throughout the grade levels, we can more mindfully incorporate these standards into our lessons and lesson sets. We can use the staircase tool to ensure that we are covering every need.

Shift 7: Focusing on Technology-Based Genres of Text

The 21st century is the century of the critical thinker. The 21st century reader, writer, speaker, and listener absorbs the informational world via screens, mobile phones, and e-readers. More than ever before, our children need to do more

than just decode words and answer basic questions like "Who is the character in this story?" Instead, our children are required to navigate a complex universe of information, a web of opinions and explanations, and an increasing and continually changing array of media. Ultimately, the 21st century thinker needs to be able to jump from genre to genre, across different types of media, to become an expert in interdisciplinary literacies—moving through the varied disciplines encountered with ease and independence.

Our students need to be able to input their own carefully crafted questions into Google and marshal the information they get in return. The questions and answers they field themselves are the ones that matter the most (Asimov & Clarke, 1997). They will become the captains of their own educations, and their questions, whether they be scientific, historical, literary, or personal, will guide them on their magical and expansive journeys of learning and emotional growth.

We now have a deeper understanding of the wide variety of complex skills that the 21st century learner must possess, but the techniques we continue to use in our schools to teach reading and writing do not match this new understanding (Partnership for 21st Century Skills, 2008).

Imagine if you enrolled your child in a soccer tutorial and for three-quarters of the hourlong practice the coach described soccer using words instead of action. In place of drills or scrimmages, players were lectured on the precise angle to hold their foot when kicking the ball, or the theory behind a good offensive play. This is how reading and writing has been taught for years in our schools. We lecture about "reading comprehension strategies" and "decoding skills" instead of giving children the opportunities to actually read from varied and meaningful resources in school. Children are independently reading less than 7 minutes a day, if that, by the middle school grades.

With this in mind, the simplest solution and the essential key to strengthening reading and writing performance is to treat every aspect of literacy as practice. Just as in soccer, where the only way to improve agility, flexibility, and speed is by continuous practice, our students need continuous practice in all kinds of reading and writing. Teachers need to reduce the amount of time spent talking about the benefits of reading and writing and allow students to sit down to read and write. It is widely accepted that math aptitude comes from working through problems and exercises—and so it is with reading and writing. The muscles for reading and writing well are cultivated and strengthened by absorbing a large number of words every day and practicing how to synthesize new ideas and new information for a new world.

For students to build the capacity to read and write beyond their current levels, they must read deeply, from a variety of texts—a video game manual, a graphic novel, a blog on a subject of interest, the back of a cereal box, a classic canonical text. They must write widely, for any purpose, for any audience. Most important, they need to read and write every single day.

Technology Should Be the Engine, Not the Caboose Twenty-first-century media are propelling us to a new era in writing and reading. We read and write differently than we did a mere 10 years ago. The act of reading has changed dramatically. Ebooks can be delivered digitally in seconds to handheld devices, e-readers, and computers. Audiobooks, in digital format, are enjoying a resurgence. News podcasts can be listened to on demand. Newspaper and journal archives can be accessed online. As adults, one of our first instincts when gathering information is to use a search engine. Writing has changed too. Blogging has created a new, accessible writing medium and a global audience for anyone who wants it. Emails are being replaced with short, concise bursts of communication on social media sites and text messages. The digital stage is dominated by informational and explanatory text. Digitization has changed the way we buy and consume text—and the way writers write it. The digital train has left the station—are you on it? Or will you be standing on the platform?

But ignore the technology for a moment, and we are reminded that our students will still need to be able to distinguish the reliable sources from the unreliable. They will need to be able to search for that information efficiently and swiftly. They will need to be able to comprehend, digest, and report in their own words what they have learned. Investing in and using 21st century technology in a smart, accessible way, integrated with the Core Ready series, will allow students to move swiftly around the digital universe in order to be college and career ready.

Just as districts and schools must prepare classroom reading collections for the Common Core State Standards, they must also carefully prepare for use of technology in both teaching and assessments. Districts are going to have to step up to the technology plate with reliable, wireless, high-speed Internet access, technology support, and appropriate hardware and software. Districts must also plan to examine and upgrade technology needs every year, as technology changes and improvements are happening at the speed of light.

Like the classroom reading collection, technology in the classroom cannot be an afterthought. One or two desktop computers for a classroom or a handful of tablets shared across the grade level is not good enough. Having one computer lab in the building that students visit once a week to work on an assignment is not good enough. Being fully integrated, as the Common Core State Standards inspire us to be, is to connect technology to every student, every day.

But I know that these are challenging times economically, and many teachers will not have access to the high-tech resources in their classrooms they need.

So while I implore the funders, the decision makers, the grant underwriters, and the gift givers to be generous in this area, I also acknowledge that getting these high-tech resources into classrooms may take a little time in some places. That's why the books in the Core Ready series have a low-tech option you can use during the transition to high tech in your classroom. But I cannot stress enough the urgency of getting our technology house in order as quickly as possible.

Let's take a look at not only how technology enhances a student's learning experience, but also how it can fundamentally shift the college and career readiness of a student into the stratosphere. For example: Student A reads a book that was chosen for him and writes a traditional book report. It's graded and put into a writing portfolio or folder for the rest of the school year. Student B reads the book of his choosing on a digital e-reader in a literature circle with Student C. They collaboratively write, record, and edit a podcast of their report on a tablet, read the report to students in a "buddy" classroom on the other side of the world and receive feedback, have a Q&A video chat with the author, and publish that podcast on a class blog for future classes to enjoy for years to come. Now think of yourself as a college or career recruiter and think about Student A and Student B. Which student is more well rounded? Which student is more hirable? Which student will have a greater chance of success on a college campus? Don't you want to set up the technology in your school so that all students can demonstrate these digital literacies of the Common Core State Standards? Let us fight together for the right of all children to have access to technology.

Bottom line: Put technology infrastructure, training, and support at the top of the priority list. Shift attitudes away from technology as an "add on" to one of technology as an essential tool for Common Core State Standards success.

To Be Literate in the 21st Century Is to Be Technologically Literate There is much talk about "digital literacies," but what does that mean in terms of the Common Core State Standards? We think that 21st century core literacies are a blend of being able to gather and manage complex streams of information, create multimedia texts, and share those texts with others around the world in collaboration, all with an awareness of the "footprint" we leave behind us. Some of these literacies are not necessarily new to the 21st century; certainly we needed to be able to do many of those things before the Internet came to households or before everyone had a smartphone. But now with the added element of "digital" that dominates the landscape, we can embrace those literacies as a guiding element in the Core Ready series.

There are four types of technological literacies, which we are calling the *21st century Core Ready literacies*. Students will need to attain these skills to be considered college and career ready:

1. *Informational literacy.* The ability to find and prioritize multiple pieces of information, sort it by relevance, evaluate its credibility, and make sure that information suits the original purpose. Can you seek, sort, and juggle this information to suit your needs?

2. *Media and visual literacy.* The ability to create a product by understanding the basic principles of visual design and media, and to become informed and critical consumers of visual information. Can you distinguish between an effective visual message and a big mess of a message?

3. *Global, cultural, and historical literacy.* The ability to value diversity, express empathy and sensitivity to other cultural groups, understand the bigger picture of yourself in the world context, and engage, connect, and participate in the larger global society. Can you make your sphere of influence bigger and more meaningful?

4. *Network literacy.* The ability to seek out, manage, and use modes of digital communication to make connections, seek information, share understandings, and have ethical responses to those connections. Can you connect with and within a group and be responsible about it?

These four literacies are quite new and different from what we knew just a few years ago. *Informational literacy* goes way beyond just going to the library, checking out a few books, and putting information together for a report. Now, having access to more sources has changed everything; it has allowed us to have so much information at our fingertips that we can become overloaded. Today's students must know how to manage all of that information and make crucial decisions with it.

Ever-changing hardware and software make *media and visual literacy* important to today's learner. In the past, students presented information by giving a typed report and maybe a simple slide presentation. They consumed TV or radio on just a few channels. Now, communicating and consuming visual information is primarily digital in nature. Students need to know how to be savvy creators and consumers of all types of media.

Before the Internet changed everything, we relied on newspapers and mail to give us information on other cultures. Now, the world is at our fingertips, providing a tremendous and powerful opportunity to learn how our everyday decisions and ability to make person-to-person connections on the other side of the globe affect the world around us. Having *global, cultural, and historical literacy* will ensure that those powerful opportunities are used for the common good.

Network literacy is truly brand new. It once meant having a full Rolodex or being able to make good conversation at parties, but now the networking landscape is infinite. Digital networks are made for sharing, connecting, and collaborating. Students will interact with this tool (usually through social media sites and applications) to shape their understanding of the world—whether we want them to or not. Showing them how to use networking to share and learn from others will be key to finding future jobs and making a mark on the world.

These four literacies will require four essential skills to take their rightful place in today's modern curriculum. These essential skills are:

- Critical thinking
- Creativity
- Collaboration
- Connection and communication

These skills do not exist in a vacuum. They pollinate one another, helping to grow and build understanding. Take a walk in your mind into a school where these digital literacies are alive every day, and revel in the possibilities.

While visiting a fourth-grade classroom, you might find students studying the early 20th century period of immigration through Ellis Island. They have interviewed their families, using digital voice recorders to record their own family histories, and now they are creating a digital family tree document. They go online to research the Ellis Island databases, perhaps finding their own ancestors. Through a virtual field trip of the Ellis Island Museum, students get an understanding of an immigrant's experiences and stories. Students use social media websites to create a profile under an immigrant "character's" name and share experiences and opinions through their character's profile, just as if that person had access to social media way back when.

A second-grade classroom down the hall might be busy taking photos for personal narrative comics. Students using digital cameras work in partnerships to plan out each other's personal narratives. They work out frames and dialogue. They print copies for their classroom reading collection and upload copies to the classroom's set of e-reader tablets for all to enjoy.

A peek into a sixth-grade classroom might catch students using tablets or laptops to create videos demonstrating how to solve different types of math problems. After creating the videos, they are uploaded to a class wiki that students can access in class or at home for help with homework or other math problems.

The laughing down the hall can be attributed to a joyful exchange happening in the kindergarten classroom. Through a video chat, children are listening and watching intently to another kindergarten class in Kenya put on a play about a traditional Kenyan folktale. Later, the Kenyan class will watch the U.S. class put on a play about the Three Little Pigs. Afterward, the teachers will facilitate a discussion with the students about the similarities and differences between the folktales of the two countries.

These classrooms are not just dreams—they are a reality for many innovative, motivated, and resourceful educators. For students to be literate, we must put the 21st century Core Ready literacies in the forefront of their learning experiences. Without them, students will be left holding an empty bag of tricks.

Use Technology Thoughtfully, Selectively, and with Purpose When working within Core Ready, we believe that technology is a tool, just like pencils and paper are tools. Students need to learn how to utilize those tools to benefit their learning. And just like a pencil or paper, technology is not the end goal—it is the means to an end. Technology should *enhance*, not distract from, the learning experience.

We envision a classroom where blogs, wikis, and online collaboration tools allow students to express themselves like never before. But, as with reading, strip away the technology . . . can students write clear, concise passages? Can they write compelling stories with a beginning, middle, and end and a "big idea"? Core Ready aims to ensure that students have the writing skills they need to write clearly and passionately, no matter the medium.

The Common Core State Standards assert that students need to be able to learn from both print and nonprint texts in media forms old and new. We must make sure that all students have access to fast, modern, and reliable forms of technology. At the same time, we must remember not to use the new media just for new media's sake. It must enhance and lift our lessons to a place of bold exceptionality. Find out more about how to help students navigate critically through technology and media literacy in Chapter 7.

Shift 8: The Student-Centered Classroom

The Common Core State Standards bring students to their rightful place in the classroom—front and center. Twenty-first-century classrooms are more diverse than ever, serving the complex needs of varied students. The Common Core State Standards enable us to assess the skills of each individual child and to devise specific sets of teaching points to meet the unique needs of each student by working with her in small groups, one on one, and even online to support her growth up the staircase of learning.

The "what" of teaching remains consistent across all educational domains, but the Common Core State Standards remind us that the "how" of teaching is very much about the individual student. This means that teachers must, more than ever before, be diagnosticians. A full and complete understanding of where each student stands on the staircase in relation to these standards is the first critical step toward creating an educational plan that will properly scaffold that student to climb higher. The teacher can no longer wait for the results of a standardized test to find out how each student is doing. Formative and performance-based assessments will give us vital information on a weekly basis. This is really a significant shift because we can no longer rely on lecture-style teaching to serve the purpose of education. This model is not keeping up with the rest of the world. Even large companies are shifting away from that top-down approach and giving employees far more autonomy to work on long-term projects, to work virtually, and to manage their own resources with the leaders coaching, guiding, and assessing, sometimes virtually and sometimes in person.

In addition, while I honor the value of close reading in our practice (see Chapter 9 for more on close reading), the triumph of contemporary resources is that we can provide opportunities for our students to be reading at differentiated reading levels throughout the day, whether it be narrative or informational text, whether it be in the English language arts classroom or in science or history class. Online reading lets our students read and watch video at the same time, browse through easier text to build stamina, and seek references and research that will prove a claim they are making, all in the same day. And best of all, during their guided practice time we can coach them to do their very best work, using resources hand-selected just for them. Core Ready offers lessons for the whole class, but the lesson itself should last no more than 15 minutes. The rest of the literacy time should be spent on the practice side. If we are teaching about archetypes in literature, all of us can do a close read using a Greek myth; then, during guided practice, one student might read *D'Aulaires Book of Greek Myths* while another reads *Harry Potter and the Sorcerer's Stone*, another reads *Oh My Gods! A Look It Up Guide to the Gods of Mythology,* and yet another reads *Percy Jackson and the Olympians.* All require different levels of reading, but all are within the scope of the specific goals of the lesson.

Assessment data is much more useful in this model. We can no longer be in the business of gathering data just to put it away. The assessment data will help us learn how to best confer with individual students as well as create small groups for targeted instruction. The data must tell new stories about our students that can really help us diagnose, coach, and lead. Core Ready offers many opportunities for gathering relevant data. Teacher observation of students is key, and a daily routine that incorporates ample time for students to engage in the real work of readers and writers allows teachers to make important notes about each student's growth. Performance-based and summative assessments accompany the lesson sets, along with tools for recording results of these assessments. This combination of data enables teachers to make informed decisions about how to properly coach students in individualized and responsive ways. The goal is for all students to arrive at the top of the staircase by the end of senior year in high school, but we all know that their routes to the top will be as varied as they are and that each step along the way we must make that route meaningful. Tools that help us tailor our instruction and leadership ensure that every student receives what he or she needs to meet the ultimate learning goals.

---

career ready **Book Editor**

Being able to write clearly and concisely and to use language precisely is extremely important, but so is an ear for rhythm. Following Strunk & White's guidelines will help anyone who doesn't have a natural sense of style write well. For editorial work, I would only hire someone who can read, write, speak, and listen noticeably well.

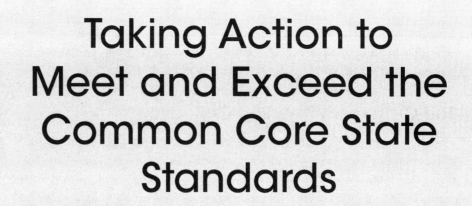

Taking Action to Meet and Exceed the Common Core State Standards

"Whatever we learn to do, we learn by actually doing it; men come to be builders, for instance, by building, and harp players by playing the harp. In the same way, by doing just acts we come to be just; by doing self-controlled acts, we come to be self-controlled; and by doing brave acts, we become brave."

—Aristotle

In this chapter, I outline key action steps that will build Core Ready classrooms and communities. Each of these can be the subject of your faculty meeting discussions, online forums, professional learning study groups, and strategy goals for the year.

Action Step 1: Establish a Classroom Reading Collection

Your first action step will be to establish a classroom reading collection that is accessible to the students, supports your learning objectives, and is reflective of the real reading and writing people do in the world outside of school.

The Classroom Reading Collection

Every classroom needs to offer students accessibility to the tools of their trade. Their trade is learning to read and write and their tools are texts. I have seen too many classrooms bereft of books, on or offline. The problem with this is that it would be like going to a gym and finding there no exercise equipment, no mats, no strengthening bars. We have to advocate for plentiful resources for our students or their reading and writing lives will not develop. It is that urgent, and it is that important. The classroom reading collection might be housed in a cozily decorated corner of a classroom in bins and baskets; it might be organized on a portable rolling shelf; or it might even be collected as folders on tablet computers or with the use of online applications.

Your classroom reading collection should:

- *Be easily and organically accessible to all students at all times.* Students should be able to make their own choices about what to use from the collection during the independent and guided practice portions of your lessons. Students should be allowed to make decisions about how to use these materials to support their work, and they should be able to readily explore literary tools and resources. If you are using print materials, consider having a basket or bin labeled for every student where he can keep his own curated mini-collection, changing it by the week. Soon enough all our

collections will go online. Still, it is crucial that our students know what is in the overall collection and can easily retrieve what they need for their independent reading. Practice, practice, practice is the key. And access is key to practice. The more readily available the texts are, the more likely students will use available time to have their eyes on texts. And that is our goal.

- *Include fresh, modern materials reflective of the type of text that is common in the world now.* Literacy is changing minute by minute. Let us keep the collections fresh, bringing in new titles, on and offline, books in hand, books online. Core Ready students must not only be familiar with the literacy of their generation, but they also need the skills to be able to consume it, to use it, and to create with it. This means that the reading and writing students do in school should match the reading and writing they do beyond school. Tablets and reading response journals can both be made easily available; to help students see the integration of reading and writing, and the reciprocity of both, keep the writing tools near the reading collection and offer students ongoing options as to how they respond to text.

- *Support the learning objectives that you have planned for the year.* Take a close look at the Core Ready lessons and suggested children's book titles in the Core Ready books that follow this one. A glorious array of titles is listed in those books. The classroom collection should feel directly related to the work you are all doing as a learning community.

Balancing Your Resources: The Literary Text/Informational Text Equation

When you think of a picture book read-aloud, do you automatically think of your favorite Kevin Henkes title? Or a classic like *Snowy Day* by Ezra Jack Keats? There's no doubt that those titles and other favorites offer educators rich and deep texts to use with lessons. But the Common Core State Standards place a particular emphasis on informational texts because students in the United States are currently ill-equipped to handle the reading rigors of college and the workplace and therefore need more exposure to expository texts in order to be more prepared for life after high school. Not only that, but as I found when I wrote my book *Best Books for Boys*, boys are longing for more informational text in the classroom. (And it is something girls will love too!) So when thinking about read-alouds for the classroom, consider rich informational texts such as *National Geographic for Kids,* or engaging informational titles such as *What Do You Do with a Tail like This?*

It can be a little too easy to fill a kindergarten collection solely with fun, character-driven titles that also make great read-alouds. But without proper scaffolding of informational texts, students will struggle with these texts in the upper grades, where well over 50% of both reading and writing activities utilize informational texts. If we want students to be college and career ready, this type of reading and writing has to start as early as possible.

Whether you already have a classroom collection or are building one from scratch, you will find that the content of your collection needs to shift to an equal if not heavier emphasis on informational texts. Notice that I use the word *texts* instead of *books*—this is deliberate. In both printed books and digital works, *text* basically means "written or printed words formed in such a way that they can be read to make meaning." The word *text* refers to all forms and types of written works. Think about how much informational text you come across each day. Your online newspaper, emails, recipes, business briefs, bank statements, instructions . . . all day, every day, we read to gain information, to lead our lives they way we want, to plan, to make crucial decisions. In our information-based economy, being able to discern what is important and what is not from an informational text is a valuable currency to employers, colleges, and households.

It is therefore extremely important that your collection has an appropriate mix of literature and informational texts. This is because the Common Core State Standards place an emphasis on a gradually higher and higher ratio of information to literary text as the grade level climbs. Specifically, in grade 4 there should be a 50–50 mix of literary to informational texts. The percentage of informational texts rises with the grades, so that by grade 8, the mix is 45% literary and 55% informational. Figure 4.1 shows the increasing emphasis on informational text from fourth to eighth through twelfth grades.

Informational texts run across all nonfiction genres, not just books. We need to make sure we have not only history and science books, but also newspapers, magazines, how-to guides, instruction manuals, CD-ROMs, catalogs, maps,

Figure 4.1 Needed Ratios of Literary Texts to Informational Texts

brochures, take-out menus, fliers, and joke and riddle books. Let the students help build this section with you. They will have the best ideas of all (video game manuals are a recent favorite; another was a first grader's request for "a whole big bin of bedtime stories").

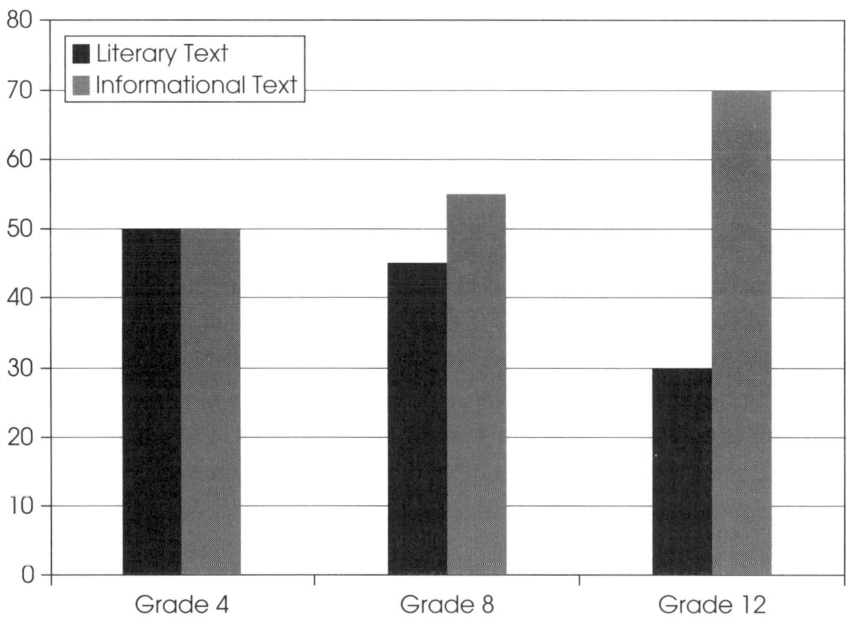

Embrace Traditional Literature in a Fresh Way

As important as informational texts are to our students' world understanding, the equal importance of approaching traditional literature in a fresh, accessible way cannot be overstated. The Common Core State Standards compel us to break away from simply "covering" traditional literature and lead us to teach it in ways that ask readers to engage in close, analytical reading of texts in ways that will truly matter to them.

Instead of covering a book chapter by chapter in a teacher-centered approach, we can empower our students as close readers by using the most classic examples of folktales, myths, and famous tales to explore with them such elements as character types, plot formulas, and themes. We can connect the examples to students' own independent reading selections. We can form small reading groups that scaffold close reading of traditional literature in new and dynamic ways. We can use these texts for whole-group shared reading experiences or interactive read-alouds. We can teach them through different modalities (e.g., musical, physical, dramatic) focusing on oral storytelling, which emphasizes the speaking and listening skills in the standards. We can use them to illuminate comparisons of modern archetypes to those found in classic text. These approaches ensure that the text can reach all learners, sustain their interest, and allow for lively and engaging discussions while still lifting them to the higher level of text reading that the Common Core State Standards require. Traditional literature is easily available online, another plus. Many of the texts are short and pack a big punch, yet another plus for teaching the developing reader.

If students in first grade can understand character as archetype in myths and fairy tales, then they will be able to grasp the same concept later when they read the Harry Potter series in grade 5, and recognize it again even later when they read *To Kill a Mockingbird*.

The purposeful shift to celebrating traditional literature in modern ways means we can cluster groupings of literature together in fresh ways to inspire our students.

The classroom reading collection is key to successful Common Core State Standards implementation and should be made a top budgetary and planning priority. The classroom collection is no longer a curriculum add on or just a place for students to browse in their free time. It is the heart of our best and greatest work because it is the cornerstone of independent practice. The collection should reflect the teaching and the teaching should reflect the collection. Classroom collections are also shifting away from being solely print based and moving quickly into the digital realm. In this way, teachers across grade levels can begin sharing titles and expanding collections. The classroom reading collection, encompassing both digital and print forms, is now the cornerstone of Common Core State Standards teaching—a vibrant and engaging tool to be used every single day in both our reading and writing lessons and in students' practice.

An Inspiring Classroom Reading Collection Will Bring Inspired Learners

Access to resources is a students' rights issue. Students need resources, and resources for reading are the foundation for all the work we want our students to do well. How can we expect to teach students reading and writing if they are not given easy access to plentiful high-quality, high-interest, and developmentally appropriate texts? We're talking about real, actual books one can find at the bookstore, in homes, and in public libraries. We're talking about tablets and digital e-readers preloaded with appropriate titles, and simple, fast access to the Internet for the latest news or student collaborations. Old, worn-out books with ripped covers below the students' current reading level and slow, buggy, outdated technology do not inspire. A classroom reading collection must have enough variety in its genres and media to appeal to all students and have the appropriate text complexity to lift students' understanding levels each year they are in school.

A Collection as Diverse as the World around Us

When building a classroom reading collection, due consideration must be given to the range of representation of ideas, cultures, gender, and information. The classroom reading collection is a chance to create an equal-opportunity vehicle that contains interests for all. The classroom texts need to reflect ideas that represent the classroom, the community, and the world. In other words, the collection of texts in the classroom should be both *worldly* and *intimate*. We are charged with teaching learners of the world, and a thoughtfully diverse classroom reading collection will open up rich opportunities for thinking beyond ourselves. Global voices and voices that represent both genders and many perspectives will add delight and knowledge to our students' reading lives.

Recent research indicates that when compared to female students, boys learn to read at a slower pace (Jones, 2005), read fewer books (Jones, 2005; Moss, 2000), have problems comprehending fiction (Jones & Fiorelli, 2003), read less fiction (Taylor, 2004), score lower on standardized reading and writing tests (Bafile, 2005; Moss, 2000), are more likely to be placed in remedial reading classes (Bafile, 2005), and read less for pleasure (Jones & Fiorelli, 2003). Building a diverse collection encompasses balancing gender equity across genres. According to the U.S. Department of Education reading tests, girls have scored higher than boys every year in every age category for the past 30 years (Scieszka, 2003). We must build classroom reading collections that break gender stereotypes of girls enjoying only literature and boys reaching only for informational texts. Conversely, to encourage more girls to become interested in the STEM subjects (science, technology, engineering, and math), we must create a learning environment in which girls can feel inspired to dive into a book about whales as easily as they pick up a Charlotte Brontë novel. These shifts must occur if we expect both boys and girls to be career- and college-ready readers. We must build classroom reading collections that will allow all students to envision their past, present, and future selves. We must not judge our students for the types of material they love and want to read, such as riddle books or books about nature. These texts will help them build stamina, for their interest propels them to read more every day. If our goal for the standards is mastery, we must use all available resources far more wisely than we have in the past. We have to take advantage of the fact that many extraordinary titles for children are available, and these titles should be an essential resource each and every day.

Create Themed Text Collections to Reach across the Curriculum

When creating or updating a classroom reading collection, think beyond the simple method of organizing by genres. Considering the Common Core State Standards' Integration of Knowledge and Ideas (Anchor Standard 9), we can now feel compelled to create exciting and engaging categories within the book baskets and on virtual e-reader "shelves"— categories that showcase the multitude of formats and styles the reading collection can encompass.

A survival-themed basket or preloaded e-reader in fifth grade, for instance, would contain such titles as *Sign of the Beaver, Hatchet, Nature Girl,* and *Number the Stars,* as well as *Survival Kid: A Practical Guide to Wilderness Survival*, storm safety pamphlets, *Backpacker* magazine, and articles from news sources that tell extraordinary tales of survival.

Reading across texts in themed baskets opens up readers' eyes to new connections to the subject matter and makes them explicitly aware of the idea of theme, which can be a difficult concept for some readers to grasp. Having a variety of texts in a themed basket or digital folder will also pique the interest of readers who might have been reluctant to browse a category simply titled "Gary Paulsen." Reading across texts and putting together themed text collections inside the classroom reading collection is a great way of making cross-curricular connections with science and social studies, as well as stimulating the interest of students who might have otherwise passed by that book box.

Classroom Reading Collections versus School Libraries: No Need to Argue

Though funding and maintaining classroom reading collections is essential, I want to make it clear that this should not happen at the expense of school libraries. One is not more important than the other. Instead, the two should have a cooperative relationship, one in which students cross seamlessly and comfortably between the two. Skills and strategies taught in the classroom can be practiced with materials checked out from the school library, and now the school library media center can be the hub for sharing online resources too. Librarians and media specialists have the training and knowledge to fill students' information needs and complement the instruction in the classroom both on and offline.

Scholastic and Yankelovich (2008) found that despite the abundance of information and reading materials, "half of all children think there are not enough 'really good' books from which to choose" (p. 14). Fifty-five percent of the children surveyed agreed with the statement "[t]here aren't enough really good books for boys/girls my age." A key reason why children ages 9 to 17 stated that they do not read more books for fun is that they have trouble finding books they like. Only 15% of children surveyed said they do not read for fun more because they "don't like to read" (p. 15). It is crucial that our students become hungry to read because they love it. People get better at things they love to do. That is the simple truth of it. And historically we have not done a great job of making reading in school fun enough for kids to want to do it. For children to really reach the standards, let alone exceed them, they have to read significantly more than they are currently reading. We must increase the minutes and increase the motivation by providing texts students really want to read.

Classroom reading collections serve a purpose that is distinctive from school libraries in several ways:

- *Students need immediate access to rich and varied texts.* While the school library does contain rich and varied texts, most students in the elementary grades visit the library only once, maybe twice a week, when the focus is on a certain "library seeking" skill. This is not enough to sustain lessons for the standards. Text has to be instantly available to students from morning until night. The media specialist and the classroom teacher can collaborate both online and offline to be sure we meet this goal of 100% access time.

- *Students need to select and work with texts of an appropriate level of complexity.* Because much of the Common Core State Standards' emphasis is on students reading and working with books that are at appropriate levels for them while also being guided through books of increasing text complexity at each grade level, it would be impossible for the librarian or media specialist to ensure that each students checks out books that meet those qualifications. The ideal collection will be online and allow students to converse with both the classroom teacher and the media library specialist about what texts they are reading. In the meantime, everyone must collaborate as closely as possible so students have access to print but are also being closely monitored and encouraged to read like reading athletes, building stamina and motivation by having books in hand that represent advancing stages of text complexity.

- *Classroom collections can be tailored to the needs of the students.* School libraries generally are not leveled; therefore it cannot be ensured that students will check out books that are at their appropriate reading levels or text complexity. Classroom reading collections should not be completely leveled either, but teachers can take care to load them with texts that are appropriately complex for the grade level and are scaffolded to help students at all reading levels achieve their goals by reading as much as possible every single day. I suggest that approximately 30% of a classroom collection be leveled. The rest should be categorized by themes, as suggested earlier in the chapter; by genres discussed in the standards; and by a wide range of intriguing texts that represent student interests and passions, as well as authors beloved by students of that age group.

The Classroom Reading Collection Is an Essential Tool

Educators are a savvy, resourceful bunch. We know how to cull through tag sales and public library book sales and how to ask parents for leftovers. We plug in our personal e-readers to the projector to create a digital "big book." Educators will always add a book to their library if they feel it brings value to the learning and to the curriculum. But should educators be essentially begging, borrowing, and scrounging to build their collections? Shouldn't a tool as essential and valuable as the classroom reading collection be given its due with proper funding of money, time, and resources? The standards are a call to action to make sure our students' lives are rich with constant access to text. Just as we would not open a gym without exercise equipment, we cannot run a school without text resources. They are simply essential.

Bottom line: Core Ready students need dynamic reading resources so their reading lives are ongoing, varied, and standards-rich.

Action Step 2: Embrace New Media

Embrace new media—anything that gets kids reading more and more
When building a classroom reading collection, be sure to plan for both print and digital resources. Considering that adults use digital resources to send and receive information on an hourly basis, it would be unwise not to outfit a classroom with Internet-enabled computers, tablets, and other devices. As adults, we are continually checking news and emails; using social media to follow favorite causes, artists, and politicians; receiving advice and expertise; applying for jobs; researching medical needs; filing government forms . . . the list goes on and on.

Starting in grade 3, the Common Core State Standards explicitly call for students to be able to gather information from print and digital resources (W.3.8). Starting as early as grade 5, students are expected to use multimedia in presentations when appropriate to enhance main ideas and themes being presented (SL.5.5). Limited access to digital resources runs counter to the main goals and requirements set forth in the standards. Are we going to help students harness their power for learning excellence? Or will digital access be merely a footnote in your school? We need it not just to comply with the Common Core State Standards, but for the sake of the children's learning.

Conversely, considering how many texts are still available only in print, it would be just as unwise to assume that an entire classroom reading collection for the K–8 set could be contained in an e-reader or another digital format. Our earliest readers still need to know basic reading skills such as left to right, top to bottom, and page by page reading (RF.K.1a). Such print concepts are a necessary foundation for students to be able to eventually read across a wide variety of text types and media. E-reader creators have also found it hard to replicate the act of browsing for books (choosing an appropriate book is a fundamental Core Ready skill), with all of its visual, tactile, and other sensory experiences, solely on an electronic device. Someday soon the devices will give us that capacity in three-dimensional ways, but for now the combination of print and online resources is our best bet.

I envision the classroom reading collection as an opportunity for both paper and digital resources to interact well and powerfully. With guidance from the Core Ready series, the teacher should be able to choose the right mix between the two types to execute effective and engaging lessons.

Bottom line: Technology is not an option; it is part of best practice and will fuel the hunger to read and write in your classroom. To speak and listen too!

Action Step 3: Use the Whole–Small– Whole Model

Teaching is like the dining room table I liken teaching to the lessons we learn in life when we first gather around our dining room table to hear from our parents and mentors, then go out into the world to practice those lessons, and then come back to regroup, share, and replenish, ready to start again the next day. In the classroom, this model helps us structure our lessons to allow for the correct balance of direct instruction and guided practice. Each lesson begins with a short direct instruction session. Students then practice that new skill independently. Finally, the day ends with a wrap-up to support the new learning and to connect with what will come the next day.

In the first part of the daily lesson, the first "whole," the teacher offers a highly focused teaching point connected to the larger purpose of the lesson set. The teaching point is within the context of lesson sets that are driving toward the achievement of standards and may involve some brief discussion and a lively connection to prior teaching and learning. As video technology improves and more children have access to online learning, I envision and advocate for a day when some of this instruction will be "flipped"; that is, your students may watch your teaching point at home and come to the classroom for more coaching opportunities from you one on one or in small groups. For now, we gather together on a rug or in a central meeting space for the "whole." It is a send-off to the independent and small-group practice.

The second part of the daily lesson, the "small" part of the lesson or "practice," lasts 10 to 40 minutes depending on the age and stamina of our students (the timing should build across the year) and involves students working in small groups or independently on the new skill introduced in your lesson. Core Ready students are engaged in the work of real readers and writers. They have ready access to the tools they need to hone this new craft, and they practice with their peers or on their own. During this time, the teacher joins in the work as the able mentor, offering strategies that will improve students' reading and writing skills. Interactions with students during this time might be formal in nature, such as a reading group or a writing conference at a quiet location in the room, or they might be more informal in nature as the teacher gets down on bended knee to check in with small groups or individuals to offer support. The teacher might use online resources such as Google Docs to help students improve their writing in a one-to-one virtual conference by working together on the document and chatting in the margins.

The final portion of the lesson, the last "whole" or "wrap-up," brings the entire group back together. Here, you are back in the direct instruction role, leading a brief summary of the learning that took place, or you are highlighting a strong example of the work. You might do a very brief summary of the day's learning, or you might opt to make a positive example of a student who put the new learning into place readily and successfully, or of a student who tried something that did not work but led to new thinking. Another purpose of this time is to link today's lesson to tomorrow's. The final "whole" is essential because it holds your students accountable to the learning you present each day while at the same time reinforcing the strong sense of continuity from one day's lesson to the next. The daily presence of this final "whole" period sends the message that you will teach something new each day and then you will check to see how successful your students were at implementing that new skill. If the final "whole" cannot be done in school, there are many online offerings that give us the opportunity to recap with our students when they return home, such as a classwide blog or teacher-managed, password-protected website that celebrates daily work.

The whole–small–whole model works best when it is in place routinely. For the most part, every element of the model will occur every day, but there are instances when the "brief" direct instruction lesson might go long, or the practice session might be cut short. This is just the nature of teaching, and if the routine stays relatively consistent, it is OK to vary the length of the elements within the routine and to tailor your teaching to the age of your students. The routine helps students settle into the work that will be expected of them each and every day. Children realize quickly that daily reading and writing practice is something that will occur every day and that active engagement is expected. Reading and writing are difficult processes in real life, and this structure helps students develop a work ethic that allows for daily improvement.

Daily Lesson Interval	What It Looks Like	Language Associated with This Interval
Whole	Teacher models a new skill to the whole class.	Teach, Try, Clarify
Small	Small groups, partners, or individuals practice the new skill in real reading or writing. Teachers confer with individuals or groups.	Independent Practice
Whole	Teacher leads a whole-group session to close the daily session.	Wrap Up

Bottom line: Front-of-the-room teaching is a thing of the past. For students to meet the standards, they need daily practice that connects to the lesson and lessons that connect to the larger goals of the standards. The whole–small–whole model brings students in, sends them forth, and brings them back in a routine that inspires independence, a key hallmark of the standards.

Action Step 4: Adopt the Lesson Set Structure

Whereas the whole–small–whole model provides the structure of your daily lessons, the lesson set structure provides the spine of your entire year   The lesson set structure requires you to group the daily lessons you will teach into rich lesson sets that involve authentic purposes for reading and writing. The Core Ready series includes fully articulated lesson sets for every grade level.

Each lesson set contains 20 interconnected reading and writing lessons that are directly informed by the standards and specific outcomes the standards demand. The direct instruction involves teaching points that relate to the overall theme of the set (themes are also directly correlated to the standards outcomes). Guided practice allows students the time to develop the skills within the set.

By grouping lessons into deeper studies, we give ourselves and our students the gift of time. Teaching this way allows us to meet many standards at once while engaging in rich, authentic tasks that enable students to process and solidify these new skills. Students work at their level of independence during these lesson sets, and we have the time to coach them as they do so, rigorously moving each student toward higher levels of performance.

Lesson sets also have clear beginnings and endings. Students benefit from knowing the purpose of every day as each lesson relates to the overall purpose of the lesson set. Students begin their lesson knowing where they are going and end with a completed project and a celebration. Too many times I enter classrooms and, while the teacher is working away on a lesson, I ask the students what they are studying. And too much of the time, *they do not know.* The Core Ready model is designed to make explicit not only what we are teaching but also why we are teaching it and what the students' roles and responsibilities are for their own learning so they can practice independently at their reading and writing every day, both in school and at home.

Bottom line: Lesson sets help students and teachers know what is being taught today and what the goals are for tomorrow so as to become truly Core Ready.

Action Step 5: Mentor Students

The mentor–apprentice model invites you to become more of a coach to your students during the majority of your language arts block   In your role as a mentor you have many essential roles. First, you are there to encourage your students in their practice and pursuits. Second, you are ultimately in charge of planning the journeys of learning your students will take. Third, you will gather and make available the appropriate tools for learning on these journeys. Finally, you will demonstrate skills and techniques and then watch over the learning to offer helpful hints and specialized teaching. Because the whole–small–whole structure allows you to spend so much time with individual students and small groups, you will be well-versed in each student's skill level and therefore in an excellent position to design teaching that matches the needs of each student. At the college level and in the workplace, a mentor guides the learning of a new employee—offering information, tools, support, and tricks of the trade. Time for the apprentice to practice and put this new learning into place is also important in this equation. The mentor–apprentice model for teaching works much the same way.

This model fits in with the whole–small–whole structure of the day. During the first "whole" period, you, the mentor, demonstrate new learning. During the "small" period, the apprentice practices this new learning independently while you encourage, coach, and offer advice. During this time frame, confer with your students individually or in small groups both on- and offline, working with your student readers and writers much like a coach works with junior athletes. Remember that ultimately, your goal is to nurture and hone the specific skills of your apprentice readers and writers. This is highly differentiated teaching because conferring can and should include individually designed lessons and practice activities that help students build their own reading and writing muscles. During the final "whole" period, lead the learning by guiding group discussion to summarize the learning and plan for next steps.

The mentor–apprentice model levels the playing field. Instead of standing on a pedestal above students, we join them in the journey of learning. This is far more contemporary and situates teaching and learning more solidly inside a 21st century framework where learning can happen any day and any time. Communicate this to your students in language such as "Let's find out together" or "Let's see what we can discover about this today." Though you have carefully planned the lessons and gathered the tools for the discovery of new information, you can still position yourself as an active member of the team who sets out to discover new things and build new ideas.

Easy ways to engage your students in a coaching role include:

1. Sharing with them your own favorite books and reading and writing experiences

2. Sharing with them times when reading or writing felt hard and frustrating and how you overcame that feeling

3. Inviting them to see you revise a piece of writing, either online via Google Docs or another venue or with marker and paper on a large chart board

4. Modeling your work as you do a close read of a text

Bottom line: The CCSS require a high level of independence from learners of all ages, but this learning happens best in the mode of accompaniment, in which every teacher becomes a co-learner, a mentor, a guide.

Action Step 6: Let Student Work Drive Instruction

Look closely at what students are reading and what they are writing, and use this as data to inform how we teach and what we teach Standardized tests, summative assessments, portfolios, and project-based assessments all provide valuable information. (See Chapter 12 for more information.) But this information only benefits students if it is used to further teach, coach, and mentor each student.

The whole–small–whole model for teaching helps this process. Once you have the results of assessments and have pinpointed the areas of need for each of your students, you can then coach individual students or small groups as they practice these specific skills. This is one way to ensure that every day of instruction includes individualized teaching.

Additionally, more time is available for guided practice in this model, so you will have ample time for observing students and engaging with them as they take on the tasks of real reading and writing. In this way, you will be less reliant on annual assessments and more focused on gathering natural data—i.e., student writing and your conferring notes, as well as records of the progress students are making in their independent reading in the course of culminating lesson sets, a much stronger and more accurate way to assess students. In the Core Ready series, each lesson set includes milestone assessments and standards-aligned rubrics.

Bottom line: Do not wait for standardized test results to know whether students are going to meet the standards by the end of the school year. Data are naturally available when you collect student writing and analyze it and when you track the progress students make in their independent reading.

Action Step 7: Make the Core ELA Standards a Family Affair

Let families in on what the standards are and how they can be part of this extraordinary movement   As a first step, commit to communicating with the parents of your students regularly and in all modes. Instead of recounting the learning that has already been done, tell what is to come in upcoming lesson sets and give tips about how parents might prepare for and support that learning. As an example, you might announce an upcoming lesson set and describe the themes and teaching points that you will cover. Use email, social media sites, texting, and group bulletin boards to get families familiar with the goings-on of the classroom and more open to other forms of efficient communication as they become available. Just because families might be too busy to come to all school functions does not mean they cannot be integrally connected to us and the work of our classrooms. Life is hard and often stressful for parents. Let them see that you will communicate with them by any means necessary, that you are all a team working together to support their children.

Give parents a list of concrete actions they can take to support learning during an upcoming lesson set. Encourage families to read the texts you will use in your instruction by providing lists of titles. Ask families to discuss the themes you explore in literature by providing easy templates for them to follow. Invite parents to extend the learning you present in informational text studies by visiting museums or by simply guiding an Internet search. Parents of your students will be thankful for concrete ideas.

Invite parents and families to celebrate newly acquired skills. Make parents aware when a lesson set comes to an end. Describe the types of celebration that will take place in the classroom and encourage parents to celebrate at home as well. For example: "We've just finished reading information books. Please ask your child about her favorite part of this lesson set." Ask parents to join classroom celebrations in person, via live online chats, or by visiting examples of student learning on a class website.

Finally, and perhaps most important, celebrate the families' children as they travel along the staircase of learning standards and **let parents know** when milestones have been reached or when a small success took place. Send a text message saying, "Today Sam really nailed it during independent practice! He wrote a beautiful piece of writing today." Or: "Sarah made exciting progress as a reader today of classic literature." Parents will be thrilled to receive a compliment on behalf of their child, and at the same time you are sending the message that this journey to standards is a community affair.

Bottom line: Parents are a vital partner on the journey to reaching and exceeding CCSS, so they need to be actively included as contributors to the success of their children.

chapter 5

Mastering Text Complexity

"The books that help you most are those which make you think the most. The hardest way of learning is that of easy reading; but a great book that comes from a great thinker is a ship of thought, deep freighted with truth and beauty."
— Theodore Parker

"I love the solitude of reading. I love the deep dive into someone else's story, the delicious ache of a last page."
— Naomi Shihab Nye

No vacation in Rome is complete without a visit to the Spanish Steps, one of the most famous staircases in the world. This architectural gateway runs from the brilliant Piazza di Spagna at the bottom to the resplendent Piazza Trinita de Monti at the top. The steps were designed by Italian architects and offer everything you'd expect of an Italian showpiece—access to some of Italy's greatest artistic treasures. Pedestrians climbing the steps admire the city—the art, the architecture, the sounds, the smells, and the people of glorious Rome. On any summer night, the Spanish steps are jammed with clusters of people sitting for hours, savoring the scene, soaking in the experience.

The Common Core State Standards advocate for a similar experience for teachers and students. Rich with treasures, they invite us to delve into the details within the larger picture. These standards were purposely designed to be fewer and deeper, and their careful construction welcomes children to stay a while in the details of quality literature—to take it all in, to really cherish the learning before climbing again. And though arrival at the top is important, the journey there is equally important.

A traditional lockstep, ankle-deep style of cramming in a ton of skills-based lessons just won't work with these standards—and that approach is not good for children anyway. Instead, let us find a step, sit, and really savor the good stuff, while never forgetting that the point is that our students are all ascending.

Different Step, Different View

The term *staircase* is used to describe the CCSS because there are two major instances in which the level of complexity and sophistication rises with each step of the child's ascent through school: (1) within each of the standards themselves and (2) in the texts used to teach those standards. The view from each step is unique, but it also relies on the firm presence and stability of the structure below.

The Standards Staircase

With few exceptions, there is a unique version of every standard for each grade level. This concept is refreshingly different from the previous lists of semi-related skills that varied greatly from grade level to grade level. In this clearly unified

format, all members of the teaching team can see exactly where the child will start on the journey and exactly where the child will need to end in order to be college and career ready, with a clear path in between.

Let's take a look at Reading Literature Standard 5 in the Craft and Structure section.

Kindergarten	Recognize common types of texts (e.g., storybooks, poems).
Grade 1	Explain major differences between books that tell stories and books that give information, drawing on a wide reading of a range of text types.
Grade 2	Describe the overall structure of a story, including describing how the beginning introduces the story and the ending concludes the action.
Grade 3	Refer to parts of stories, dramas, and poems when writing or speaking about a text, using terms such as *chapter*, *scene*, and *stanza*; describe how each successive part builds on earlier sections.
Grade 4	Explain major differences between poems, drama, and prose, and refer to the structural elements of poems (e.g., verse, rhythm, meter) and drama (e.g., casts of characters, settings, descriptions, dialogue, stage directions) when writing or speaking about a text.
Grade 5	Explain how a series of chapters, scenes, or stanzas fits together to provide the overall structure of a particular story, drama, or poem.
Grade 6	Analyze how a particular sentence, chapter, scene, or stanza fits into the overall structure of a text and contributes to the development of the theme, setting, or plot.
Grade 7	Analyze how a drama or poem's form or structure (e.g., soliloquy, sonnet) contributes to its meaning.
Grade 8	Compare and contrast the structure of two or more texts and analyze how the differing structure of each text contributes to its meaning and style.

This standard thread starts small and begins the foundation for understanding the common structures of fiction. The kindergartner need only understand that different types of texts exist. She climbs a step to first grade, where she explores two *specific* types of texts—those that tell stories and those that inform. She climbs another step to second grade, where the seeds of story structure are planted. On her climb to third grade, the child explores the language of literature and discusses it using words such as *chapter* and *scene*. She climbs once again, to fourth grade. Here, she has an entire year to savor the elements of poems and plays and to become comfortable talking about their differences. She climbs to fifth grade, where another layer of story elements is added and where the child uses her academic vocabulary to discuss them. Here, her study grows more sophisticated as she considers the ways in which these elements fit together to support the overall structure of the story. Her step up to sixth grade again provides her time to closely examine small yet significant pieces of text—a single sentence, a paragraph, or a chapter—and consider the impact they have on a story. In seventh grade, she draws on what she has learned about story structure in the earlier grades to analyze how that structure contributes to the overall meaning of a piece. One final step and she has arrived at the top, ready for the final push. Here, she uses all she has gained for the most sophisticated of literary tasks: comparing and contrasting two stories and considering how their structures contribute to their meaning and style.

Like any staircase, the strength of each step is dependent wholly on those below it. Teaching any of these concepts without the foundation of those intended to be taught before them weakens the structure. Teaching each of those steps well and solidly supports the child's firm footing as she ascends confidently and boldly toward her future.

The Text Complexity Staircase

The concept of text complexity is also presented in the Common Core State Standards by way of a staircase model. As we noted in Chapter 3, one major paradigm shift associated with the Common Core State Standards is the push to include more complex, high-quality texts in the reading curriculum. Indeed, *every* child has a fundamental right to experience complex, high-quality text, the gold-standard literature that invites deep analysis and conversation. "Just as it's impossible to build muscle without weight or resistance, it's impossible to build robust reading skills without reading challenging text" (Shanahan, Fisher, & Frey,

2012, p. 68). Every child's arrival at the top of the core staircase armed and ready for college or career depends on the development of this reading "muscle."

Yet we cannot possibly disregard the zone of proximal development (Moll & Greenberg, 1990) or the need for proper scaffolding. Children need time to read texts they love and explore texts that feel comfortable for them in order to build their strength. We can and must protect independent reading with appropriately leveled text while responding to the Common Core State Standards' demand to increase the complexity of the texts chosen for close scaffolded study.

While adjusting text levels to better prepare students for the demands of college and career is a necessary pursuit, doing so requires critical understanding of effective methods for teaching literacy. For this reason, I offer six core principles for responding to the Common Core State Standards' demands for increased text complexity.

Core Principle for Text Complexity 1

All Students Need Exposure to Complex Texts

Students need rich and rewarding opportunities to work with complex texts. Studies suggest that students currently arrive at college and in careers unable to read college- and career-level text (National Governors Association Center for Best Practices & Council of Chief State School Officers, 2010). To better prepare students for college and the professional world, schools must commit to purposefully incorporating complex, meaningful texts into their curriculum, even for students who may not yet be ready to read these texts independently. This is best done with a combination of whole-group sessions, small-group instruction, and shared reading sessions where there is supported facilitation for analyzing difficult text.

Many Ways to Climb

One size surely does not fit all when educating children. Core Ready acknowledges that there are many ways to climb this staircase, and as many ways to guide students to the top where they have full access to college- and career-ready texts. Children come to us in all shapes and sizes; with various backgrounds and experiences; and with unique genetic, financial, social, emotional, and linguistic influences. It is inappropriate to expect that every child make this climb at the same pace in the same manner. But we can expect more from our students. We must not say, "They don't have what they need at home; therefore they can't make the climb." We can't say, "My school has no resources; therefore my students can't make the climb." All children deserve to get to the top. We want to give students what they need to be able to relish these complex texts—to really experience all they have to offer. We want to scaffold students in just the ways they need to help them access texts that may have once been held back from them because the texts were too hard. Core Ready makes use of the body of research that identifies successful methodologies for teaching reading and writing and uses combinations of strategies to guide students on their ascent toward full access to college- and career-ready text.

Core Principle for Text Complexity 2

All Schools Should Employ Effective Teaching Practices for English Language Arts

Ineffective teaching practices cannot be remedied simply by adding more complex text to the classroom. In fact, adding complex text to a classroom without focusing on effective teaching practice will actually hinder learning. Layering more complex texts on top of ineffective practices will improve nothing. If students are not successfully reading less complex texts, using the same strategies with more complex texts will not have the desired effect. Effective teaching practice combined with complex text will achieve the goal.

Critical Elements of Effective Literacy Instruction

In their piece *Every Child, Every Day,* Allington and Gabriel (2012, pp. 10–15) combined years of reading research to identify six elements of instruction every child should experience every day. These elements of instruction are simple and inexpensive, but for one reason or another are absent in many classrooms across

the United States. Core Ready rests on this methodological foundation, believing that access to complex, high-quality, grade-level texts begins here.

1. *Every child reads something he or she chooses.* "In a 2004 meta-analysis, Guthrie and Humenick found that the two most powerful instructional design factors for improving reading motivation and comprehension were (1) student access to many books and (2) personal choice of what to read" (Allington & Gabriel). Student choice makes students active. Instead of waiting to be instructed, students become real readers who develop opinions and preferences for what they read.

2. *Every child reads accurately.* "The last 60 years of research on optimal text difficulty—a body of research that began with Betts (1949)—consistently demonstrates the importance of having students read texts they can read accurately and understand. In fact, research shows that reading at 98 percent or higher accuracy is essential for reading acceleration. Anything less slows the rate of improvement, and anything below 90 percent accuracy doesn't improve reading ability at all" (Allington & Gabriel, 2012; Ehri, Dreyer, Flugman, & Gross, 2007). Teachers must plan for time every day for students to practice with texts that are appropriately leveled for them regardless of grade level.

3. *Every child reads something he or she understands.* All too often, reading interventions focus so closely on isolated reading skills that struggling readers are denied the opportunity to experience the sole purpose of reading, which is to understand a message. Various studies in neurology and instruction support the idea that instructional practices that accelerate reading skill devote at least two-thirds of the time to real reading and rereading.

4. *Every child writes about something personally meaningful.* "Those who do have the opportunity to compose something longer than a few sentences are either responding to a teacher-selected prompt or writing within a strict structural formula that turns even paragraphs and essays into fill-in-the-blank exercises" (Allington & Gabriel). When students are given the opportunity to write about things they care deeply about, they produce high-quality work because they are invested in the product. Worksheet-based writing instruction is simply not effective and need not occupy valuable classroom time.

5. *Every child talks with peers about reading and writing.* "Research has demonstrated that conversation with peers improves comprehension and engagement with texts in a variety of settings (Cazden, 1988)" (Allington & Gabriel). Giving students the opportunity to talk about reading will also aid students by further scaffolding their access to more complex texts. Conversations can be casual. They can take the form of a "turn and talk about . . . " session or a whole-group coming together to discuss a rich text.

6. *Every child listens to a fluent adult read aloud.* "Listening to an adult model fluent reading increases students' own fluency and comprehension skills (Trelease, 2001), as well as expanding their vocabulary, background knowledge, sense of story, awareness of genre and text structure, and comprehension of the texts read (Wu & Samuels, 2004)" (Allington & Gabriel). Reading aloud to students, no matter the age, should happen on a daily basis. This provides a model for successful reading of college and professional texts and helps students clearly see their ultimate goal.

Core Principle for Text Complexity 3

All Students Need Practice with Instructional Texts

Students must have opportunities to work with texts at their specific reading levels. Without this foundational practice, there is no other way for students to progress as readers. During independent practice and in small-group collaborations, all students need to work with texts they can read with a high level of accuracy and comprehension (i.e., at their developmentally appropriate reading level) in order to significantly improve their reading (Allington, 2012; Ehri, Dreyer, Flugman, & Gross, 2007). Complex text is one of the texts all students must read, but it cannot be the only text.

Balancing Direct Instruction and Independent Practice

In the whole–small–whole model, discussed in Chapter 4, there is time in every session for both direct instruction (teaching your whole class at once)

and independent practice (students practicing reading on their own). The types of texts you choose and the corresponding complexity of those texts might be different in those two scenarios.

The shift toward more complex texts can be primarily addressed in the direct instruction portion of your day or week, as this is the place where you can scaffold these interactions the most. Demand a lot of the texts you use in direct instruction because you can expertly model the access points needed to understand them. Feel free to slow down with these texts. Get your students talking, feeling, noticing, thinking. Read and reread the same text and invite your students to do the same. With you at the helm, these rich and complex texts should provide exceptional examples of the topics of study in your lessons and lesson sets.

While the standards call for more complex texts to be used for close reading, text matching to a student's independent level is still essential. As Allington and Gabriel (2012) state, research is clearly in support of students getting ample time to independently practice their reading skills with appropriately leveled, quality texts. Including this practice does not preempt exposure to text that is of appropriate complexity, but rather adds another layer of practice to the reading instruction.

A healthy combination of whole-class close study of complex text and independent practice with appropriately leveled quality text is the optimal scenario for students. The Core Ready reader needs and deserves both. He needs an able expert (you) to demonstrate, describe, and model these sophisticated core skills. He also needs time to explore these concepts in books at his level of comprehension. Finally, he needs opportunities to discuss all of this with his peers.

A Broad Range of Texts

To build a foundation for college and career readiness, students must read widely and deeply from among a broad range of high-quality, increasingly challenging literary and informational texts. Through extensive reading of stories, dramas, poems, and myths from diverse cultures and different time periods, students gain literary and cultural knowledge as well as familiarity with various text structures and elements. By reading texts in history/social studies, science, and other disciplines, students build a foundation of knowledge in these fields that will also give them the background to be better readers in all content areas. (National Governors Association Center for Best Practices & Council of Chief State School Officers, 2010)

Think about the texts you have chosen for read-alouds and whole-class lessons and the individual texts your students have read. How broad is the range of texts? Are multiple cultures represented? Are topics and genres varied? Do they cross disciplines? Are texts representative of all the different reasons why children read (for example, to learn jokes, to find out more about animals they love, to memorize a poem)? We cannot always select the texts we read with our students just because of our own emotional attachment to them, and our text selections cannot be haphazard or last-minute. Choosing the body of literature to which your students will be exposed will take some forward planning and a commitment to including a broad range of texts.

You can ensure that your classroom reading collection includes a broad range of texts by including the following:

- Various genres and formats, including many different informational and explanatory titles, as well as e-text

- A wide range of authors and styles

- Multiple cultures, including those represented by the children in your classroom

- Topics from multiple content areas

By exposing students to a broader range of texts, you help widen their perspectives. You open their eyes to the world. A broad range of texts invites students to become citizens of the world as they travel to faraway places and climb into the lives of people unlike themselves. A broad range of texts touches topics in the content areas and pushes students toward new understandings of the world. Most important, a broad classroom reading collection sends a clear message that a world of discovery is awaiting them in text. A tired collection sends the opposite message—that there is really no point in picking up a book.

Increasingly Complex Texts

We have to acknowledge that to be optimally college and career ready, people need the ability to rise to the challenges of those roles. The ability to read, comprehend,

and apply sophisticated text like college textbooks and training manuals is necessary for high achievement in school and work. Sadly, those who cannot read these materials are tremendously disadvantaged, as they are not only less likely to get into college or find a job, but also more likely to fail once there.

To identify a book's level of complexity, you should consider its:

- Quantitative features

- Qualitative features

- Reader and task objectives

Quantitative Features of Text

There is great debate in education about the best way to quantitatively measure the readability of text. Many measurement devices make attempts at identifying the level of readability by measuring word length, word frequency, sentence length, word familiarity, text length, and even how cohesive a text might be. You may already have a quantitative system in place in your school or district that assigns levels or scores to specific texts. Consider the possibility that the leveling system you are using could be underestimating the complexity of text because it is looking through only the quantitative lens and not taking into account the subtlety and nuance of the qualitative qualities of the text.

Quantitative features of text relate to decoding and fluency skills. Reading instruction should include attention to building these skills—the muscles all students need to develop that enable them to decode unfamiliar texts. Constant exposure to the correct levels of text, both complexity and instructional level, and purposeful instruction with these texts will help students to develop sight word vocabularies, to decode unfamiliar words, to recognize simple and complex sentence structures, and to increase their reading vocabularies—all skills that will positively affect fluency. It is equally important to remember that this is only one part of this three-part equation for text complexity, and that reading instruction should not stop here (though it very often does).

Core Principle for Text Complexity 4

All Educators Need to Use Comprehensive Methods for Determining Text Complexity

Text complexity is not accurately quantifiable. While I recognize that systems such as Lexiles assign numbers or levels to text, most of these systems reduce text to sentences and words rather than giving due consideration to thematic complexity, nuances of literature, and the reader's developing knowledge of the world. For this reason, all quantitative systems must be combined with an opportunity also to view texts through a qualitative lens to best account for such important, nonmeasurable indicators as literary devices, inference, and language use. Just because a child has the ability to read a text does not mean it is automatically an appropriate text for that child. And just because a text has a Lexile level below a child's reading ability does not mean it should not be read by that child. Theme and meaning must be factored into the calculation of text complexity and appropriateness.

Qualitative Features of Text

The *qualitative* features of text are largely subjective and are best examined through a skilled lens. The Common Core State Standards offer four qualitative factors that can help you identify the complexity of a text. Asking some key questions about the texts you are considering within each of these factors can help you narrow your focus as you choose texts for your classroom reading collection.

Levels of Meaning and Purpose

- Literature
  - What are the levels of meaning in this story?
  - What themes or lessons exist in this story?
  - Are the levels of meaning simple, or do they require some deeper analysis to access?
- Informational
  - What is the purpose of this piece?
  - Is the purpose obvious to the reader, or is it hard to figure out why it was written?
  - Who is the intended audience for this piece?

Structure

- Literature
  - What is the structure of the story?
  - Is this story told in a simple, chronological format?
  - Does this story use a more complex structure such as nonsequential storytelling or take liberties with manipulating time?
- Informational
  - Is the information presented simply, without regard to specific formats unique to certain disciplines?
  - Is the information presented according to the complex structures of specific disciplines?
  - Is the structure common to the subgenre of informational text it represents?
  - Are multiple structures included?
  - Are the graphics easy to access or do they require more complex knowledge?

Language Conventions and Clarity

- Is the language in the piece casual and easy to understand?
- Is the language in the piece more academic or professional in nature?
- Is the vocabulary in the piece complex or simple?
- Is the language in the piece more literal, or are there heavy doses of figurative language?
- Is the language in the piece modern or archaic?

Knowledge Demands

- What tasks are required for interacting with and fully comprehending the text? Are they straightforward or do they take more analytical thinking?
- Does the text assume a high level of cultural knowledge?
- Does the text assume a high level of literary knowledge?
- Does the text assume a high level of content knowledge?
- Is the text rooted in common, everyday experience or does it rely on fantasy or imagination?

Whereas the quantitative features of text relate to decoding and fluency, qualitative features of text relate to comprehension. Command of these text features ensures not only that students decode fluently, but also that they understand what they are reading in a way that enables them to deeply consider the content within, add it to their existing knowledge base, and apply it to their own lives. Without command of qualitative features of text, students will miss out on the best parts of text—the meaning.

Reader and Task Objectives

The third part of the text complexity triad includes those specific tasks that are required for a reader to fully and deeply access the texts they are reading. All texts, no matter the type, are more successful with an audience that is prepared to read them. Readers who understand the particular genre will attack a text more successfully. Readers with some background knowledge about the content will more clearly understand the messages in a text. Readers with the appropriate attention span and maturity for a text will better enjoy its contents. The

complexity of this set of skill requirements for a text dramatically affects the complexity of the text itself.

The Common Core State Standards invite you to use your own professional judgment when matching texts to individual students. Ultimately, you are the best judge of the complexity–student match. We know that all readers benefit from independent reading of text that is matched to their independent reading level. We know that struggling readers need more practice with text that is less complex, and more sophisticated readers need the challenge of exposure to more complex text. The Core Ready series includes plenty of time for leveled text reading and encourages you to use your own knowledge of literature and your familiarity with your students to do so in a way that best supports learning.

When you choose a text for independent reading, consider the cognitive abilities of your student, the purpose for the reading, and the demands of the text and ask yourself—is this a match? Does the student have the appropriate attention span for the text? Does the student have the ability to visualize and to infer, if required? Can your student hold the correct number of details in memory that might be required to fully access the text? Does this reader have the level of motivation needed to do the hard work to engage with the text? Does she have the right background knowledge in place to be able to access the meaning in the text? Is this reader interested in the content of this text? Does this reader have the language skills needed to understand the vocabulary in the text? Also give some thought to the purpose and outcome of the reading. Is the purpose of this reading for the student to learn something new, to skim it lightly for specific information, to enjoy a story? Can this reader perform that outcome task independently? Matching the right text to the reader can make a huge difference in the impact the act of reading has on her skill level.

A best fit match means that the task and purpose for reading are matched to both level and motivation. We must recognize that the levels assigned by various publishing companies can be subjective indeed, so even with that information printed on the back of the book, we must be critical readers of the levels. Don't panic! Instead, let's include our students in the assessment of text levels. Asking the students their best estimation is often a thousand times more accurate than any "expert" adult. It is also very helpful to include our students in these discussions so they become fully able to select their own best fit reads for themselves, with or without us.

Reader and task considerations about text relate to *reading processes.* As we create a comprehensive reading curriculum, we must include careful and explicit teaching into these reading processes in our lessons. Core Ready purposefully includes many opportunities for students to build reading process skills such as increasing stamina, understanding genres, and building individual reading identities—skills that will enable all students to successfully access complex texts.

Core Principle for Text Complexity 5

All Educators Need a Thorough Professional Knowledge of Literature

Administrators, curriculum developers, teachers, and anyone else planning lessons must become intimately familiar with children's literature to assess text complexity on all levels. Core Ready provides texts for every lesson selected to meet the new demands of increased text complexity as well as the interests and developmental needs of the children who will read them. Create opportunities to meet as a faculty or to gain knowledge from others, taking time to peruse texts and identify their levels and layers of complexity. Involve the children in these conversations.

Use Appendix B of the Common Core State Standards as a Tool

You may find it helpful to calibrate your concept of text complexity with the exemplar texts provided in Appendix B of the Common Core State Standards. These exemplars are not included as mandatory reading lists; they are provided as samples of what complex texts generally look like at every grade level. You do not have to include these texts in your classroom reading collection to be Common Core State Standards compliant. Instead, use the exemplar texts to guide your decisions. Obtain a few of the texts and read them analytically. Collaborate with other educators and your students to note the quantitative, qualitative, and reader and task features of these titles. This process will help you become appropriately critical of texts you might include in your lessons and help calibrate your thinking in a way that

will most align your classroom reading collection with the Common Core State Standards text complexity requirements. "Gone are the days when text was judged as difficult solely on the basis of sentence length and syllable count. We now know that many factors affect text complexity. With this increased understanding, teachers do not have to rely on intuition to figure out which books their students can handle. Instead, teachers can select texts worthy of instruction and align their instructional efforts to ensure that all their students read complex, interesting, and important texts" (Shanahan, Fisher, & Frey 2012). However, this means that teachers and curriculum coordinators must have a heightened working knowledge of the intricacies of text complexity.

put it to use

Calibrating text complexity is a powerful professional development opportunity when done in small grade-level groups. Ask each member of a grade-level team to bring one book or text to the meeting that he or she considers to be appropriately complex for the step on the staircase. Together as a group, critically analyze the text complexity of each book. Ask the qualitative questions listed on pages 73–74 and discuss them together. Compare these texts to a few of the exemplar texts listed in the Common Core State Standards.

Be a Ravenous Consumer of Children's Literature

The 21st century student deserves a 21st century teacher who knows children's literature. Although the Core Ready program provides calibrated texts in the units, you will still need the skills to choose appropriately complex texts at appropriate levels for your students. Read as much children's text as you can get your hands on. Become familiar with what is available. Find your favorite authors. Obtain lists of award winners. Find out what new titles and even new genres are hitting the scene. Know what your students want to read and bring it to them. Give yourself the gift of time to really get to know children's literature and the nuances, contexts, and trends that influence it, because your students' ability to closely read and understand grade-level text will depend on your intimate familiarity with it.

Consider some suggestions for immersing yourself in current children's literature, informational text, and e-text:

- Follow children's book review blogs.
- Follow awards news: Caldecott Medal, Newbery Medal, Young Reader's Choice Award, Children's Media Awards, Teacher's Choice Award, the Jane Addams Award, and more.
- Sign up for listservs from the American Library Association.
- Explore children's magazine websites.
- Observe the favored methods of communication of your students.
- Talk to a children's librarian.
- Sign up for emails from book distributors such as Amazon, Scholastic, or great local bookstores.
- Regularly visit e-text websites for children's books offered online, such as www.wegivebooks.org and others.

Invite Your Students to Take a Seat and Enjoy the View

Increasing text complexity at every grade level and acknowledging that every student has a fundamental right to fully access complex texts requires creative methodology by knowledgeable teachers. As though they are visitors

Core Principle for Text Complexity 6

All Students Need to Develop Strong Personal Reading Identities

Reading is more than rote skill. It is a dynamic combination of decoding and comprehension skills, stamina, and independence building. For this reason, it is crucial that students be given ample opportunity not only to read complex texts, but also to discover who they are and where they need to go as readers. Help them discover their reading preferences, joys, and passions. Elevate their awareness of their thinking and processes as they read. Encourage them to reflect on their strengths and needs as readers, and guide them to set and work toward personal goals as readers. All of this, combined with engagement with appropriately complex texts and the skills within the Core Standards State Standards, will help students become truly independent college- and career-ready readers.

to the Spanish Steps in Rome, we want to give our students the opportunity to enjoy the view while ascending at their maximum capacity. We need to structure our time and strategies in ways that meet the text complexity demands of the Common Core State Standards, but we also need to understand research about what works in reading instruction and be sure we are both raising expectations and being humane and realistic all at the same time. We can do it all.

chapter 6

Mastering Argument and Evidence

"Research is formalized curiosity. It is poking and prying
with a purpose. It is a seeking that he who wishes may know
the cosmic secrets of the world and they that dwell therein."
— Zora Neale Hurston

Though the word *argument* is already familiar and ingrained in our vocabulary, we sometimes forget that it is still important to ask the question, "What is an argument?" Like many words in the English language, *argument* can be interpreted in countless ways depending on who is giving the definition. For instance, children might commonly associate this word with verbal altercations regarding which is the superior genre of music or who has the bigger slice of cake. With respect to the Common Core State Standards, we want to eliminate any negative, combative connotations that might be conjured with the word *argument*. Instead, our students will define writing an argument as an invaluable way to express to the world what they find truly important, what matters to them.

The Pen (or Keyboard) Is Mightier Than the Sword

Writing well and being able to express our ideas articulately is how we present ourselves to the world. It is how we form relationships, stand up for justice, communicate well with others, and effect real and lasting change. It is also how we feel understood and connected to the world—or misunderstood and misinterpreted. Our students have no shortage of opinions, passion, and enthusiasm and we want to teach ways to harness this emotion into a well-structured, meticulously researched piece of work. The Common Core State Standards ensure that our children develop techniques to capture the ideas in their wonderful brains and relate them effectively to an audience. They learn the difference between writing to inform, writing to persuade, and writing to narrate, and come to understand the value of using their writing as an outlet to command the world's attention.

Before they begin to write their own arguments, students must obtain a sense of flavor and structure by reading a wide variety of persuasive and argumentative texts. The goal is for students to quantify what it is about a particular argument that resonates with them and understand that the author has chosen her language carefully and with purpose to deliver impact with each word. The text complexity dictated by the Common Core State Standards highlights that an argument can take many different forms and transcend genres. Persuasive essays overtly appeal to our emotions and unabashedly declare an opinion, whereas commentary and opinions can be offered in a more subtle manner, even in poems and picture books. Pablo Neruda's "Ode to My Socks" is a persuasive text. Never before in the history of literature has such a compelling case been made about the power of one tiny clothing item!

In this exploratory phase, students are not passively reading each word just to get done. They are dissecting what an author is really trying to say and investigating the underlying message of a text. They are attempting to pinpoint why one text seems to resonate with them more deeply than another. They will respond to the material, quantifying how they feel about it. We **want** our students to wrestle with a text—not to build frustration, but to savor the excitement that reading brings when we attempt to answer all the different "whys" that surface when reading.

The following are examples of open-ended questions that guide students in their search to uncover the meaning behind a piece of writing:

1. List the three most important events. Which of these events is the most important? Why?

2. Why did the author write about this topic? What else would you want to know about this topic?

3. Think about how the character (or narrator) changed over time. Predict what will happen next.

4. How does this reading reveal this author's attitudes and beliefs?

5. What evidence does the author provide for his statements?

6. As used in this text, what does this phrase "_____" mean?

7. What is the central idea of the passage?

8. What is the theme of this passage?

9. What do you think the author's point of view is?

10. How would the story be different if it were told from another point of view?

11. Why do characters make the choices they make?

Writing to Be Heard

Consider how many magazines, newspapers, blog posts, and books exist in the world—billions. With so many options available to a reader, students must command attention to have their voices heard. This is accomplished by having a solid grasp on how the elements and structure of an argument ensure all paragraphs answer the fundamental question "Why am I writing?" Before a student begins to write, he should take the time to outline his argument. In addition to succinctly answering why he is writing, he must flesh out a list of arguments in favor of his point of view and potential counterarguments or rebuttals.

An argument consists of an introduction, body, and conclusion, with each part containing a unique structure and layout. The introduction must grab a reader by her shirt collar with both hands and compel her to listen. The more technical term for this is a *lead*. Making a bold statement or giving a brief anecdote are effective tools that could be used. Next, the reader is given a preview of both sides of an argument, succinctly capturing why debate exists about this issue to begin with. The final element of the introductory paragraph is the claim, a concise sentence summarizing the author's stance on the issue and what the remaining paragraphs will attempt to prove.

The body paragraphs should each tackle one supporting point and cite specific, relevant, and meaningful evidence collected from research. A strong argumentative writer assumes she is addressing a skeptical audience and that the burden of proof falls on her shoulders. Therefore, the student must devote the body of the text to her argument, supported with facts gleaned during research.

The following is a persuasive essay written by a grade 5 student that resonates emotionally while incorporating evidence and backing. Take some time to identify the elements listed at the end of the previous section and evaluate whether the author is effective at communicating his point of view. Does the introduction grab your attention and compel you to keep reading? Does the author use logical arguments supported by evidence? Does he refute counterarguments?

Smoking (Wheeze) Is (Cough) Bad by Nick P.

If murder is illegal then why isn't smoking illegal?

Every day after school I walk past a huddle of Hastings High School kids on Mt. Hope Boulevard. They hide between two cars; the boys are wearing leather jackets and jeans, the girls shivering in their short skirts and parkas. I hold my breath, start my engines, and run past them. They're smoking. Yick! Why do they do that? I guess it probably feels cool to smoke. The high schoolers sure think so, 28% of high schoolers smoke nationwide!

How many movies have you seen in your life? How many had characters smoking in them? Why do movies have to have smoking to be cool? Can't they just not have smoking? Let's say you idolize a movie character and that movie character smokes. You want to be just like him. So what the movie did was convince you to smoke and basically kill yourself. If smoking was illegal that couldn't happen. You wouldn't be able to advertise smoking. How come it is against the law to advertise smoking in T.V. commercials, but you can advertise it secretly by making cool characters smoke in movies and on T.V. shows. Isn't that wrong?

I loved my Grandma Anne so much, but smoking took her away from me. I was only five when she died at 54 of lung cancer. My whole family was miserable. 400,000 people die from smoking each year; that's more than AIDS, car accidents, murder, and alcohol put together. Yet

3,000 kids start smoking every day. Eighty-nine percent of people who smoke, try cigarettes by the age of 18. But seventy percent of teenage smokers say they wouldn't have started smoking if they could choose again. Maybe if we can convince kids to not start smoking, then there won't be smoking in our future, and our loved ones won't die.

While I am sad that people die from smoking every year, it isn't just the smoker who can get sick. People who breathe in second hand smoke damage their lungs too. Smokers have a choice not to smoke, but the people around the smokers don't. Second hand smoke is even worse than smoking. Did you know that second hand smoke has more than 4,000 chemicals in it, and more than 60 of them are known to cause cancer? I interviewed my classmate Jared, age 10, and asked him what he thinks about smoking. He said, "I think smoking should be illegal because it kills other people and they don't have a choice not to breathe in second hand smoke." Also he said, "If I ran into a smoker I would cover my nose, blow out my cheeks, hold my breath, and make a big impression that smoking is bad."

People usually start smoking when they are kids. They think it is cool from movies and T.V. and it's not illegal, so they think there is nothing to worry about. But there is. Smoking can kill you. It can kill the people around you who breathe in your smoke. And if you die from smoking, the people who love you will have to suffer too. So, I hope that if you were considering smoking, you've changed your mind. For the good of mankind.

More Than a Feeling

For most students, just hearing the word *research* can feel boring. However, to have any credibility with an audience, students must justify their claim with evidence. Without a doubt, there is a very personal nature to a piece of argumentative writing—after all, if a child were not truly invested in the topic, then she would not be writing to sway the audience. This emotional element is crucial, but an audience will not be convinced to accept a point of view that is backed up with "Because I said so!" More important, it is possible to uncover evidence that changes one's own opinion. First and foremost, a student must have an intimate, in-depth understanding of all sides of an issue to convince herself that her stance is truly the best stance.

Highlighting the importance of research is also an effective way to build students' confidence as they prepare to share their opinions with an audience. It can often feel daunting to openly declare one's beliefs. We worry about the reaction of those who disagree with us. The antidote for this insecurity is research. Thorough research leads to an in-depth understanding of an issue and exposes children to the many perspectives and intricacies attached to their subject matter. It is much easier and far less stressful to defend an opinion if a student has taken the time to analyze the topic from many different angles and can anticipate counterarguments and readily validate his position with proof. Like rehearsing for a play or studying for a spelling test, research leads to successful outcomes. Undertaking full-bodied research goes hand in hand with another key idea: not allowing a single story to shape our entire viewpoint. To form conclusions that have any hope of persuading an audience, students must gather evidence from multiple sources encountered during vigorous research.

To avoid the feeling of information overload, the following tool is a simple way for students to catalog evidence and organize their thoughts. This can bring to light which information is relevant to an argument and which isn't.

Fact	Source	Explanation	My Thoughts	Counterclaim

It Looks Like a Duck, but Best to Make It Quack Anyway

Paired with research comes the task of identifying credible sources. With all the different digital and print resources available, students need to understand when information is reliable and can be considered an acceptable academic reference and when it is merely an author's opinion. Students should know, for

example, how Wikipedia differs from a scholarly journal or a personal blog and what purpose each of these serves when students are learning about a subject.

In many instances, information can be presented in a physically pleasing manner that seems plausible. However, Core Ready learners will pay attention to their sense of skepticism and look past the superficial appeal of written material to identify when information has been skewed to suit a particular agenda. Again, this is a skill that students will perfect with practice that comes from reading constantly and engaging in relevant discussion. Students will learn to assess the overall treatment of data and decide if it is a fair representation of facts, or if it requires further investigation.

Opponent Is Not a Synonym for Enemy

As satisfying as it feels to place the final period at the end of the concluding sentence of a written piece, this is not the end of the story. The entire purpose for writing a persuasive or argumentative piece is to appeal to an audience and communicate an idea that ignites a discussion. For some children, it might feel daunting to offer their lovingly crafted piece to an audience that may level critiques and counterarguments. Indeed, great vulnerability comes with taking a strong stance. However, we must instill within our students the idea that opposing views are not personal attacks but instead learning opportunities. This should start with whole-class discussions about what it means to argue respectfully and how to have a productive, meaningful debate. It is hard, especially when an issue feels personal, to remember that unlike our early ancestors—or our early selves—we cannot resort to hair pulling, name calling, or clubbing the other party over the head with a rock. Once the class has agreed on certain guidelines to structure their discourse, they can disband into smaller groups to begin deconstructing one another's arguments. It is natural that children may still feel timid or uncomfortable, but with continual practice, sharing and debating will transform into enriching experiences in which every voice can speak freely without fear of being attacked or demeaned.

Think about how remarkable it would be if grown-ups subscribed to this mentality. Consider the last political debate you watched on television. How did the candidates behave? Did you leave feeling informed or frustrated? Did the candidates seem open to discussion or closed off, ready to defend their speaking points by any means necessary? Often they deflect a direct question with an attack on their opponent's voting history or simply answer in such a convoluted manner that the initial question is forgotten. In the current political climate, it is seen as a weakness for a candidate to acknowledge strength in an opponent's argument and respond critically. Of course, it is also a matter of pride. Since we cannot force grown men and women to go back to elementary school and graduate through the Common Core State Standards, we can view these standards as an opportunity to raise a generation that is better at arguing and debating—one that will adhere to higher standards.

But Wait! There's More

Do you ever feel, as you wait in line to buy the latest technological gadget, that by the time the cashier hands you the receipt a newer version will emerge from the stockroom? We live in an age of information, but as the information changes, our greatest strength is knowing how to research and use evidence to bolster our opinions. Research is continuous. It should be happening all the time. Students must make it a routine to revisit their arguments and opinions, not only as new research is published, but also after participating in discussion with peers or receiving feedback from other sources. Core Ready students will absorb new information and decide how it affects their current argument. Do they need to reformulate an argument or does the current evidence remain strong? Perhaps the main points are valid but need to be explained from a different angle to have a greater impact on the audience.

From the Very Youngest Age, Argument Begins

Our youngest students can practice their skills of argument from the very youngest age. They are natural researchers, natural builders of ideas, and naturally passionate. Through the power of the read-aloud, they can be encouraged to have opinions and seek evidence from the pictures in the text. "How do you know the character is feeling sad?" we might ask. And the response can be: "I noticed on that page that the character is not smiling." Through our modeled thinking, we can demonstrate to them many more examples of this kind that are organic to a great read-aloud. In writing, even our youngest students have their own topics, questions, and interests. My student Fiona, who is 6 years old, was preoccupied because her grandfather had to go to a nursing home. She first pursued this concern by researching nursing homes, finding out how many there are in the United States. Then she did her primary research by asking her grandpa how he liked it there. He said he liked it because the food was pretty good. She used this as the cornerstone of her argument, which was to say that nursing homes were not so bad after all and that an old person could get good care there. As adorable as this is—and it is!—the real point here is that Fiona at age 6 could go through all the processes a writer goes through, starting with a

question or idea that drives her writing, researching to gain information, building a claim or an argument, and then proving it with further evidence. Fiona did all that in first grade. The staircase of complexity is waiting for her to ascend it. She can take those skills used early in her Core Ready classroom and carry them with her as her opinions and perspectives grow and change, until the complexity of her understandings and her writing coalesce to create ideas and compelling arguments that could indeed change the world.

---

colleague conversation   **Be the Student!**

Select a topic that matters to you: gardening, cooking, history, sports, etc. Now fill in this chart, and share with a colleague.

My Topic
....
....

What I Know about My Topic
....
....

My Argument
....
....

Evidence That Bolsters My Argument
....
....

What I Want to Share with My Colleagues
....
....

chapter 7

Mastering Technology and New Media

"For I dipped into the future, far as human eye could see, Saw a vision of the world, and all the wonder it would be"
— Alfred, Lord Tennyson

"I'm interested in the way in which the past affects the present and I think that if we understand a good deal more about history, we automatically understand a great more about contemporary life."
— Toni Morrison

As a teacher, you already know that new media is constantly revolutionizing ideas about reading and literacy in general. But what are best practice methods for teaching new media literacy? What do you need to know about how students are already interacting with technology? In this chapter, I outline key precepts about new media learning and how it is reflected in the Common Core State Standards.

"Traditional notions of literacy, based squarely on the printed word, are rapidly giving way to multiple ideas of what constitutes literate activity. It is now common to use the plural—literacies— to refer to a range of concepts, including visual, digital, and others" (Robinson & McKenna, 2007, p. 253). Our students need to navigate an ever-expanding technological landscape. Thoughtful, carefully considered teaching will help them greatly along the way.

We often equate the word *innovation* with technology and new media, but simply putting technology in our rooms or giving our students access to YouTube does not necessarily constitute innovation. The new era and the Common Core State Standards have an expectation that we bring technology and new media into our classrooms in a thoughtful manner to maximize the students' ability to use these new tools to communicate in new and different ways. *How* we communicate and *what* we communicate using the new technology are at the heart of the new digital media. Instruction should foster the critical thinking skills students need to navigate technology and to integrate media into the life of the classroom. This can all be creative, fun, and truly innovative—or it can all feel as lifeless as a worksheet of vocabulary words. The latter is not the intention of the Common Core State Standards.

Take a simple pencil. It too can be either a tool for innovation, or a tool to merely reiterate old ideas. A pencil can be used to create great ideas and deepen

thought, or it can be used to fill in the blanks. The same is true of a computer. Technology can cause imagination to deteriorate or to blossom. If it is used in a rote manner, technology will not only fail to increase critical thought, it will hinder it.

But when technology and innovation meet the inquiring, active mind of the student and the open and flexible mind of the teacher, the reaction can be dynamic and thrilling.

One major development in media literacy education is that the teacher is no longer the gatekeeper—the sole guardian of all the information to be passed down to the student. Now the student has access too. The learning can be co-created and co-constructed. We should not be afraid, nor should we try to hold or control information too tightly. It is time to make use of all forms of media and campaign for access to the technology it requires to gain access to it, to help us learn to teach in new ways and to become more fully a part of the students' lives outside of school.

Student Uses of Technology and Media

If we are to mirror what students are doing outside of school as innovative experimenters with technology and new media—and also set an example they can follow—we need to identify how they are using technology and new media in their lives and be conscious as to what they are doing to feel purposeful and successful. In my ongoing conversations with students of all ages, I have determined three major ways students seek to use technology and media to enhance and uplift their lives.

1. To Communicate and Collaborate with Others

Our students learn to use technology and new media to *collaborate* with one another, and beyond that, to *network* far and wide, both down the hall to their friends in another classroom and across the world to their friends in Kenya.

As you know, email, Facebook, LinkedIn, Google Docs, Twitter, and other tools—including the new tools that come on the scene every day—provide ways to get in touch, be in touch, and stay in touch. But soon enough there will thousands of new tools to connect us. The teacher should serve as a co-facilitator and curator of the many resources available for bringing people together. Your students might collaborate on a project with students in Europe, they might post videos of school performances, they might watch live broadcasts of momentous political events. The Bricks in Space program has astronauts assemble Lego sets at the International Space Station in microgravity, as students around the globe watch and analyze their findings. During the 2011 uprising in Egypt, teenagers posted live updates on Facebook and Twitter, making sure that the rest of the globe could witness what was happening. Online communication has the ability to do tremendous good.

Technology can help students form meaningful connections by, for example, Skyping with children at a partner school on another continent. It can also weave connections within your own classroom. You might create an online forum about a class project or email students comments on their essays. The goal in all of this is to make communication stronger, clearer, and wider.

2. To Consume and Create

Our students learn to use technology/new media to *absorb* something new, to *consume* ideas and content, and to *create* their own new information and ideas. Students can chase their interests across the Internet, perform research online, encounter wonders and curiosities, and construct their own ideas.

A young friend of mine recently found an online archive of real letters written home by Civil War soldiers. Another stumbled on the work of Jacques Henri Lartigue, a French photographer and daredevil who built his own airplanes.

Learning online might take the form of leisurely exploration or hyperfocused research. Similarly, sharing ideas might mean submitting an essay to an academic website or simply creating a Tumblr account.

Navigating blogs, websites, YouTube, Wikipedia, and databases requires strong literacy skills because our students are not only absorbing information, but also making qualitative decisions about what to keep and what to let go, as well as what they like and do not like. By being active online—adding to, challenging, or agreeing with what they encounter—our students develop their writing voices. In the Core Ready series, I place a strong emphasis on opinion and argument, not just to align with the Common Core State Standards as they are written, but also because in this lively and chattering world, students have to be confident and self-assured as they navigate this unprecedented flow of information, deciding what they want and need from it and finding their own place.

3. To Curate and Collate

Our students *aggregate* and *organize* their data, ideas, and frequently visited sites. Even the youngest children are already learning to do this, and want to do it. Students use tools to contain and manage a wild and seemingly endless bounty of information, becoming selective and thoughtful in the process. Here they can like, share, and pronounce something a favorite. They are constantly sifting, culling, and making decisions.

We all crave systems to enhance our lives and learning and to warm up what could otherwise be cold and impersonal technology. Organizing systems help us think about technology and media as forms of sharing, teamwork, innovation, and inspiration. We save links to our favorite blogs, follow certain people on Twitter, share photos on Instagram, and create scrapbooks on Pinterest. Such sites and applications are systems that help us organize our thinking, reading, writing, speaking, listening, and viewing. Without them we would be lost. Students can do a great deal of self-directed learning in this process, but we need to guide them toward mastery.

The gaming expert Jane McGonigal presented a TED talk (a speech at a Technology, Entertainment, and Design conference) in 2010 on the power of online gaming as a source for inspiration for young people (McGonigal,

2010). She said the average teen spends 10,000 hours gaming by the age of 21, the exact amount of time students spend in school from fifth grade to high school graduation—an entire parallel track of engagement and motivation that students experience outside of formal school. McGonigal identifies four areas of strength she has observed in young people as they engage in online gaming:

1. They all have a sense of "urgent optimism," confidence the outcome will be productive and a feeling that if they focus, they will be rewarded, leading to high levels of self-motivation.

2. The online community helps them "weave a tight social fabric"; they learn to trust people, play by rules, and build strong social relationships.

3. They are "blissfully productive"; having meaningful "work" makes them happy and feels fruitful.

4. They see themselves as creating "epic meaning"; that is, they are building the world of a story and producing something in the playing of the game.

I like how these young people are describing their experiences. Do not get me wrong—I am not advocating the replacement of reading a glorious book aloud with incessant video game playing! I do, however, believe we have something to learn from these findings and that what they are telling us can and should have an impact on our work. The Common Core State Standards prompt us to reconsider the purposes for reading, writing, speaking, and listening so that they can more deeply and effectively connect with one another and be sincerely motivated in their work. Learning to read, write, speak, and listen *should* be all about urgent optimism, social fabrics, productivity, and creating epic meaning together. If you think about the purpose and value of reading and writing in this way, it really is about learning optimism, creating community, being productive, and creating stories that have epic meaning. Children can do this from the start. Kindergarteners know better than anyone through their play in a dress-up box what it means to build community and create epic meaning. The tools they use as they grow should continue to further those strengths.

The National Association for Media Literacy Education (2012) has many wise words to share on the important subject of how we can help our students become masterful readers, writers, speakers, and listeners in the supercharged space of the Internet. I recommend a visit to the association's site, www.namle.net.

Talking Points for Faculty Meetings

As you discuss these crucial issues with your colleagues, here are some key talking points for you to use in your faculty meetings when discussing some of the main ways education in general is changing and is going to change even more over the next few years. Use these as jumping-off points for larger discussions in your learning communities—conversations that don't feel riddled by anxiety, but rather feel empowered by the changes yet to come.

1. *Your students are consumers and producers of text outside of school, so they must be consumers and producers of text inside of school.* Media literacy education includes both consuming and producing text online. The dynamic exchange online is a give and take, a breathing in and out—much like reading, writing, speaking, and listening themselves are. In this way, the dialogue is always a transaction. The media viewer/reader/listener is taking in and absorbing the universe of ideas. The media creator/writer/speaker is engaging with the universe of ideas and adding some of his or her own. Even the youngest child is creating online, making new ideas, drawings, and messages. It is a give *and* take, right from the beginning. This is a great motivation for our students; they can see themselves in an interactive world where one day they can write a story for a friend and the next day they can get information on giraffes from another friend a long, long distance away. It is nearly miraculous.

According to O'Mara and Laidlaw (2011), this generation of students has a much different understanding of text than did previous generations. Though in the past we have thought of text as fixed and constant, 21st century students come into school with a very different mindset. The 21st century student clearly understands that text in this modern world is dynamic and must be viewed critically. The dynamism of modern text is what has shifted. Traditional text was presented to the reader by a creator/authority in a linear manner to dispense knowledge, with the writer as creator and the reader as recipient. The new text, though, is valued not just for what it says, but also for what it symbolically represents and how it interacts with and acts as a catalyst for other textual experiences the reader has. "Text is designed by producer and redesigned by reader. . . . [I]ts value is in its potential usefulness" (O'Mara & Laidlaw, 2011, p. 156).

2. *Your students are constantly learning how to use new tools outside of school, so we too must learn them, so we can all use them inside of school.* As the tools evolve and our understanding of them evolves, our teaching is going to have to evolve along with them. It will not be enough to learn how a new technology tool works and then stick with that. The world is moving much too quickly. What is new today will not be new tomorrow, and while that can seem exhausting at times, it can also be exhilarating. Use your own personal passions as a guide for you to learn about the latest tools and resources. Whether it is gar-

dening or cooking, fixing cars or reading poetry, find something and explore it online. Seek out all the new ways people are sharing ideas about this passion. Play around with what tools really work for you in supporting your passion. Then bring those tools into classroom life and into the ways you interact with your students between home and school. The website Pinterest started as a forum for people obsessed with home decor to share ideas with one another, and by 2011 had become a powerhouse tool for individuals to share everything from fashion to design to education. Similarly, Twitter started out as a charming, yet somewhat fringe, resource for people who wanted to say clever things about celebrities, but its importance as a medium has grown so much that it is an absolutely integral part of the 2012 presidential campaign. You never know where these tools will lead, but be part of the game. Use faculty meetings to share your favorite passion and what

new tools you are experimenting with that might have great potential for the classroom.

I campaign for much greater access in schools to online resources and sites that facilitate sharing. It is becoming troublesome and a huge barrier to the open-air forums representing the best in education these days to prevent access. But with that openness comes a tremendous responsibility, and we can only prepare our students to use the Internet wisely through thoughtful, regular practice in which we coach and assist our students in making good decisions and in navigating the complex terrain of the online world.

3. *Your students are growing up in a global society and the use of technology and new media promotes global citizenship.* "Media Literacy Education explores representations, misrepresentations, and lack of representation of cultures and countries in the global community" (National Association for Media Literacy Education, 2009, p. 5). The CCSS also emphasize a future in which every career- and college-ready student must be well prepared to play on the global playground, in which we understand one another through literature, informational text, dialogue, discourse, and debate; and how we can reach out to one another through all the channels now at our disposal. Our children are going to grow up in this global community. They most surely will work alongside, albeit virtually, neighbors from Baghdad to Bangkok, from New York City to Nice, from Shanghai to Shreveport. Media literacy education lays the groundwork for the world to come, teaching our children about people near and far by sharing information through viewing, reading, writing, and listening.

As Luke (2007) suggests, "children need to be educated as 'global cosmopolitan citizens' who are growing up processing multiple digital information sources at once, in their time outside of school, and as a result are developing abilities that may be less familiar to the adults around them." (O'Mara & Laidlaw, 2011, p. 157).

4. *The very nature of technology and new media turns us all into learners; let yourself learn something new every day about how reading, writing, speaking, and listening can be applied differently with the new tools at our disposal.* Modern technology calls for more fluid exploration and approximation. Even the most sophisticated programmers are still guessing about what will work and what will not. The dot-com mentality is very much one of an entrepreneurial spirit. Let's bring this to our teaching and to our students' learning. Working in tandem with students and remaining open to what they might contribute to lessons that involve technology and new media—letting go of the idea that we need to be in full control all the time—can have the positive effect of inviting additional opportunities for discovery for both student and teacher. Educators "might turn to their students to learn through observing young peoples' competencies with these technologies and then working these into their pedagogical practices with their students as collaborators" (O'Mara & Laidlaw, 2011, p. 152).

Making It Fun

I end this chapter with some really straightforward tips for how you can best accompany students on this journey toward Common Core State Standards success via the information superhighway. At the end of the day, I very much want you to have fun with this. Yes, that is right—fun! Good, deep work should feel a lot like play, and with technology and new media, we have a chance to make the work we do in reaching the goals of the Common Core State Standards feel like a whole lot of fun. And here they are, Pam's Tips for How to Have Fun but Take It Really Seriously:

1. *Be explicit.* Though in many cases students may know more about technology than you do, do not assume they have it all figured out. They may not. They are learners and explorers too, and even if you are a co-facilitator more than a guide, that is OK. You can ease the process for your students by modeling your reading, writing, *and* navigation skills.

   We cannot assume all of our students know how to navigate through various sites, research effectively online, craft the best question, wade through a complex website, or find their way back to their original point of entry. Though they may know how to *use* technological devices, they may not have fully developed critical media literacy skills that allow them to sort information or make connections that are valuable. A 3-year-old can turn the pages of a book, but this does not mean he is critically literate. Having access at one's fingertips does not mean the student is an "expert reader" of that modality. Because of this, we must allow time for addressing media skills specifically. This work can be easily done during reading and writing time because it is so much a part of it. Reserve 5 or 7 minutes a day and call it "media work." Use this time to create a sample search question or topic to explore. Then together with your students craft new questions, explore new information, and navigate across different sites. Let each session be a quick case study. In this way, you inspire high levels of motivation and a sense of mutual discovery in your learning community. The technology is going to be ever-changing; it is not going to stay static. So media literacy is not about learning how to use one tech tool or the other; it is about learning what to do with what we have and how to make what we have feel rich and meaningful for all of us. And if you do not have it? If your school has not yet bought computers, or you are blocked from gaining access to most of the incredible sites teachers are using? You have to fight for it all. Access to the Internet and available resources is part of the issue of student rights and what it means to give all kids a quality education. We must get a lot more feisty than we currently are. Look at the nicest private schools. Do they skimp on technology? Do they ban mobile devices from the classroom? I can assure you they do not. Remember the core values of the Common Core State Standards. All children deserve a level playing field. And that is what technology and new media can help to give them.

2. *Give up some control and join students as a co-explorer.* Provide opportunities for students to follow their own passions and interests with the tools of technology and new media. This is the way they would interact with technology outside of school, so it should be the way they interact with it inside of school too. Offer chances for students to use technology in the same ways you would—to explore a topic of interest, to find something out, to challenge an opinion, to declare something about themselves. Interactions

with technology in school should not be so limiting as to create a mismatch between the activity and the power of the tool itself. Browsing the Internet is not a finite activity. We never know what we will find when we enter a topic into a search engine. In those 7 minutes a day of "media work," let students practice getting really good at crafting a question for a Google search. In those minutes, give them the opportunity to swim in the sea of their very favorite subject, whether it is dogs or soccer or flavors of ice cream. No topic is too small to browse and explore online, and that is exactly the fun of it. Haven't you had moments of sheer glory when you have come up with the name of that actor in the TV show from the 1980s you and your friends were trying to figure out over dinner? That is exactly the point! Seek out questions you and your students together want answers for, not just predetermined questions that might bore all of you a little bit.

Invite students to share their favorite online resources. What are their favorite apps and why? What do they use most frequently at home? What games do they play? How do they communicate with their friends? What sites do they visit for information? What are the most popular ways they use technology and new media to relax? I have found dozens of truly fun apps and sites through my young friends in schools, from kindergarten on up. They are delighted to share the information with you and even more delighted to see you trying them with the community.

3. *Help students to view technology as a tool that delivers text, not as the text itself.* In too many classrooms, technology instruction is tacked on to the curriculum as yet another subject. I do not see it this way. Instead, we need to think of media literacy as an integral part of the literacy curriculum and technology as a tool for delivering those lessons. It should be wholly integrated in all that we do as we address reading, writing, speaking, and listening with our students. We would not think of teaching "book use" as a comprehensive approach to reading instruction, and we should not feel as though teaching "computer use" constitutes the teaching of technology and new media literacy skills.

Media literacy involves many more literacy skills than turning on a computer or navigating a website. Students can access many different types of text through the window of technology, so they need to develop the skills

to recognize, read, navigate, and create these types of texts. This requires an understanding of the purposes of these texts, their benefits and limitations, their intended audiences, and the requirements for their composition.

4. *Model respect and care for the tools themselves as deliverers of valuable gifts.* The rules around the handling and care of the tools should reflect that the device should be treated respectfully but not differently from how one would take good care of any other tool. According to O'Mara and Laidlaw (2011, p. 156), "any 'rules' for usage [should be] based on very practical concerns where the aim is very clear—taking turns with a sibling, taking care with the device so as not to break it, putting it away when done—all practices that tend to be very similar to practices around use of toys and other materials in the home, and thus these do not stand out as 'special' rules for a 'special device.'"

Whatever your feelings are about technology, it is not only here to stay; it is evolving by the minute. The e-reader today will look quite different tomorrow. For these reasons, we need to take regular time and be patient with helping our students know how to use the many new tools and to introduce them to the new features. When you feel your students are not getting easy access to the tools at home, be sure to assist them in school in teaching them handling skills and to show them how you regard the tools with the care and reverence such important devices require. Just because they are cold and look technical doesn't mean they do not carry the same kinds of gifts the front and back covers of books did in the days of yore. Your reverence for the tools helps students value what is inside them too.

Be Core Ready: The Worldwide Web of Interconnectedness

Being college- and career-ready means that our students must be fully prepared to study and work with people they may never meet and who may not share their language. Through new media and technology, they will be able to collaborate and connect. Now that our students can easily engage in a worldwide dialogue from as early as kindergarten, it is all the more critical that we educate them, and help them to educate themselves about what it means to be a global citizen. By researching and exploring the cultures and lives of people near and far, our students strengthen their curiosity and empathy. The Core Ready program in the series that follows this book honors the lives of people around the world through the extraordinary resource of children's literature, exposing them to the stories and cultures of people who live far and wide, near and close. The program also studies the evidence and facts of histories and cultures so that our students grow knowledgeable about people and ideas of different perspectives. Poets such as Naomi Shihab Nye and Pablo Neruda have taught us that the global voice represents the voice of humanity. Technology and new media help all of us get closer to these goals of the Common Core State Standards by making it possible for our students to actually interact with people everywhere, not just to read about them. The series offers both high- and low-tech options for lessons, because although this chapter is a call to action, I know we are not quite there yet. You will see that even without the latest tool, you can introduce your students to the high-level thinking skills outlined in this chapter.

We can no longer see literacy—reading, writing, speaking, and listening—as one or two dimensional. It is three or four or five dimensional. It refracts across space, casting a dazzling, powerful net. It is mixed up, chaotic, and, best of all, completely sensible.

chapter 8

Implementing Core Ready Lessons

"Practice means to perform, over and over again in the face of all obstacles, some act of vision, of faith, of desire. Practice is a means of inviting the perfection desired."

—Martha Graham

What Are Lesson Sets and How Can We Best Use Them?

I have long advocated that teachers organize their English language arts teaching within a yearlong calendar of preplanned topics of study in which students have extended time to explore big ideas critical to becoming successful readers and writers. In my earliest years of teaching, I created for the teachers with whom I worked what I called "Seasons of the Year," my very first attempt to organize a structure for my lessons. The teaching of reading and writing seemed so amorphous and I was trying to see how I could create a flow to the year, rather than jumping from isolated skill to isolated skill as the spirit moved me. As I clustered lessons around important ideas, I found myself feeling more confident and bold in my teaching, knowing that I was framing my teaching around major outcomes.

A Core Ready lesson set is a specific cycle of deliberately connected lessons that relate to a specific topic. Teacher and students are clear about the goals and why they are engaged in learning. The teaching within lesson sets feels authentic; the learning feels natural. Teacher and students work side by side, journeying together, exploring, mining new discoveries. The activities within the lesson set relate back to the goals and focus student efforts on practicing and achieving these goals for an extended period of time. Lesson sets offer students a clear beginning and ending, and students enjoy the cyclical nature of the year—a new beginning, hard work, and an ending celebration that gives way to another new beginning.

Well-planned, cohesive lesson sets represent effective teaching practice by providing students with optimal learning conditions needed for becoming college and career ready. In 1988, Brian Cambourne described eight conditions for optimal literacy learning based on his extensive research. Turner (1995) built on this foundation by providing a similar set of conditions for motivating learners in an English language arts classroom. This research was summarized and expanded by Morrow and Tracey in 1998 and may be seen in Figure 8.1. The Core Ready lesson sets rest on this research. Let's use Cambourne's conditions for learning to frame the description of how the Core Ready program represents effective practices.

Figure 8.1 Activities That Motivate Language Learning

- Purposeful, participatory lessons: Give students a role in their learning by letting them know the long-term goals of lessons. Lessons should be motivational and interesting, and should provide clear pathways to deeper understandings.

- Opportunities for collaboration: Students learn best when truly engaged in the relationship of learning—working with a teacher in individual conferences and small groups, as well as working alongside peers to create meaningful products and outcomes.

- Creation of work done independently: Give students time to practice and develop the skills being taught. Make sure they have access to relevant materials and supportive coaching when needed. Work done by the student both at home and in school that is fully created by the student leads to a sense of self-worth.

- Accomplishable goals: The learning should challenge the students but be achievable, leading to the kind of exhilarating success that comes from striving and completing realistic goals.

Source: Based on D. H. Tracey & L. M. Morrow (1998). "Motivating Contexts for Young Children's Literacy Development," in *Word Recognition in Beginning Literacy* (J. L. Metsala & L. C. Ehri, eds.).

- *Immersion.* Each lesson set begins with introductory lessons, which provide students the opportunity to explore what the lesson set is all about right from the beginning. Whether in a study of character development, cause and effect, or elements of fantasy, students activate prior knowledge and begin to build foundational understandings of the lesson set topic and how it relates to their world. Across the entirety of the lesson set, students are fully immersed in the topic and invited to become inquisitive about it. Tools and opportunities are provided for this quest, such as quality literature, explicit models of what students are expected to produce, and purposeful talk about the focus of study.

- *Demonstration.* Every day, Core Ready teachers show students explicitly what good readers and writers *do*. Teachers model and reveal the inner thoughts of an effective reader or writer, highlighting the processes of *how* successful reading and writing is done. Think-alouds, text excerpts, graphic organizers, writing samples, charts, and visual aids are just a sampling of the tools used to demonstrate the skills and strategies students need to achieve the goals of the lesson set.

- *Engagement.* The key to achievement in any endeavor is practice. The Core Ready lesson structure reminds us as teachers to "get off the stage" when the demonstration is done and allow the students plenty of time to actively engage in the reading, writing, listening, and speaking behaviors we have modeled. A sufficient amount of practice time is essential for students to develop the capacities of English language arts literacy. The lesson set structure and daily activities include ample time for students to practice the essential skills they need to meet the Common Core State Standards. This is the most critical time within which teachers can assess and coach progress and differentiate instruction to meet the needs of the diverse learners present in every classroom.

- *Expectation.* Each Core Ready lesson set suggests standards-aligned, developmentally appropriate expectations for student performance. Standards-aligned milestone assessment checklists and rubrics for reading and writing provide teachers with guidelines for what and how to assess as students work to achieve the objectives of the lesson set. All instruction is planned with these expectations in mind, and teachers keep a close eye on who is making steady progress and who needs additional support or reteaching to achieve the lesson set goals. Across the lesson sets, teachers consider the diversity of learners in classrooms and how to scaffold achievement to help all students reach their potential. All Core Ready lesson sets provide specific suggestions for how to do this.

- *Responsibility.* Responsibility is one of the conditions most closely connected with independence, our ultimate goal for our young readers

> 66 *Launch out on his story, Muse, daughter of Zeus, start from where you will—sing for our time too.*
>
> — *"The Odyssey," Homer* 99

and writers. Students on the road to independence must be able to make decisions about their own learning. With our coaching and guidance, students in our classrooms have opportunities to choose books with purpose, select topics wisely, manage their own time, and seek out mentors and support from one another. They reflect on and report back about their own learning regularly. Students are provided with opportunities for recognition of growth in their own literacy.

- *Approximation.* Teaching within a lesson set allows students time to try out new learning and hone their skill over the course of several days. Like a middle school band or peewee baseball team, students in Core Ready classrooms are not expected to perform at a Carnegie Hall or Yankee Stadium level of play right away. Rather, we anticipate and embrace students' imperfect attempts to replicate what they have seen in the work of professional authors or in our classroom demonstrations. Plenty of time for this experimentation and growth is provided in our lesson set framework. No matter where students are in the continuum of learning, we point out what they are doing well already and build on these strengths to coach them to the next level. It is important to note that approximation does not mean we have low expectations. To the contrary, trying and drafting, practicing and honing, are crucial steps to exceeding expectations. I have very high expectations for all students. It is not enough to do just the minimum. All students across the world should be held to high levels of possibility and accomplishment. Watching a child kick a soccer ball again and again, making mistakes as she goes, involves dedication to improvement. Approximation is not about being careless; it's about practice, practice, practice.

- *Use.* Use is absolutely essential to student development of independence. According to Cambourne (1988), learners are most likely to engage when

- *Response.* In the spirit of cognitive apprenticeship (Collins, Brown, & Newman, 1989), we recognize that learners benefit from timely feedback and genuine response from a knowledgeable coach. The Core Ready lesson sets offer many chances to make such coaching readily available to students because they assume a mentor–apprentice relationship between teacher and student. Self-reflection and peer feedback are also extremely important varieties of response. While these elements are present in many places across a lesson set, they are perhaps most evident in the final lessons, which allow students opportunities to present their work, reflect on their progress, and seek feedback from others. The combination of expert and peer feedback and self-reflection in Core Ready lesson sets propels student growth as language learners. In addition, organizing curriculum in lesson sets allows teachers an excellent opportunity to grow their expertise as they plan, teach, and reflect on the effectiveness of their instruction within a focused context over an extended period of time.

they see that the learning at hand will further the purposes of their lives. If it appears useful, it is more interesting. In the Core Ready lesson sets, we expose students to how reading, writing, listening, and speaking are applicable in the real world as well as in school. We also connect students with authentic audiences for their work. We recognize that our students live in an interconnected world in which new technologies have changed the way they learn, what motivates them, and even the definition of literacy itself (Coiro, Knobel, Lankshear, & Leu, 2008). I suggest practical and engaging ways for students to use technology to enhance how they acquire, analyze, and share knowledge. The use of technology must be strategic as well as authentic. The student in the 21st century asks, "Why am I using this tool?" "How will it enhance my output?" "How will it teach me something new?" Nothing is passive; everything is active. We use literature and technology in this busy, multifaceted world, where we are interacting and interconnecting in a myriad ways, with literacy as the guiding force for how we make sense of the world and of one another. It is how we, as E. M. Forster so wisely said, "Only connect."

The Reading and Writing Lesson Sets—Strategically Connected

Reading and writing go together; that is, what our students study in reading is directly related to what they study in writing. Several researchers and authors have cited the benefits of integrating reading and writing instruction (Duke & Pressley, 2002; Durkin, 1988; Hiebert, Pearson, & Taylor, 1998; Moffett & Wagner, 1983; Shanahan, 1990). Core Ready builds on that foundation by integrating rich opportunities for reading, writing, listening, and speaking in all lesson sets.

The confluence of reading and writing within Core Ready lesson sets benefits both students and teachers. Each skill is dependent on the other, closely relying on each other as the reader writes and the writer draws on all he has read. A reading experience helps students gain knowledge that then develops and enhances the content and structure of connected writing tasks. As students read folktales, they gain a sense of the literary elements, author's purpose, and craft techniques they will need to consider as they write folktales. Likewise, a close study of how to write folktales raises students' awareness of what to expect in this genre, causing them to be more confident and perceptive readers.

Teachers intuitively understand that such connections help students, but curricular materials often do not align reading and writing lessons. Core Ready's integrated reading and writing lesson sets make it easy for teachers to help students see important connections clearly and immediately: "In reading yesterday, we talked about how folktales usually include magic and fantasy. Today in writing, you begin to imagine how magic and fantasy can be an important part of your original tale."

Because of the close relationship between Core Ready reading and writing lesson sets, I strongly recommend that they be taught side by side. Is it possible to teach just the reading lessons or just the writing lessons? In most cases, with some adjustments, this could be done, but again, I recommend that reading and writing be presented simultaneously to maximize the benefits for students and teachers.

How the Core Ready Lesson Sets Are Arranged—A Purposeful Sequence

The lessons within the Core Ready lesson sets are arranged in a strategic way that reflects respected models of how students learn, such as the gradual release of responsibility model (Pearson & Gallagher, 1993) and cognitive apprenticeship theory (Collins, Brown, & Newman, 1989). Across the lesson set, the teacher guides the students toward increasing levels of independence.

There are four stages in a Core Ready lesson set that stand proudly on the shoulders of research: Introduce, Define, Extend, and Assess. I use the acronym I.D.E.A. to refer to this structure. Each stage of a lesson set may extend across one to several days and includes activities that are designed specifically in the spirit of that stage. Each stage of a Core Ready lesson set is described in the following paragraphs.

Introduce

The first stage of a lesson set involves activities that introduce the topic and goals of the study. The Introduce lessons activate students' background knowledge and build a big-picture understanding of the new subject. The learning experiences in the Introduce lessons are constructivist in nature, allowing students time to become immersed in the new learning and to question, discover, and build a collaborative understanding of what the topic of the lesson set is all about. Introduce lessons help to build students' confidence and motivation to engage in the learning that is to come.

Stage of a Lesson Set	Description	Actions Associated with This Stage
Introduce	Lessons that immerse students in and invite inquiry about the new topic.	Notice, explore, collect, note, immerse, surround, record, share
Define	Lessons that provide students with essential understandings, skills, structures, or information needed for success with the topic of study.	Name, identify, outline, clarify, select, plan, define
Extend	Lessons that invite students to apply and refine new understandings related to the topic of study.	Try, experiment, attempt, approximate, practice, explain, revise, refine
Assess	Lessons that enable students and teacher to recognize and celebrate new knowledge related to the topic.	Reflect, conclude, connect, share, recognize, respond

Examples of activities in the Introduce stage of a lesson set include the following:

- In a folktales lesson set, the class will read and examine authentic examples of the genre, making notes of what folktales seem to have in common.
- In a lesson set on cause and effect, students will search for real cause and effect relationships in their lives. This builds a concrete foundation of the concept of cause and effect on which to build as they explore cause and effect in reading and writing.

Define

The Define lessons provide students with essential knowledge, terms, and structures that will guide their learning about the topic across the lesson set. They may also provide students with a clear picture of or plan for what they will be expected to achieve and produce during the lesson set. It is in this phase of the lesson set that the teacher's role as content expert comes to the forefront. Students are novices to the study, relying on a mentor to provide them the road map they need to guide further exploration.

Examples of activities in the Define stage of a lesson set include the following:

- In a lesson set on fantasy, the teacher will outline the universal elements of the genre that students can expect to find in any fantasy they encounter.
- In a lesson set on reading and writing informational text, the teacher will guide students to identify and explain the relationship between key ideas, people, and events.

Extend

If one can compare the types of lessons found in the Define stage of the lesson set to a road map to learning, the Extend lessons might be likened to a series of guided day trips designed to help students become increasingly independent travelers. This is the phase in which students apply and refine the skills and strategies they need to achieve the goals of the lesson set. The teacher serves as coach and guide as the students build their level of expertise and independence within

the topic of study. With appropriate practice and support, the young apprentices extend themselves and their capacities to reach new levels of achievement.

Examples of activities in the Extend stage of a lesson set include the following:

- In a lesson set on reading drama and prose, readers practice determining the theme(s) of their reading by using a variety of clues.
- In a lesson set on interpreting poetry, students experiment with using expression and body language to convey the poem's message.

Assess

The Assess lessons wrap up each lesson set in a meaningful way intended to encourage students to recognize how they have grown as readers, writers, listeners, and speakers. During this phase of the lesson set, the class takes time to share and celebrate the good work they have done with one another and interested audiences. They reflect on the journey they have taken and articulate what they have learned and how this experience has changed them. They consider how this learning is meaningful to their own lives and commit to "holding on" to the new capacities and understandings they have developed.

Examples of activities in the Assess stage of a lesson set include the following:

- In a lesson set focusing on evaluating favorite authors and series, the students will make future reading plans to continue to discover more favorites in the reading world.
- In a lesson set on poetry, students reflect on their prior and current thinking about poetry to see if the lesson set learning experiences have changed their views.

A Day in the Life of a Lesson Set

Just as the school year comprises thoughtful and rich lesson sets that incorporate Common Core State Standards skills into authentic study, a day in the life of a lesson set is similarly potent. A Core Ready lesson set spans the course of 3 to 4 weeks, including many daily lessons, all of which are tied directly to the goals of the study. This takes the randomness out of teaching and unifies all the different parts. No longer should we see unrelated daily lessons haphazardly splattered across the plan book.

In Chapter 4, I encouraged you to adopt the whole–small–whole model for daily lessons. Core Ready uses this model. All Core Ready lessons include these three steps, whether they appear in the Introduce stage, the Define stage, the Extend stage, or the Assess stage. This is effective teaching practice according to the existing body of research.

Every Core Ready lesson includes the following instructional segments.

Direct Instruction (Whole)

Direct instruction is a whole-group lesson during which the teacher demonstrates a single teaching point. This first whole typically involves the teacher at the front of the class instructing, modeling, or demonstrating a new skill that relates to the lesson set. Students listen, taking in the instructions or information in preparation to use it when the direct instruction is over. This session is usually quite short (5–10 minutes) but flexible, depending on the subject matter being covered. There are four segments within the whole-group lesson: the Warm Up, in which the teacher hooks the students and draws them into the new learning; the Teach portion, in which the teacher models, demonstrates, or gives instruction; the Try portion, in which the students are asked to give it a go; and the Clarify portion, in which the teacher resolves any confusion about the concept.

Practice (Small)

The students then move out of the direct instruction segment and into the practice portion of the daily lesson—the most important and effective time spent in terms of students becoming independent. As in sports practice, after a quick demonstration, the teacher provides practice time for students to try out their new skills. This is the bulkiest portion of the daily lesson—from 30 minutes to an hour, depending on what is needed and what is developmentally appropriate. During practice, students work independently or in small groups while actively engaging in reading, writing, listening, and speaking. The teacher might conduct conferences or small-group lessons to address the teaching point or other targeted needs at this time.

Wrap Up (Whole)

After practice, the class comes together again to share some of their work on the teaching point, to reflect on how things played out for them during practice and why, and to make plans for future learning. The Wrap Up mode is casual conversational. It may include a child who was successful during practice demonstrating this success for her classmates. It may involve a simple conversation starting with the teacher asking, "How did it go for everyone today?" Timing is flexible here too, but it's usually short (5–15 minutes). It can be very easy to fall into the trap of rushing off to the next "thing" directly from the practice portion of the lesson, thereby omitting this final segment when the schedule is tight, when lunch sneaks up on you, or when there is an assembly or picture day on the calendar. But the Wrap Up session sends a clear message to students that the daily work is expected. It holds students accountable and makes each of them an important member of a community of learners that is working together for collective goals.

Lessons: The Day, the Set, the Year

Core Ready is purposeful in its use of effective methodology, which I see as imperative with the Common Core State Standards. They are rich and deep and cannot be taught in isolated, shallow lessons that do not relate to one another. Making use of lesson sets helps us to gather related reading, writing, listening, and speaking skills from the CCSS into inspiring and interesting quests on which we can travel with our students. Learning has never been so fun.

> Children have to be educated,
> but they have also to be left to educate themselves.
>
> —Ernest Dimnet

Example of a Daily Core Ready Lesson

From Core Ready Lesson Sets for Grades 3 to 5: the Shape of Story: Yesterday and Today

▼ Teaching Objective

Readers understand that folktales have common elements and often explain something that happens in nature or convey a certain truth about life.

▼ Standards Alignment

RL.3.1, RL.3.2, RI.3.10, SL.3.1a–d, SL.3.6, L.3.1, L.3.6

▼ Materials

- *Why Mosquitoes Buzz in People's Ears*
- *The Ant and the Grasshopper*
- *Chart paper or interactive whiteboard*

▼ Procedure

Warm Up Gather the class to set the stage for today's learning

Revisit the definition of a folktale you began with the class yesterday.

Teach Model what students need to learn and do

Tell the class that one of the most important elements of a folktale is that it often offers an explanation for something that happens in nature or conveys a lesson about life. An important purpose for creating these tales was to share these explanations and lessons with other people. Use *Why Mosquitoes Buzz in People's Ears* as an example.

> Think about *Why Mosquitoes Buzz in People's Ears*. That folktale offers an explanation about why mosquitoes buzz around and bother everyone in the summer—they're trying to see if everyone is still mad at them for what

happened to Owlet. The story gives us an explanation about something that happens in nature. Now think about the lesson we learned about our actions. Who can remind us what we learned?

Have a student or students recap the lesson learned from this folktale, citing specific moments from the text to support their thinking. Reiterate that this folktale happens to have *both* elements—it offers an explanation about something that happens in nature and teaches us a life lesson (there are consequences for our actions). As your students watch, begin a three-column chart. Label the first column "Title," the second column "Explanation about Nature," and the third column "Life Lesson." Chart what you have discussed so far.

Example Chart What Have You Learned from This Folktale?

Title	Explanation about Nature	Life Lesson
Why Mosquitoes Buzz in People's Ears	Explains why mosquitoes buzz around and bother people	Teaches that telling lies can cause lots of trouble

Try Guide students to rehearse what they need to learn and do in preparation for practice

> Now let's give this a try together. Let's think about *The Ant and the Grasshopper*. Who can remind us what happened in that folktale?

After recapping the folktale, ask the class, "Did that folktale explain something that happens in nature?" Allow students a moment to discuss and realize that this folktale does not offer an explanation of an event in nature. Now ask, "Does this folktale reveal a truth about life?" Provide students a few minutes to sum up the lesson that there is a time for work and a time for play. Be sure to push your students to use specific evidence from the text to support their thinking. (Note: Allow your students to sum up this lesson in their own words. Using their own terminology or way of discussing big ideas is powerful teaching.) Add to the chart.

Example Chart   What Have You Learned from This Folktale?

Title	Explanation from Nature	Life Lesson
Why Mosquitoes Buzz in People's Ears	Explains why mosquitoes buzz around and bother people	Telling lies can cause lots of trouble
The Ant and the Grasshopper	None	There is a time to work and a time to play

Clarify   Briefly restate today's teaching point and explain the practice task(s)

> When we read folktales, we can expect to discover an explanation for something that happens in nature or learn a lesson about life. Today, when you're reading, look for these elements and jot down an example to bring back to the carpet.

Practice   Students work independently or in small groups to apply today's teaching objective

Students will continue to read folktales independently. As they read, students should choose one folktale that illustrates either an explanation of something in nature or a life lesson. Provide students with a method for jotting down their thinking to bring back to the meeting area.

Wrap Up   Check understanding as you guide students to briefly share what they have learned and produced today

Call students back to the meeting area, reminding them to bring the folktale they've chosen to share with the class. Ask your students if they'd like to share what they discovered during their reading. Remind students that teaching lessons and explaining things about nature were main reasons that folktales were told over and over again in many cultures. As students share their thinking, add it to the class chart. Graphic organizers are useful tools to help ELLs record their thinking and see these ideas connect around folktales. If needed, you can add visuals (e.g., make a small copy of the front of the book under the title, sketch the thought). This offers a visual support tied to the written thought.

chapter 9

Mastering the Art of Close Reading

"If I have seen further, it is only by
standing on the shoulders of giants."
—Sir Isaac Newton

" . . . much like a tree growing new branches,
everything we remember becomes another set of
branches to which memories can be attached. The more
we learn and retain, the more we can learn and retain."
—David Souza, How the Brain Works

Going Deep Really Matters

Our days are full of the assorted and lively business of our lives. We rush to finish our tasks, to absorb new ideas, to engage in relationships that matter to us. Our reading lives can feel the same. We rush to answer emails, to finish work-related reading, and to engage with friends and colleagues via the printed word in ways that matter to us. But in life as in reading, there are moments when we must slow down and go deep. A novel demands untangling, or a problem at work requires close attention to a document. Although sometimes this may feel challenging, I also relish the struggle. I know the puzzle will bring me closer to full realization of something new. The struggle is part of the journey and the journey into a problem or an idea brings me pleasure when I break through.

Close reading of the world is essential to our well-being. Looking deeply at anything, whether it is the flower growing out of the sidewalk or your mother's hands, creates new ways of thinking. When I give myself the chance to dive beneath the surface, I remember, I wonder, I imagine, I observe, I admire, I critique.

Taking time to read deeply conveys the same kinds of gifts. Close reading too gives us both pause *and* power. By knowing something well, we gain power. We *master* it. Though the world is full of things to read, there are crucial times when a reader slows down and goes much longer and deeper into the world of that particular chapter, paragraph, stanza, section. "Close reading is akin to watching fine architecture grow from blueprint to final brick. It allows us to walk within a literary structure and ponder the brilliance of the creation intimately and holistically" (Lockett, 2010). In a world driven by speed, where technology has made everything almost relentlessly fast, helping our students learn how to purposefully slow down and examine a sentence, a paragraph, or a chapter gives them strategies for living a meaningful life.

In the teaching of writing, I advocate using mentor texts to show our students well-crafted language and the glory of writing that serves a purpose, whether it is to make us laugh or cry or understand something better. From picture books to informational articles to examples of glorious poetry, I carry with me always a short stack of favorite books to convey teaching points. I ask students to model their own writing after the great authors they love, both narrative fiction writers and informational text writers. All of this *is and always has*

been close reading. It is not a new idea, but the technique and practice of close reading are due for a fresh look; that is what this chapter is all about and what the standards encourage us to do. To start, here are my Top Five Big Ideas about Close Reading:

1. Close reading should *inspire* our students to go deep. By this, I do not suggest we institute a punishing schedule of revisiting some uninteresting text again and again so that our students throw up their hands in despair and nod over their desks in sheer boredom. Let us instead create a sense of wonder for seminal texts that is positive, open, and reverential of the excitement about what it means to know text well and to fall through the pages of the words and into deeper understandings.

2. *Model* close reading for your students with "in the air" thinking. Let us use whole-class direct instruction to show what we as readers do when we look closely at text, and not leave close reading as something our students do in isolation, without seeing how people actually do it.

3. Use close-reading strategies to teach *both reading and writing.* The teaching of writing requires models and knowledge of text. When Ernest Hemingway was asked how to become a great writer, he said, "Read *Anna Karenina,* read *Anna Karenina,* read *Anna Karenina.*" As students get to know specific texts really well, they emulate their qualities of writing in their own work.

4. Close reading can be done by very *young children.* Have them practice with photographs and art, glorious picture books and paintings—the youngest children are the very best at looking closely.

5. Be open to your students' *interpretations.* Do not get stuck on the need for right or wrong "answers" when doing close readings with students. You will miss all the fun. Your students will develop some amazing ideas if you make the environment safe for them to discover what they are thinking. Let us also not be sticklers for staying too close to the text either. Some have said that we must not give our students background information on the text used for close reading. That is ridiculous! It is impossible in this day and age, when we as lifelong adult readers are happily jumping from source to source as we read, to say to children that to do a successful close read they cannot leave the single page. We can help our students become

really good at close reading while still allowing them the enormous pleasures of seeing the connections among different books. The world of other texts and ideas and context will help make their close read stronger and more dimensional.

The Core Ready Text Trees

In wanting to make the work of close reading joyful and interesting, I created a visual for Core Ready that would really work to help teachers organize their thinking. This is how I developed "text trees," as seen in Figure 9.1. Think about a text, any text at all, as a tree. The solid trunk is the place you cast your reading eye first. You read down the lines of that tree, perceiving at least something about its age and its history just by looking at it. Now, it is only in your mind's eye that you can envision the roots; you cannot see them, but you know they are there. They represent history and culture and the deep underpinnings that caused the text to grow.

Now picture the glorious green of the leaves and the branches sprouting up from the trunk, from the text itself. Let us consider them as a metaphor for *your* ideas as a reader. They have grown from the solid foundation of the text and the roots that fed that text. But what emerges and spreads itself to the sky are the ideas you create from them.

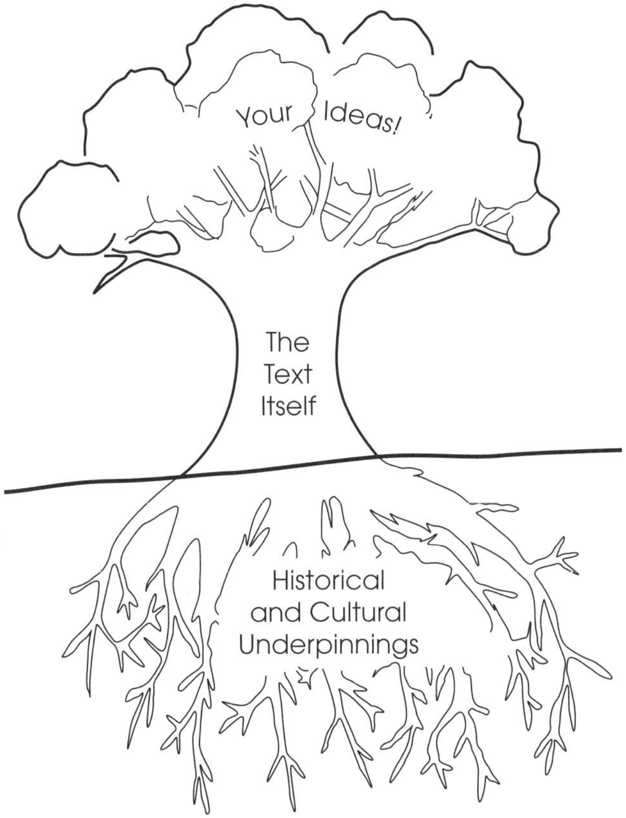

The Power of "Absorbedness"

The reader is absorbing new information, ideas, and stories all the time. As he grows, the college- and career-ready student slows down and speeds up, depending on the purpose of his reading. Sometimes he is reading more than one thing at once, especially if he is online. When he slows down, he is often looking at the sentence or word level and moving in and out of the text much the way a photographer uses a zoom lens. He can see things big and small. It is crucial that the reader can do both fluidly, sometimes at the same time. It is absolutely transcendent when he can do this not just well but profoundly, and with the

Figure 9.1 Core Ready Text Tree Sample

Your Ideas!

The Text Itself

Historical and Cultural Underpinnings

"absorbedness" Donald Hall talks about—when it becomes so natural for him that he reaches new heights as a reader.

Thomas Newkirk (2012) writes: "[w]e read for pleasure and meaning—and to do so, we must be able to control the tempo of our reading. And . . . by slowing down, by refusing to see reading as a form of consumption or efficient productivity, we can attend to word meanings and sound, building a bridge to the oral traditions that writing arose out of. We can hold passages in memory, we can come to the view that good texts are inexhaustible, to the belief that the white spaces always invite us to reflect and expand" (p. 197).

Modeling Close Reading Is Not about Standing in Front of the Room

In Chapter 5 I defined complex text by exploring the quantitative and qualitative features as well as reader and task objectives. As I have said with regard to text complexity, deep reading and fostering text understandings must be rooted in effective teaching practice. There is a danger when we see the words *close reading* that we will be tempted to return to the days when a teacher stood in front of a room and lectured for days about the same set of chapters. That is not what we are advocating here. In this era, that kind of teaching and reading is obsolete. It simply does not fit with how our students are living and experiencing their world. They are living in a mashed-up, dynamic worldwide community where learning can happen every second of the day, where world-renowned lecturers can appear before them on a screen after they have watched a baseball game. The idea that students come into school to passively "receive" important information—and that school is the only place they can get it—is completely outdated.

But as educators, we can advocate for the simmering experience of diving deep into text. Instead of dryly teaching the text, we can teach the processes for consuming text in a way that feels contemporary and honors what we know about teaching and learning. Today's students are used to having their opinions regarded, respected, and heard and seen all over social media! Expecting them to come into class for your expertise as though they are empty vessels is not going to work. Our students have to co-create understandings of text with us through examples of close reading.

In the Common Core State Standards and now the Core Ready program,

> "*Contentment is work so engrossing that you do not know that you are working. . . . [C]ontentment (is) absorbedness.*"
>
> —Donald Hall, poet and author of the classic children's book Ox Cart Man

close reading is woven into all stages of a daily lesson (direct instruction, practice, and wrap up) so that students are not merely listening but getting ample time to practice these processes. Close reading also threads throughout all of the Core Ready lesson sets (in the activities described and further in the Questions for Close Reading feature) because, after all, the whole point of our teaching is to help kids do close reading on their own. The ultimate purpose of the staircase of complexity is to create readers who are experts by graduation, so whether their college close reading is a piece of glorious literature or the text of a math problem, they are fearless. And when they enter the workplace, whether their reading is an email from a client, a patient's health report, or a colleague's research paper, they can, as poet Donald Hall said, find "absorbedness" in engagement with that text. It is powerful to have control over text and to read it masterfully.

A Celebration of the Qualitative Features of Text

We in our profession have sometimes had an unfortunate preoccupation with quantitative features of text alone, as if a reading is some kind of scientific experiment. This is impossible and wrong, as anyone who loves to read knows. As teachers and as leaders, you must educate yourselves about what people are trying to sell as definitive measures for how texts are quantified. We could quantify *The Great Gatsby* at a fifth-grade reading level through a Lexile system that takes into account only quantitative measures (and it has been done). While that system might look at the length of sentences or the numbers of challenging vocabulary words, it does not take into account the exquisite nuances of character development in that book, or the reverberating themes, or the uses of metaphor, or the profound way Fitzgerald describes the vulnerability and loss of innocence of all the characters. And how to quantify grammar from a qualitative point of view? Is that writing meant for a fifth grader? Please! In his classic book on writing, *The Elements of Style,* the great writer E. B. White says, "The approach to style is by way of plainness, simplicity, orderliness, sincerity" (p. 100). He also wrote *Charlotte's Web,* whose indelible first line reads, "'Where's Papa going with that ax?' said Fern to her mother as they were setting the table for breakfast." The writer Eudora Welty wrote of the book, "As a piece of work it is just about perfect."

Charlotte's Web is likely on a third-grade reading level according to the measurements by Lexiles, but that first sentence is one many of us only wish we could write. From the grammatical point of view, it is lovely. Even the simplest word conveys power. For example, the word *going* is active and gives the reader a strong picture of the immediacy of the moment. The second clause implies a further sense of urgency because it sets the stage for what Fern and her mother are doing right that minute. There are no adjectives in the entire sentence. The sentence is not long. But it also does not stand alone. It is the gateway to the story. It does the job of getting our hearts beating a little bit faster right from the start. It is deceptively simple quantitatively but hugely meaningful qualitatively. The close reader will look to both, of course. But the deep dive gives the reader a chance to investigate all the layers even further.

Let us refresh how we read deeply through the metaphor of looking through a lens. Sometimes I isolate one lens and look through just that one, as if I am viewing the text under a magnifying glass. Other times, I want to blend the lenses and think at a higher level about the text I am reading.

In this book and in the following Core Ready series of lesson sets in reading and writing, I advocate close reading of texts in ways that are designed to increase the reader's capacity for reading at higher levels, and nurture deeper understanding through the use of lenses. I share them here and then I encourage you, with your faculty team, to select a text and practice doing close readings with one another.

The Core Ready lenses help students become investigators in the literary world. When examining a piece of writing, it is important to understand the many different ways of looking at a text. In order to truly "go deep" into a text, readers must understand how a text can be broken down. Each of the following questions helps readers look at a text in a new way. Going through a text using one lens at a time will help readers understand how all of the elements in a piece of writing work together to give the text a deeper meaning.

The Personal Lens

The personal lens is uniquely yours. This lens is influenced by your own history, your gender, and your socioeconomic, religious, and political status. You cannot approach a text without this lens, and it is through it that your opinion of a text grows. The branches of your own text tree will look different from those of another who reads that same piece, because you are looking at it through your own personal lens. There are those who say that the close read has to be objective, that we have to read as if the text and only the text appears in front of us. But this is denying the whole miraculous truth of reading: that it is life changing—that you bring yourself to the text, as the reader, and change the text by reading it. For years I have read certain texts again and again. I am always curious about how I read them differently at various ages of my life. The "me" that read Virginia Woolf's *To the Lighthouse* at 18 years of age is very different from the "me" who read it last summer. That is curious to me and delightful and deep and profound. I simply cannot separate myself completely from text and the meaning of text. I would be lost if I did.

Guiding Questions for the Personal Lens

- What is your purpose in reading this text?
- How will you go about reading this text?
- What do you already know about this subject that will influence your transaction with this text?
- Who was this text written for? Are you that audience?
- What are you thinking about as you are reading this text?

The Linguistic Lens

"With so much reading ahead of you, the temptation might be to speed up. But in fact it's essential to slow down and read every word. Because one important thing that can be learned by reading slowly is the seemingly obvious but oddly underappreciated fact that language is the medium we use in much the same way that a composer uses notes, the way a painter uses paint" (Prose, 2007, pp. 15–16).

In our hurried lives, we barely notice trees. We zoom by them on our way to our next meeting. But in a quiet moment, we might lay a blanket down under one, lie back, and marvel at its branches, its leaves, its rough bark, its age. There is a time and place for scanning and skimming text, but well-crafted texts merit a closer look. Using the linguistic lens, we can examine the purposeful choices the author has made—choosing a word with incredible care, or choosing to tighten a sentence, or choosing to lengthen it. Close reading provides an opportunity to teach grammar **by example.** And that example is in the text itself. Lingering over a sentence from a speech by Abraham Lincoln, we take a moment to marvel over the deliberateness of his choices, even down to the order of his adjectives, to convey his larger meaning.

Guiding Questions for the Linguistic Lens

- What does the author's use of syntax suggest?
- What is the tone of this text? What does the tone communicate?
- What do we notice about word choice?
- What imagery does the author develop? Why?
- What does the length of the sentences indicate about the author's message?

The Semantic Lens

Semantic understanding is grasping the meaning of the text and the interplay between the language itself and the meaning on the page. Punctuation and paragraphing both assist with meaning. Our students become experts when they can see everything in the text as codes toward meaning. By reading at the superficial text level, skating over the surface of our reading, we see only words. The semantic lens brings the deeper message into focus.

Guiding Questions for the Semantic Lens

- What is the gist of this text?
- What are the fundamental concepts presented in this text?
- What questions arise as you read?
- What ideas are connected in this text?
- Are there words in this text that mean something more to you than their dictionary definitions? Words that have specific connotations for you?

The Analytical Lens

Through this lens, readers combine what they know about the historical context of the text, its meaning, and their own personal impressions, and they draw conclusions about its implications. Analysis requires holding several ideas in one's mind at once. But even young children can do this, especially when using pictures in children's literature to begin learning about analysis.

Guiding Questions for the Analytical Lens

- What patterns do you notice developing across the text?
- What response does the text elicit?
- Why was the text written?
- What important conclusions or big ideas can you draw from this text?

The Context Lens

The context lens helps us draw meaning from the historical, political, and social world in which a text was created. This lens helps us look at how and why the text was written, how it survived, and the impact it has on the world today. We are more aware of the profound power of the Gettysburg Address when we understand that Lincoln was standing on the very ground that was forever marked by the deaths of so many soldiers. Reading in context changes the text. There are some who say close reading means there should be no context, but I firmly disagree. I want reading to always be as closely connected as possible to the kinds of real reading real readers do in the real world. We cannot forget about context.

Guiding Questions for the Context Lens

- Who wrote this text? How does this knowledge inform your reading?
- In what time period was this written?
- What is included? What isn't included?
- What are the other points of view or perspectives on this topic?
- What are the greater implications of the information presented in this text?
- Why was this text written?
- What does this text want us to do?

The Metaphoric Lens

The great writer Octavio Paz said that metaphor is the greatest invention of mankind and what separates him from all the other animal species. Even the very young child can begin to experience metaphor. When I once read Pablo Neruda's poem "Ode to My Socks" aloud, a kindergartner said to me, "I know why he wrote about socks." "Why?" I asked. He said, "It means he loves his mom for washing his socks." All humans are hardwired for metaphor. Reading together, especially in the close-reading journey, we illuminate what it means to have one thing stand in for another.

Guiding Questions for the Metaphoric Lens

- What is the author using as a stand-in for a big idea?
- What images might mean something larger?
- Are there small metaphors that illuminate a big idea?

The Critical Lens

This is a very important lens and the one that is most often forgotten in our teaching when we are trying to present information. But in the world today, having a critical lens is arguably the single most important skill we can cultivate in school. Our students can get their information from just about anywhere. It is the sharpness of their critical lens that will both protect and fortify them as they manage what they see, hear, and read. They must ask, Is this true? Do I believe it? Do I even like it? What is my perspective?

Guiding Questions for the Critical Lens

- What does the author do well in supporting his or her theme?
- How does the author help you connect to the characters?
- Compare this text to another text. What do they have in common?
- Do you like this text? Why or why not?
- Are you sure you trust the authenticity of this text?

Multiple Lens Reading

And so, we read. Ultimately, the goal is to put it all together. The standards do not ask us to keep things separate. There is a steady focus in the standards on integration, connections, synergies, and cohesion. They put a premium on independence. The Core Ready learner is an independent learner. A true lifelong reader is always making connections, finding synergies, integrating understandings, and achieving cohesion. We read every day with multiple lenses. This is the goal. And it is never too early to start. Even the very youngest child, awakening to the world of literature, listening to *Goodnight Moon* or *The Snowy Day,* is squinting at the text, listening with her deepest self, trying on her little magnifying lenses as she comes to a place of understanding through rereading and through listening, time and again, to that very same story. Even as a listener she is already practicing her deepest reading. It is why our youngest children so want to hear stories again and again and again. They are close readers of text because they seek to understand them at their deepest level. **Rereading matters.**

The Gettysburg Address is a profoundly beautiful text, miraculously both literary and historical at the same time. "The world will little note, nor long remember, what we say here, but it can never forget what they did here. It is for us, the living, rather to be dedicated here to the unfinished work which they who fought here have thus far so nobly advanced. It is rather for us to be here dedicated to the great task remaining before us, that from these honored dead we take increased devotion to that cause for which they here gave the last full measure of devotion. . . . " The expert reader of the Gettysburg Address is reading it on many levels: linguistic, historical, semantic. Endlessly, the expert reader layers his and others' thoughts and ideas onto the text. I cannot read this text without the reverberation of the great companion text Garry Wills wrote called *Lincoln at Gettysburg.* In this book, Wills explains the context and the metaphor, the semantic and the linguistic lenses. His is arguably one of the greatest examples of close reading of all time.

Through Wills's text I am able to observe that Lincoln uses various forms of the words *devotion* and *dedication* to bring us close to the dead that lay around him at the scene of battle. He writes about *us,* not *them,* because he is creating unity between us and those who sacrificed their lives for us. Lincoln's writing unifies us now—and did the same then. We share responsibility for the work the "honored dead" have done for us. I am moved by those two words in the same sentence, by the crisp clarity of his sentences, by the repetition of the language that makes it feel like poetry. Doing a close read makes me feel powerful, like I have mastered this text. I want my students to love it too.

While reading, I dive deep and am submerged. I am not afraid of the deep dive because I practice it again and again, and I have mentors, like Wills. The purpose of close reading is to practice boldness. But in this 21st century, remember, we as readers, as listeners, as viewers, are voracious. The purpose of our Google visits is the "search and find." We range across a wide variety of media and genre all in the space of seconds. The strong reader needs the opportunity to practice both the deep dive and dipping in and out of a variety of texts. The Core Ready classroom is balanced. It offers our students both ways to read. In this way, we raise lifelong readers.

Close Reading, Fearless Writers

By modeling close reading with our students, we help them to become better, stronger writers, in addition to better readers. We are, in effect, helping them to read like writers. In a close read, we pay close attention to the author's moves, to her decisions, to her deliberate and often exquisite decisions to choose a word or to *not* choose a word. The act of close reading helps our students learn to be simultaneously both reader and writer. Reading is like breathing in and writing is like breathing out. They are always better when they happen in conjunction—in fact, they are essential to the life of a student and to the life of the forever learner. The writer becomes our mentor, and we use those mentor texts to model our own writing lives. Students can access writing as a tool to dig their way into the meaning of a text, strengthening and deepening comprehension (Harvey & Daniels, 2009) or to learn subject matter (Gallagher & Lee, 2008; Lane, 2008). Here are my top five tips for how to do close reading so that it also helps your students improve their writing:

1. Use the language "Notice" and "try": "Notice how this author does _____. Today, we can try the same in our own writing."

2. Express admiration. "I love how this writer uses _____. I'd love for you to try that."

3. Be specific. "This writer uses short sentences, perhaps to express the urgency of the moment. Would you like to try this in your writing?"

4. Show that simple is good. The best writing is often quite plainly written. Think of Margaret Wise Brown, E. B. White, F. Scott Fitzgerald, or Langston Hughes. As teachers, we tend to point out the merits of long sentences or of a paragraph with lots of adjectives. But in real life and also in examples of great literature, simple, clear writing is best.

5. Read aloud. Sometimes the best way to see great writing is to hear it first. Let your students enjoy the pleasures of great writing by listening to you read it aloud. Then look at the text together. By sharing your own appreciation of the piece, you will set the stage for great discussions of the text and for emulation of its best parts in the students' own work.

How to Do a Close Reading

Modeling close reading is not easy but it can be really and truly exciting to learn how do it well. Here I share with you two examples of close reading, one for primary and one for upper-grade students. Use these examples to guide your thinking in faculty meetings or in professional study groups. The lenses should help you practice how to do a close reading, but they are by no means intended to be stifling. You will find your own voice in close reading; encourage your students to find theirs. The lenses are intended as scaffolds: supports for you to gain your footing and master the art of close reading. I also provide you with an example of how to do close reading on a photograph, so our youngest readers or students who are struggling or new to the English language can also be introduced to the power and joy that close "reading" brings.

Close Reading for Primary Students

Let's take a look at the piece for younger readers on page 110. Use each of the lenses in the earlier part of the chapter to practice close reading, in this case of a fairytale. The following is my close reading.

Using the Personal Lens   This looks like a fairy tale. I have always loved reading fairy tales, and so I settle in right away. It is a comfortable form, and it reminds me of reading when I was little. The word "once" is a kind of gate, as in "Once upon a time." We enter through it, and we are in the land of fairy tales.

Using the Semantic Lens   As we go through the story, we learn more and more. First, we can build the setting in our mind. Where does the story take place? What does it look like there? If you were going to illustrate this story, what colors would you use for the landscape?

Then we learn about the people in the village and the troll. How do the villagers feel about the troll?

And finally, we have a scene between the young girl and the troll. Does their friendship change how you feel about the villagers' actions in the beginning?

Using the Linguistic Lens   I notice that the language is simple. The sentences are often short and conversational. This makes sense to me, because lots of fairy tales began as stories that people told aloud for many years before they were written down.

Another thing I notice is that the language paints a picture of the weather in the story. We are in "a very cold country." The river is "icy" and the mountains are "snow-capped." "Snow-capped" is a funny word: it means that the mountains

The Troll

There once was a village under a range of tall mountains, in a very cold country. All of the villagers worked in the mountains. They herded goats, and picked wild herbs, and cut slabs of ice that they sold in town. A path ran from the village high into the snow-capped mountains, but first it passed over a river. A troll lived under the bridge.

The troll was large and ugly. His beard was so long it dragged in the water, and his clothes were old and ragged. He sat in the shadows under the bridge, and whenever the villagers had to cross, they ran as fast as they could from one side to the other. They never looked down. At night, they brought torches, which they jabbed under the bridge to scare the troll, and threw handfuls of rocks at him.

One morning, a young girl went up to the mountains to watch the goats. As she crossed the bridge, she dropped her golden ball into the water. It was her only toy, and she began to cry.

When the troll lumbered out from under the bridge, the girl screamed.

The troll held the ball up to the girl, and she leaned down to take it from him. In the sunlight, she saw that his eyes were clever and kind.

"Hello," she said. No one had ever spoken to the troll before.

"Hello," he said. No one had ever stopped on his bridge before. "Why did you scream?"

"I was scared."

The troll nodded. "I wish you no harm," he said.

The girl continued up the path into the mountains. But on her way home, she brought the troll a pitcher of goat's milk and a bunch of yellow wildflowers. From then on, the girl and the troll were friends.

---

have a cap, or hat, of snow. Why do you think the author talks about the weather so much? I think describing weather brings you into a story: you can feel the hot sun, or the chill of the wind, and it is like you have stepped into another world.

Action words also have meaning. Can anyone point out an action word? One is that the troll's beard "dragged" in the river. To me, that makes the troll seem like he moves slowly, while the villagers "ran" up and down the bridge. They "jabbed," or poked, their torches under the bridge, which is also a fast, rushed gesture. To me, that shows that the villagers were in a hurry, that they never slowed down to really notice the troll.

But the girl slows down. She has to lean down to get her ball, which brings her closer to the troll, and then she can see what he is really like.

I love picking out colors when I read. What colors do you notice in this story? I only see two, the *golden* ball and the *yellow* wildflowers, which are two shades of the same color. Maybe that shows how the girl is repaying the troll's gift with something similar.

Using the Analytical Lens   When the girl and the troll first speak to each other, their language is exactly the same: "'Hello,' she said… 'Hello,' he said." I think this is one way to show that they are not as different as they look. "No one had ever spoken to the troll before." Doesn't that seem silly? Why do you think the villagers were scared of the troll, if they had never talked to him?

Using the Context Lens   This is just a small story, but it has very deep roots in history. Stories about trolls have been around for hundreds and hundreds of years. In Old Norse mythology, trolls lived far away from humans, in mountains and caves. In Scandinavia, there are legends that some rocks are actually trolls that turned to stone in sunlight.

In fairy tales, trolls often live under bridges. They are usually large and slow, and are frightening to humans. This builds context, so when you come across a troll in a story, you remember all the other trolls you have read about. Can you think of any other creatures who appear in fairy tales again and again? I can think of a few: goblins, elves, witches, and giants.

Using the Metaphoric Lens   Fairy tales are often simple stories, like frames, that can be set around countless variations. This story could be moved to any country in the world, set in present times or thousands of years ago. The blueprint would remain the same—a troll and a human meeting—but the colors and textures and tones could be anything.

To me, this story means that you should not judge someone based on how he or she looks. A troll could be anyone, and the only way to learn that he or she is clever and kind is to stop and listen.

Close Reading for Upper Grade Students

Let's take a look at the following poem by Emily Dickinson. Use each of the lenses in the earlier part of this chapter to practice close reading.

XXIII.
IN THE GARDEN.

    A bird came down the walk:
He did not know I saw;
He bit an angle-worm in halves
And ate the fellow, raw.

    And then he drank a dew
From a convenient grass,
And then hopped sidewise to the wall
To let a beetle pass.

    He glanced with rapid eyes
That hurried all abroad, —
They looked like frightened beads, I thought;
He stirred his velvet head

    Like one in danger; cautious,
I offered him a crumb,
And he unrolled his feathers
And rowed him softer home

    Than oars divide the ocean,
Too silver for a seam,
Or butterflies, off banks of noon,
Leap, plashless, as they swim.

Here is my own close reading, my own deep dive. I select the lenses I want most.

Using the Semantic Lens   I begin reading this poem verse by verse, summarizing the action. The first four verses focus on a single bird going about its normal activities: eating a worm, drinking water, avoiding a beetle, checking out its surroundings, and then flying off. Although the focus is on the bird from the first line, the narrator introduces herself in the second line by explaining that the bird does not know she is watching him.

As I comb through each verse, paraphrasing the bird's activities, I notice I am feeling contrasting emotions. The author manipulates the tone of this piece with her word choice. I tighten my grip on the linguistic lens and zoom in closer to these words. The opening scene is at first the innocent observation of a bird that we have all seen from a porch or window. Yet in the third and fourth lines, we are in for a shock. Although it's a commonplace act for a bird—or any living thing—to eat, the poet describes it as an act of violence: *bit, halves*, and *raw.*

Using the Linguistic Lens   How does the poet describe our main character, the bird? She uses only three adjectives (*rapid, velvet, frightened*), instead relying on metaphors and similes. In the lines, "He glanced with rapid eyes / That hurried all around," she treats "eyes" as if they are a creature or animal, separate from the bird itself. Imagining eyes moving rapidly, hurrying all around, helps us identify with the bird's nervous fear. The next line, "They looked like frightened Beads," reinforces the fear with a simile comparing the bird's eyes to beads. Why would Dickinson compare eyes to beads? What do beads look like; how do they feel? If beads are lifeless objects, how can they have an emotion like fear?

Using the Analytical Lens   As I progress through the poem, I notice a pattern emerging. The poet uses the word *then* twice in four lines. It is as though she is reminding us that the world is constantly alternating between the harmless and the dangerous: "then" this happens but "then" something always follows to negate it.

Using the Context Lens   In the fourth verse, as the narrator approaches the bird to offer a crumb, the word *cautious* is placed so that it could describe either the narrator or the bird. We know the bird should be cautious, but why would the narrator be? Is she afraid the bird will attack her or block her path? I notice that the author has left out some information. Does it seem as though the bird has taken the proffered crumb or that he proudly flies off, leaving behind the human who cannot soar? It is up to each of us to answer this question, looking through our personal lens, reflecting on our past observations and interactions with birds.

Using the Metaphoric and Critical Lenses   The last stanza is less straightforward. Dickinson uses a stunningly vivid and beautiful metaphor to compare the sky to the sea. She sets up the sky–water analogy at the end of the third verse with the words _unrolled_ to evoke unfurling sails and _rowed_ instead of _fly_. How is rowing like flying? How is it different? The final verse continues the comparison, as the "rowing" (or flying) bird becomes a butterfly that is "swimming" (or flying). As we consider the idea of swimming/rowing, we realize that flying is more serene and less noisy, "plashless" and "softer."

So why did the poet use the watery metaphor? Humans, at least, can swim or row or sail. But isn't there a universal longing to take flight? With "Banks of Noon," we enter the most metaphorical territory of the poem: time as a river. Is this an entirely new theme for the poem? Perhaps it connects to the contrast of groundedness/flight, joy/fear, gentility/violence, human/nature: Dickinson provokes us to think and feel deeply. Making flying seem like swimming or rowing makes the reader aware of how the world is intertwined, the same way perhaps the narrator and the bird are related, or how being high above or deep below the earth combines excitement and fear in equal measure.

Debrief

As experienced readers, we do not follow a prescribed procedure for a close reading of Emily Dickinson's poetry. We read the poem, perhaps multiple times, and naturally gravitate to certain words or phrases to begin our analysis. We are patient and kind with ourselves, enjoying the process of investigating the meaning behind words, understanding that when the text feels foggy under one lens, switching to another might bring clarity. Even when we think we have a verse clearly focused, our experience and intuition tell us that bringing in yet another lens will bring greater meaning. This process of holding text up to the light to illuminate the subtle nuances allows us to be continually surprised by our findings. It is our reward for rereading a favorite or forgotten text. But it is a process. Sometimes full comprehension of a text eludes the most masterful reader and thinker. When this happens, as it is bound to, we can supplement our efforts with research, seeking out interviews with the author, or reading the commentary from others who have spent time with the text.

When Do We Do Close Reading?

We can practice close reading and model it for and with our students in three different ways:

- Through a read-aloud
- Through shared text in small groups
- Through whole-class direct instruction using a text that everyone can see

Do not save close reading only for whole-class instruction. The smaller setting of group work will give your quieter voices a chance to shine. The read-aloud is an excellent way for you to demonstrate what a close read feels and sounds like without the pressure of students having to negotiate written language on their own.

The Primary Student Masters Close Reading: A New Approach

I have worked with children in primary grades for more than 20 years. There is no more astute reader than the youngest child. When I read aloud, I am always stunned by how much the young child notices in the illustrations, the texture of the piece, and the sound of the text. But of course the young child has unique developmental needs, and we must be aware of them. Those of us who are early childhood and primary grade experts want always to be sure that our environments for teaching are humane and kind, as well as rigorous and dynamic. For this reason, I recommend two specific ways to practice close reading regularly with our youngest students:

1. *Through the read-aloud.* Make sure there is time every day to read to your students. Not every read-aloud should be a close read, but those that are should be the chance for you to model your thinking aloud. Let your students see you grappling with text, trying to understand, savoring language, looking for clues. Invite your students to join you. Use the metaphor of the magnifying lens to talk about close reading and let them try out a few of the lenses (even if you don't use all those big terms!).

2. *Through photos, art, and other visual images.* We can model what close reading looks and feels like. For example, have your students take a look at this photo with you.

Then, with the same kind of analogy, talk about using "lenses" to really "see" the image. This also works well with our special needs and ELL students. They are practicing the art of close reading without text. It really helps to build their capacities for observation and for using multiple lenses to "see" text.

career ready   Attorney

I began working as a lawyer at a small firm in New York City. There were five attorneys and I was the fifth. This meant that I was the most inexperienced person in the group and therefore had to learn everything. (A law degree is a license, not a skill.) Being lowest on the totem pole, I would generally get the most menial assignments. This required reading thousands of decisions rendered by federal and state courts and administrative tribunals. What I learned from my reading of hundreds of thousands of pages and millions of words was the importance of discerning the key facts and the law being considered. Even one fact can make the difference in how a matter is resolved.

Reading cases carefully requires painstaking effort. This was a labor of love. I saw each of the cases as stories, fascinating human stories. I love stories about people confronted with strange problems and difficult situations. I enjoyed learning and understanding the facts and the law. All the work is bearable if one has the energy to read hour after hour. It is even more bearable if one is excited about learning new words.

I do believe the nicest compliment ever paid me was that a few people said I was the most intense listener they had ever met. The explanation by the person I was chatting with was simply, "You make me feel there is no one else in the room while we talk. You listen and think about only what I am saying."

I believe, with pride and a little humility, that I have had some success developing positive client relationships. I also believe I have succeeded because the client or prospective client was convinced I was totally concerned about them and their problems. By listening intently and giving sensible, practical, and aggressive advice, the client was happy regardless of whether we succeeded in the end.

Have students respond to the following questions with a partner, in a small group, or in writing:

1. What do you think about in your own life when you look at this photo? (Personal lens)

2. Where do you think this photo might have been taken? Why might this matter to the "story" of the photo? (Context lens)

3. What do you think about or wonder about when you look at this photo? (Analytical lens)

4. What ideas do you have when you look at this photo? (Semantic lens)

5. What would you be inspired to write or to tell when you look at this photo, using beautiful language? (Linguistic lens)

6. What big story could you tell about the world by looking at this photo? (Metaphoric lens)

7. What are you thinking about when you look at this photo? (Critical lens)

For all our students, looking closely is powerful and profound. Viewing should be part of the literacy loop. It's so much a part of how we "read" our contemporary world that, in fact, this activity is not just for our primary students anymore.

A Special Note

In the Core Ready series, you will find a Close Reading icon in each of the lesson sets where I either show an example of close reading or suggest it is a good place to do one.

chapter 10

Empowering ELL Core Ready Learners

"It is really hard to be lonely very long in a world of words. Even if you don't have friends somewhere, you still have language, and it will find you and wrap its little syllables around you and suddenly there will be a story to live in."

— Naomi Shihab Nye

The typical, vibrant U.S. classroom includes myriad students from different ethnic, cultural, and language backgrounds. In 2008 there were 5.3 million English language learners (ELLs) in the U.S. school system, kindergarten through grade 12 (Migration Policy Institute, 2010). In a time like no other, the opportunity exists for all of us in education to benefit from the many assets this diversity offers. As teachers and administrative leaders, we must consider the gifts these students bring to our classrooms, and more important, we must also root all we do in the firm belief that English language learners are capable of performing at the same cognitive levels as their peers. *All* students should be given the supports necessary for them to do complex, challenging work.

Remember that English language learners can carry out many communicative tasks with their so-called flawed language, and one of the strongest aspects of the Common Core State Standards is that they focus on creating strong communicators—readers, writers, listeners, and speakers who efficiently use language for specific purposes. Through consistent exposure to rich text, ample opportunities to discuss and argue, and opportunities to write for real purposes (the very same instruction recommended for English-speaking students), ELL students can reach and exceed standards. They may need more or different supports to get to the same place, and their produced language may include errors, which is perfectly acceptable (van Lier & Walqui, 2012; Understanding Language, 2012). As long as the tasks they are asked to perform are on par with the rest of the class, and they are given appropriately adapted instruction to enable their performance, their progress will be evident.

Language is more than vocabulary, grammar, and pronunciation—it is communication itself, a tool to accomplish meaningful activity. If we want ELLs to reach the standards, we cannot focus only on teaching them the discrete pieces of language, because those parts alone will not add up to communicative competence (van Lier & Walqui, 2012; Understanding Language, 2012). We have to support English language learners in reaching the skills that the Common Core State Standards define for everyone, because when paired with basic social language, these skills provide the building blocks of language proficiency.

Core Values to Guide Our Thinking about ELLs

Here, I identify five core values for our work with ELLs (and all children).

Respect

Let us honor the backgrounds of our ELL children and acknowledge the inspiration of their families and culture. This may be obvious to some, but the discourse of "what to do with ELLs" sometimes has a tone of arrogance and superiority, as though these children are deficient because they are from another country or their parents do not speak English. Consider their languages and cultures as gifts to your classroom and set out to discover everything you can about what these children already have in place. "Students with diverse linguistic and cultural backgrounds bring a wealth of experiences from their culture to the classroom. These students have unique experiences to share. You can take advantage of this natural resource and use diversity to teach your mainstream students to value the many distinct cultures of the world" (Haynes, 2007, p. 46).

Children coming to us from diverse backgrounds have plenty of rich knowledge—and it may be more varied than that of their peers. The lives these

students have lived prior to entering the American school system may be filled with rich details of travel, adventure, struggle, hard work, difficult choices, hopes and dreams—ingredients that can make for extremely compelling stories.

Studies show that ELLs may also have specific advantages over their English-only peers. They are indeed fortunate to be growing up bilingual or trilingual or more in today's society. In fact, the researcher Yudhijit Bhattacharjee writes: "Speaking two languages rather than just one has obvious practical benefits in an increasingly globalized world. . . . Being bilingual, it turns out, makes you smarter. It can have a profound effect on your brain, improving cognitive skills not related to language and even shielding against dementia in old age" (Bhattacharjee, 2012).

Working from this affirmative foundation, one way we can begin understanding our ELLs more fully is to create student profiles, in which student assets can be collected. Through these profiles, you can get a richer view of your ELLs by gathering positive information about the students' experiences, family, knowledge, and personality—information that can later become the anchor for the harder work done at school. We may tend to group ELLs together, but the reality is that the challenges (and strengths) of ELLs will come from very different places. For example, prior schooling can be a huge variable. Some of our ELLs arrive having excelled as students in their native languages. Others come to us with fractured school experience. The immigration experience itself can represent certain challenges to students. Children may have experienced traumatic events before and during their departure from their home countries. The acclimation to a new country may have been another stressful cog in the process (Ovando & Collier, 1985). ELLs' home lives are also vastly different and should be mined through interviews with the families. Find out what families' aspirations are for their children and what kinds of supports the child will receive at home to do homework and supplemental practice.

Access

Share the English language in authentic and natural ways but with abundant support in vocabulary that can help ELLs climb the same staircase of learning and text complexity as their peers. Often, ELLs are not "below" the level of their peers—they are somewhere left or right of the language and communicative practices of other students and need to be given additional skills that align with U.S. schooling expectations in order to both obtain academic English and maintain the language skills of their families and communities. We should not water down the curriculum to provide access, but should instead add more supports and scaffolding to the work to make it possible for our ELLs to thrive. At the same time, we must provide a rich array of reading resources for all our students so they can read to build not only decoding skills but also stamina, fluency, and comprehension. These other three components are as important as decoding skills.

This does not mean, of course, that students should be left to sink or swim in a sea of grade-level content completely above their heads. Long explanations of words such as *tuffet, curds,* and *whey* to a kindergartner who is hanging on for dear life to comfortable phrases such as *good morning, how are you,* and *I am fine* may not make much sense. So how to decide when and what to do to calibrate these students' experiences? We must meet students where they are and ensure that language and content instruction are always contextualized and made sensible. The truth is that all of us are at times "struggling" readers. I seldom understand every single word I read. Stopping to define every vocabulary word diminishes our return on investment when we read aloud. Letting the story or the poem or the nonfiction text wash over students has its place too. Provide exposure to quality literature in school and at home. Direct students' attention to online resources that allow them to listen to books online. It is helpful to have the children hear and read different versions of the same stories so they can absorb new vocabulary in comfortable and familiar contexts.

As the standards say, let us utilize technology strategically and capably. There are great language apps for our ELLs that allow them to record their voices and make animations speak, reinforcing an experience through simple language and providing ELLs the opportunity to practice new vocabulary words. You can also record a video of you doing a read-aloud or shared reading for students to take home and practice. All of these tech tools make it possible to capture and customize snippets of relevant learning.

Stories

All children carry with them the richness of their own stories, no matter their age. Their lives are full of sorrows and joys, the daily miracles of life, and the struggles they face. The world of childhood is a complex place. In my work around the world when I travel for my organization LitWorld, I use the power of the personal story as an essential tool to provide access to language and to build fluency. There is nothing more powerful than the child's own story to motivate both the teller and the listener to read, write, speak, and listen. Everyone wants to be heard, and everyone has a hunger to connect with others. We find out how universal our hopes and dreams are when we share stories, and also how particular our experiences are, how precious. In LitWorld LitClubs, students share their stories online, marveling at how while one of them has never seen a beach, another has never tasted an avocado. They grieve that one has to walk miles to get water for cooking, while celebrating that another of the girls has just graduated middle school, the first girl ever in the history of her village. Use the students' personal stories to extend their emerging literacies, supporting the stories through drawings, photos, and wordless picture books to start; as the students gain skills, make books together based on these stories that matter so much to the children and to their families. Students can record their stories in their native language and then translate them through a translator or translation website, or you may see them write in a combination of their native language and their emerging English language skills. Encourage them to be in their comfort zone, but at the same time set up many opportunities for them to share their work publicly with speakers of English. Their motivation to improve their English language skills will increase if they are seeking to communicate with authentic audiences who care about their lives and their stories.

Culture

Let us truly and deeply honor the cultures of the students we have in our classrooms. Know not only the countries from which our students come, but also smaller locations within those countries that provided them with their beginnings. If you

do not already know, ask families to describe what life was like for them in their home country and why they came to the United States. Be genuinely interested and open to what they have to teach. Approach these questions with sensitivity in case some families will not feel immediately comfortable sharing, and make every effort to have people available to speak with the family in their native language. Celebrate culture by having bulletin boards in the room or on your online sharing venues to help everyone in the community know more about everyone else: food, flags, customs, family traditions, language, dialects. In Kenya, for example, although Swahili is the country's most commonly known language, there are many more "mother tongues" spoken throughout all of Kenya. The child's knowledge of language is an opportunity for us all to learn about the nuances of language and culture.

Realize, as well, that families may come from cultures where support for children's schoolwork looks very different from what it is presumed to look like for Americans. In some cultures, parents will see academics as the school's job; their job is to check that their kids did their homework and to earn a living to keep their children safe and well fed, not to read books or drill multiplication facts or go to back-to-school nights. There are many ways of caring and we need to recognize them all, and then figure out both how to teach children with different home experiences and how to nurture and support families who would like to begin to get more involved in new ways with their children's schooling.

Love

Share your love for the child and for all her stories, your love for language, and your love for the open door the English language will provide her. Children growing up in homes with multiple languages around them have so much to offer us, and while they may seem quiet at first in the bustle of the classroom, they are full of the grace and joy and passions that will motivate them to learn. What I find ironic is that we are so proud of students who are born here and grow up here with English as their first language when they learn a second language, or a third, yet we too often discourage English language learners from using their home languages, especially in school. Why shouldn't our approach be the same with children who begin their lives with languages other than English? Love them for all of who they are. They are rich with assets. Convey to them the love for learning and for language, and not just for one language, but many—convey to them a love for literature. Love the child's own stories, which will compel him to want to write and to communicate. The love is essential for our work, to increase the student's capacity to go the distance.

Steps to Promote Equity in Our Learning Environment: Making Core Ready Lessons Work for ELLs

I advocate a "glass half full" approach to the teaching of our students who do not fit the requirements of what it means to be "in the middle." This approach is not a deficit model; it is about what is possible. More than that—it is about realizing ELLs already have many assets in place, and if we don't recognize and build on those assets, we are wasting precious resources and time. With more than 5.3 million English learners in the U.S. school system and this number growing each year, the number of children in our classrooms whose native language is not English has the potential to exceed the number who are native English speakers. This need not feel overwhelming. The standards give us the platform to demand equality for all students.

Many researchers, including Jim Cummins (2010), have indicated that a multilingual, multicultural class is a great way to turn challenges into opportunities. There are several ways for students, especially ELLs, to feel more comfortable in a multilingual class, especially starting a new year, a new class, or a new school. Many ELLs are not able to express their personalities or com-

municate their knowledge or mastery of basic concepts because of their lack of English language vocabulary. Researchers such as Cummins (2010) feel that educators need to assist in making input comprehensible for ELLs, as well as make an extra effort to understand ELLs' own output.

The critical distinction here is that the responsibility is placed on the teacher to bring the Common Core State Standards to the student by identifying the supports needed to make the input comprehensible to the student. What will help a child understand? What will help the student with context? How can you put those supports in place to encourage students to participate in the lessons with their classmates rather than performing different tasks that isolate and marginalize them?

ELLs may feel less confident and secure in class and will need more support and encouragement to feel acknowledged. Messages we as teachers communicate in the classroom can be affirming to students, especially when we acknowledge that they are making an effort. Provide ample support to boost their confidence as learners. By setting up a classroom culture that accepts "flawed" language as the trade-off for eager participation, for example, we acknowledge the efforts of our ELL students and boost confidence—a trait needed for further risk taking. By taking the emphasis off perfection, we place the value on the more important cognitive interactions students perform. Happily, deeper authentic participation will support language development—even that flawed subject–verb agreement—in ways that correction and drill usually cannot.

We can include these learners more deeply in the class community by asking them to share their culture and experiences acquired in their new environment. Students from different backgrounds and cultures bring personal knowledge into the classroom through their experiences. Children's literature is a rich tool for learning and appreciation because it is a wide body of work with multiple perspectives. Authors such as Carmen Agra Deedy, Frané Lessac, and Allen Say all contribute much needed voices and views.

Adaptations that are designed to support ELLs should run parallel to the expectations for the rest of the class. For example, the Common Core State Standards ask us to be sure students can take notes to record big ideas, create opinions, and use supporting evidence (W.3.8, W.3.1, RI.3.2). Let us offer alternate ways for some of our diverse learners to record their ideas: through an acceptance of their developing writing skills; through sketches, diagrams, and drawings instead of sentences; and by using their native language skills. They can most surely practice these essential skills, even if their products do not look fully conventional at first. Their writing practice can aim toward the important ways writers are thinking, and they can begin formulating opinions right from the start. The key thing to remember is that the standards value critical thinking and writing to shape ideas and to build meaning. We cannot let mechanics stop our ELLs from trying out what it feels like to write big ideas. These actions, too, are a crucial part of language development.

This section details specific principles that will help you differentiate instruction to support your ELLs. Some of the suggestions are derived from Cummins (2010), and they are written to deliberately incorporate the values listed earlier in this chapter. Every Core Ready lesson in the lesson set books that follow have specific supports connected to these principles, and opportunities for differentiation and adaptation for ELLs are highlighted.

Good Language Arts Instruction = Good English Language Learner Instruction

I once met a young woman who had immigrated to the United States from Korea when she was about 8 years old. In her new classroom, students were reading books, writing about them, and working on exciting projects—but she was given a large packet of worksheets and was told to work on them by herself instead. At the time, she assumed this was necessary, that her teachers must know best, and that it was right for her to be stuck doing solitary drills until she learned English. It took her until adulthood to question the wisdom of this approach. At the most basic level, what we know to be good instruction for mainstream students is good instruction for ELLs. Just as our English-proficient students need to explore literature, read daily, write for meaningful audiences, and engage in rich discussion in order to be Core Ready, our ELLs need the same, and even more of it. Students who are acquiring English may need extra supports as they engage in literacy experiences, as they will be developing language at the same time that they develop content knowledge, but they do not, by any means, need an entirely separate curriculum. In fact, rich literacy experiences are the best ways for them to develop both literacy and language. Here are some specific tips:

1. Explore the richness of language.
   - Read aloud every day.
   - Post new language online and on classroom walls.
   - Visualize vocabulary (through stock photos, your illustrations, or their illustrations).
   - Find words that are complex and joyously explore their meanings together.
   - Sing, chant, or read poetry (all ages—and I mean it!).

2. Expose the student to the diversity of genre.
   - Provide the ELL child with an individualized take-home book baggie with multiple genres.
   - Provide books in the native language, when possible, or provide translated versions of English books so that the student has copies in both languages.
   - Read aloud from all genres. The read-aloud should not be in fiction alone, but also in poetry, informational texts, jokes, snippets from the Internet, and so on.
   - Invite the child to respond through drawing, drama, and play to readings in nonfiction, poetry, and fiction.
   - Deepen the child's vocabulary knowledge in a variety of content areas (for example, *experiment* or *hypothesis* in science) as well as in academic cohesion words such as *because, therefore, in addition to,* and *in conclusion.*

3. Help the student read deeply.
   - The ELL child is most likely to be pulled from the classroom for intervention or ESL services just as the community engages deeply with text. We need to take care she does not miss key literacy experiences. Even if her vocabulary knowledge is not strong, keep her in the conversation. Let her hear what her peers are saying; let that explanatory language also be part of her language acquisition process. We learn language best from proficient models (speakers and texts).

- Give her books with a lower text complexity, but inspire her to talk about them in deeper, higher-level ways so she is not trying to practice two things at once: decoding and meaning making. The simpler text is a platform upon which English language learners can practice more complex critical reading skills, learning about metaphor and subtleties without the added struggle of decoding.

- When reading aloud, give the ELL child a chance to respond to the text in ways that are comfortable for her, and not just in the large group. When possible, let her respond to you one on one via writing online or in a drawing journal until she gains confidence, or orally in a way that does not feel too public.

4. Ensure that the student writes and speaks for real audiences and for authentic purposes.

- Publishing ebooks and sharing with the wider world means the student can connect to others who speak her language.

- Persuasive writing on topics that interest the student and the entire class will be great motivators for writing for purpose.

Look Past the Surface of Language

The study of ELLs has progressed to include a greater emphasis on the cognitive tasks students can do as they acquire language and increase their language proficiency rather than on what kind of vocabulary they know or what verb tense they use. Just as the Common Core State Standards have moved us from grammar exercises to deeper analysis of language and text, so too has the body of ELL research moved us to view the stages of language acquisition less in terms of the building blocks of language and more in terms of the various uses of language students demonstrate as they move toward mastery. After all, language use is less about performing for a teacher or performing flawlessly and more about performing various tasks and accomplishing real work. As teachers of English language learners, we should be in the business of helping our students perform the core tasks necessary for them to become college and career ready (van Lier & Walqui, 2012; Understanding Language, 2012).

How does an ELL student use language? Can he argue? Justify? Evaluate? Analyze? Infer? Instead of focusing on the smaller building blocks of language (which we certainly should continue to incorporate into our lessons), we now need to be sure we are teaching in a way that encourages these essential core skills. As we help students develop language, we must bear in mind that language acquisition comes primarily through these performative tasks, and that students will learn those nitty-gritty pieces (grammar, vocabulary, pronunciation) at least as much through context as they once did through drill, and probably more so as these elements of language will be included in meaningful contexts. Constant correction is likely to cause ELL students to lose confidence that their contributions have value, and may lead them to withdraw from participation entirely, delaying their language development. We may still draw ELL students' attention to these discrete aspects of language, but we must never let that focus dominate their instruction to the exclusion of real reading, writing, and discussion for real purposes (van Lier & Walqui, 2012; Understanding Language, 2012).

Identify and Communicate Content and Language Objectives

Our content objectives may include embedded language demands that do not faze our English-proficient students but that can completely block ELLs from grasping the lesson. As teachers, we need to closely study our lessons for language challenges—not just vocabulary, but also grammar and structure challenges.

As teachers, we must account for academic English in our lessons. Academic English (AE) can be viewed as part of overall English language proficiency, which also includes more social uses of language both inside and outside the school environment. It is referred to as a variation of English, a register, or a style, and is typically used within specific sociocultural academic settings. In the broadest sense, AE refers to the language used in school to help students acquire and use knowledge (Bailey & Heritage, 2008; Chamot & O'Malley, 1994; Schleppegrell, 2004). Keep in mind that academic English goes well beyond vocabulary, encompassing particular sentence types and conventions about text structure, for example (Schleppegrell, 2010).

There are two scenarios in which students can learn academic English: through interactions in the classroom and through exposure to text. Research shows there is a gap between the acquisition of conversational English and the acquisition of academic English. Strategies to teach academic English (not just new vocabulary) should be implemented consistently in order to improve academic language acquisition as well as provide extensive opportunities for students to participate in academic reading and writing (Anstrom, DiCerbo, Butler, Katz, Millet, & Rivera, 2010).

As discussed in an earlier chapter, all students learn language socially, so they need ample opportunities to interact with one another while using academic language. Build in daily chances for students to talk around reading and writing. Partner work, group work, and sharing with the whole group should be common occurrences in the reading and writing blocks. Help define for students what the expectations are during these interactions, and give them the tools and structure needed to make it happen. You can also engage in sentence-analysis discussions with all your students or just a small group of ELLs: lift challenging excerpts from class texts and take them apart together, figuring out the everyday meaning hidden in the complex language. Making scary sentences transparent will help students tackle such sentences in their own reading (Fillmore & Fillmore, 2012).

Research also shows that it takes very different time periods to reduce the gap between conversational and academic English acquisition due to factors such as individual differences and the language environment to which the student is primarily exposed. It can take as little as two years for students to be able to comfortably speak conversational English, but academic language needs at least five years to catch up to native speaker fluency (Cummins, 2010).

Build Schema

As human beings, we generally need to be able to connect new learning to something we already know. Knowledge presented without any context is rarely entirely sensible and is very difficult to remember. Students need a place to hang their new learning in their minds. You can get them ready to read an unfamiliar text by both activating existing prior knowledge and building the background knowledge that they will need to understand the content. Think about how to preview text and make connections to increase the relevancy of the lesson. Of course, this is a good strategy to use with all students, but students from non–mainstream cultures, like most ELLs, are more likely to lack some of the background knowledge presumed in the stories used in U.S. schools. Optimal schema building includes helping students develop a mental context for understanding the lesson and providing key vocabulary that will be included (Akhavan, 2008). On the other hand, supporting a child with schema is sometimes overdone and too much time is spent trying to explain things rather than letting the students be part of the experience of purposefully acquiring new information. Another common mistake teachers make is to preempt the text or provide a summarized version of it before engaging in the lesson, when in fact this denies the child the opportunity to do the harder work of making meaning of the text on her own. Instead, provide the prerequisite tools all students will need for success. Ask yourself, "Am I providing the ELL student with a genuine experience, or is my concern about loading her up with the 'right' information taking over?"

Provide Comprehensible Input

Think about how to represent the information you are teaching in ways that make its meaning more transparent. Use visuals, graphic organizers, audio recordings, and hands-on learning. Plan by viewing the lesson through students' eyes, and take into account the range of learners and learning styles that you have in your classroom. Ask yourself these key questions as you plan:

- Does my student have a "buddy" he can turn to in case he has a quick question? (This structure is immensely helpful when you have several ELLs in your classroom.)
- Am I considering all modalities for learning, such as the read-aloud or visual supports, when conveying text information to my students?
- Am I providing ample opportunity for independent practice so I can follow up my lesson with conferences with my ELLs to solidify their understandings?

Technology can play a crucial role. For example, you can use the website www.visuwords.com to build a word web for students who need a visual with definition support.

Online resources can be extremely useful aids in showing books in different, interactive ways. For example, the website www.wegivebooks.org is an interactive website where students can read books and have books read to them online (Figure 10.1). This is a great home–school connection for students with Internet access at home, especially for families who may not speak English or may have low literacy levels.

Enable Language Production

Include the entire literacy loop in your lesson: reading, writing, speaking, and listening, and my new addition: viewing. Design for listening, speaking, reading, and writing, and increase interactions between all modalities. Offer various

Figure 10.1 We Give Books Website

Source: Retrieved from www.wegivebooks.org. Reprinted by permission of the Pearson Foundation.

groupings for students to interact and learn from one another. "The relationships among listening, speaking, reading, and writing during development, then, are complex relationships of mutual support. Practice in any one process contributes to the overall reservoir of second language knowledge" (Peregoy & Boyle, 2001, p. 108). When students assist one another, the classroom atmosphere is a busy buzz, the literacy loop is alive, both students and teachers are constantly modeling, discussions are encouraged, students have constant opportunities to interact, and student work can be immediately displayed (Vogt, Echevarria, & Short, 2011). Teachers offer a lot of support in the initial stages of a new or challenging topic, and then scaffolding is gradually removed.

Plan for intentional groupings such as partnerships to support language development and model language (e.g., one Spanish speaker, one bilingual student, one English speaker to form a triad). Peer groups are powerful because they offer different models of language use as well as motivation through the need to share with peers (Gibbons, 1991).

Assess for Content and Language Understanding

Think about all the different ways to assess students, from formative and summative assessments. Alternative approaches to assessment should always be sought to gauge the effectiveness of instruction. More informal and authentic assessments as well as peer and self-assessment are essential to build a rich understanding of the English language learner in action. Assessment is useful when it occurs during lessons. While students are writing, talking, or engaged in a task, we can record the students' performance using rubrics or rating scales. These notes then inform our instruction and help students understand where they are and where they need to go.

Assessment of ELLs with regard to language use should include a focus on what the student is trying to do well. Look through the errors of the English learner's language use to understand her reasoning. Is she constructing an argument backed with reasons? Is she drawing on multiple sources and making generalizations? Identifying what she is capable of doing will help identify what she needs next. Her problems may be only with those discrete parts of language; watch closely, as she might be understanding the content just fine (Moschkovich, 2012). On the other hand, when a student is *not* showing mastery of content, observe carefully to find the root of his mistakes: Does he truly not understand the content? Or does he not understand the language of the questions, or not have the language to really show what he knows? You may need to adapt an assessment to get a clear picture of what an ELL really knows when language makes formal tests hard for him (Abedi & Liquanti, 2012).

Portfolios, which include writing samples, teacher observations, and teacher anecdotes are extraordinarily helpful in helping us talk to families about a student's growth and in helping us keep close track of our students year after year, passing this information on to every teacher that student has. Cross-content area case study groups with multiple professionals doing assessments give ELLs a broad range of feedback across their subjects (Hamayan, 2010).

Technology can play an integral part in how students can show what they know through performance-based assessments. The dynamic array of online resources gives us the opportunity to teach our ELL students in ways that do not isolate them.

Podcasts that teachers or students create can be a great resource for ELLs, as they can be downloaded and listened to repeatedly, building language skills every time. Students can create these digital stories with sound effects and add video that can be shared online. Podcasts assist all learners through verbal, kinesthetic, visual, interpersonal, and intrapersonal intelligences. Delivering book talks via podcasts is a great way for all learners, especially ELLs, to improve their speaking skills. We can use them to assess understanding as well as speaking and listening abilities.

Many poets and authors are experimenting with multimedia interpretations of their works; these can easily be found online. For ELLs to see multiple interpretations of text helps them frame ideas, more actively learn new vocabulary, and embrace highly complex language structures.

Ebook creation apps and sites give ELLs an opportunity to create their own books and work at simpler language levels without sacrificing or compromising their dignity. Being "published" feels great and, for the emerging English writer, satisfies the desire to do so without a feeling of deficit. Using images from the Web helps ELLs not to feel that their first forays into written English are "babyish." Photos as supports for text look sophisticated and grown-up. Visual images can also help the writer go deeper into more complex writing much more easily. There are so many opportunities now to share writing with new friends from around the world. And many of these readers are learning English for the first time too! The simple texts your ELLs publish will get lots of readers online if we connect them to students in other schools around the world. There is nothing more motivational for a developing writer than to have a real and appreciative audience.

English Language Learners with Exceptional Learning Needs

Some students with disabilities are also English language learners. Sometimes, though, ELLs with individualized education programs (IEPs) are overrepresented in the classroom. This overrepresentation of ELLs in special education classes suggests that educators may have difficulty distinguishing between students who truly have learning disabilities and students who are not progressing because they have not been given the time needed to acquire the language (Yates & Ortiz, 1998).

To ensure that students are properly identified, we must communicate with other building experts to implement interventions and instructional scaffolds before students are identified as having disabilities. After identification, we need to use the supports to scaffold instruction. The instructional supports in the Core Ready lessons for ELLs and students with special considerations will help you meet the needs of all learners to achieve the highest levels of literacy demanded by the Common Core State Standards. When planning for the special needs of ELLs with IEPs, it is important to include co-planning, co-brainstorming, and communication with support providers who also work with the students (English as a second language teachers, special education teachers, related service providers such as speech and occupational therapists, etc.), because every person working with these students has unique expertise in how to best support them. In co-planning instructional considerations for students, everyone is able to offer scaffolds that can be added to the bag of teaching tricks that may work for an individual child. "All students benefit when their teachers share ideas, work cooperatively, and contribute to one another's learning" (Thousand, Villa, & Nevin, 2008, p. 16).

Additionally, bear in mind that ELL students can also be highly advanced learners and may qualify for gifted and talented services. It is not necessary to know a particular language to be gifted and talented, but ELL students have traditionally been underrepresented in such programs because language is often part of the testing process—consider that a gifted child in the United States would not initially appear so if plopped down in a Russian school. Some districts now use nonverbal tests to ensure that they identify students who may still be developing English but who also have exceptional academic abilities. Teachers should collaborate with gifted and talented specialists or paraprofessionals to ensure that gifted ELLs get the challenging academic course work they need, even when their language skills may mean that they initially have low literacy levels (Cohen, n.d.).

When we work together to think deeply about our ELLs, we can understand which skills we need to factor into lessons or small-group structures to support their work toward and beyond the grade-level standards. Core Ready lessons provide a menu of ideas to discuss with related providers as a way to customize instruction, scaffolds, and assessment that will best meet the needs of each student with special considerations.

Be Core Ready: The English Language Learner Meets and Exceeds Standards

Each Core Ready lesson is equipped to help you scaffold instruction to meet the needs of all learners in your room. Your English language learners bring special considerations and positive influences to deepen and enrich the learning environment of your classroom. Through the ELL icons woven through each lesson in the Core Ready series, you will identify opportunities to enhance the teaching you do specifically for your ELLs. The Four Doors to Core Ready—The Journey to Meaning, The Shape of Story, The Road to Knowledge, and The Power to Persuade—offer dynamic teaching opportunities that no ELL should miss. The content is deep, rich, and complex, yet engaging for every student. Gone should be the days when ELLs get special slowed-down lessons or watered down content. Now let's be committed to equal access to language arts content for ELLs and to providing dynamic opportunities for them to learn alongside their peers every single day.

Teaching children whose languages are diverse can seem daunting at first, but viewing these students as bringing gifts of language and culture to the classroom changes the paradigm—believing every child can reach and even exceed standards is gratifying and uplifting for everyone.

chapter 11

Differentiating
with Passion and Purpose for
Special Needs Students

"If a man does not keep pace with his companions, perhaps
it is because he hears a different drummer."
—Henry David Thoreau

"It's not that I'm so smart; it's just that
I stay with problems longer."
—Albert Einstein

Someone once asked famous sculptor Michelangelo how he created his beautiful statues from stone. He said, "Every block of stone has a statue inside it, and it is the task of the sculptor to discover it." This is true of teaching too. We are responsible for finding the potential inside every child. It is our good hard labor to chip away at the stone on the outside and find the magic within that will compel the most struggling or special needs reader and writer to become powerful.

However, you may ask: How can I do this hard work of finding what is different about each child when I have so many children to care about? Classrooms are made up of 20 to 30 or more unique students. They all learn differently and at separate paces. This is understandably a source of anxiety and sometimes frustration for teachers. We always want to see our students succeed, and when some of them struggle it is a struggle for the entire education community—parents, teachers, principals, and peers. However, at our core we can never waver from this belief: *All students can succeed.*

In previous chapters, I describe in detail what a Core Ready learner looks like and the benchmarks that the Common Core State Standards set at each grade level. The same principles apply to the instruction of special needs learners. However, the end products may look different. Each child may chart a different course to realize the educational goals that fit with what he or she can realistically accomplish. Recognize and celebrate progress and achievement in their diverse forms.

Teaching is a constant refinement and a constant balancing. Use faculty meetings and case study professional development sessions where you look closely together at one special needs learner to really assess and inspire your work in this area.

In this chapter, I will offer support for your teaching of special needs students. Some are concrete strategies, like turning your classroom into a calm, well-organized space and gathering the resources necessary for differentiated instruction. But we will also discuss those subtler ways to calibrate your teaching for different students, such as offering affirmations and authentic praise. And we'll cover the building blocks of reading—stamina, fluency, and comprehension—and how they may vary according to students' needs. Our goal here is the same as in all teaching: to foster engaged, independent, and joyful learners.

This chapter focuses on those children who preoccupy us most, those who keep us up at night worrying. They also may become the students we remember with joy for the rest of our lives.

Build a Positive Space for Learning

To start, there are three ways we can make sure our classrooms are well established for differentiation and meet the needs of our special needs students

1. Environment
   - Have a whole-class meeting area, small-group meeting areas, and independent work spaces that are clearly designated and well organized, not overstimulating.
   - Try to avoid paint colors on walls that are overly vibrant. Use soft colors most commonly found in nature, as these have been shown to be more soothing and calming for easily distracted and excitable children.
   - Hide or avoid clutter. For the child who needs structure, or even one who is just sensitive to stimulation, clutter is a real negative. If you struggle with a tendency to collect clutter, purchase fabric and drape it around tables to the floor, and then hide clutter under the tables, out of sight.
   - Consider purchasing a small fountain. The sound of running water helps to keep a sense of calm in the room during independent reading and writing time.
   - Used wisely and thoughtfully, music can be an incredibly powerful organizing force for your most sensitive students. Use it for transitions. Use it to create a sense of calm during independent practice time. Use it to get everyone motivated to clean up. Use songs as a trigger—for example, use a specific song to signal that it's time to clean up. For the child who is likely to ignore your voice calling for order, the music is a signal that it's time to make a transition.

2. Structures: Whole Group–Small Group–One to One
   - Differentiation cannot happen if all we are doing is teaching to the whole class. The structure should feel like an accordion: It is open to the

whole class, then folds partway in to the small group, and then in even closer to the one on one.

3. Resources
   - We need to have texts at all levels in the classroom that are easily accessible to every reader. Although we can anchor in to some key texts together, readers who are reading well have to have many books at their fingertips. The same is true at the other end of the spectrum. Special needs children must have a variety of literature in every genre to meet their needs.

In this chapter, I lay out the opportunities and the realities of differentiated instruction. We must be both realistic and aspirational. A child who has had a disrupted educational history for several years and appears in your fifth-grade classroom reading at a low level may struggle initially, but clear and steady progress is what we seek and what we must continually strive for. There is something cruelly unrealistic about expecting every single one of our special needs students to leap incomprehensible barriers to fly over several grade levels in a matter of months. And yet, of course, we do want every child to succeed. We want to be sure they have every possible chance to do so. In this chapter, I am saying that we will do whatever it takes to humanely get every child as far as he or she can get. But expecting a child who is struggling mightily with text at low levels to read *To Kill a Mockingbird* simply because he is in the eighth grade, and that is the book everyone thinks he ought to read, is ridiculous—and worse, it is harmful. The child who struggles deeply will struggle even more and lose faith. We must surely work toward the idea that every child must be given an equal opportunity, and we must also provide realistic goals and resources for every child. Let us provide the kind of environment and support necessary for every student to achieve according to his richest potential. But we must also do no harm.

Educational psychologists and literacy experts agree that even if a child is challenged in some way, her surrounding environment—school and home—has a profound impact on how much she learns and how she progresses in school. We have control over the school environment and so we have to make our core values explicit, not only to have the maximum impact on all our children, but also to model for families what those values are from the minute the child enters school. Then we can work together to achieve success.

Highlight Capacities and Aspirations of Special Needs Children

Students who struggle in one area are often brilliant in other skills or subjects. Unfortunately, like a car with a tiny scratch in the paint that otherwise functions perfectly, we usually focus on the scratch. The way students feel about themselves as learners hugely affects their mental and emotional development. We have to make sure that we are approaching them with a positive outlook, because everything we say and do is deeply meaningful to them and can shape their sense of identity for years to come. This requires conscientious effort on our part to select our words carefully to ensure that we are building students' self-esteem. We have the opportunity to dispel any notions children may have that they are deficient or somehow the source of their own struggles, notions that are one of the greatest impediments in the quest to overcome learning obstacles. Reframing the child's understanding of himself from a deficit understanding to an empowerment understanding is a crucial move. The language in the following list can help us practice this affirmation. The prompts are concrete enough to always feel authentic. Make sure (and even keep track) that you give your special needs students at least one affirmation every other day. Take your time in a quieter time of the day to make note of what you want to say.

- I admire when you . . .
- I noticed that you . . .
- It makes me proud when you . . .
- I want to compliment you for. . .

Many of our children at extreme ends of the learning spectrum are quite insecure about what people think of them because they are not fitting into the norm—not in school, not at home, not with family, and not with their peers.

The Highly Introverted Student

For example, the child who is highly introverted is often not highly valued and is sometimes bullied in the classroom. We tend to look for the child who is the first to raise her hand, when it may be that the child who needs additional time to think through an idea is thinking very deeply indeed. Maybe the child who is extremely shy and would never speak in a large group would be delighted to share with you via online exchange. Or the child who rarely speaks in a group is a chatterbox when you have a writing conference with him. These children require differentiated instruction. They may have different reasons for their reserve, but it is not necessarily a bad thing.

As Susan Cain (2012) has said, "[A]t school you might have been prodded to come 'out of your shell'—that noxious expression which fails to appreciate that some animals naturally carry shelter everywhere they go, and that some humans are just the same" (p. 6). Her perspective is helpful when considering classroom responses:

- Reimagine the classroom environment so that there is space for reflective introspection as well as group talk and collaborative projects.

- Embrace mobile technology that can help students be heard in different media. Texting responses to a SmartBoard, working together on documents online, and blogging or podcasting all offer the introvert a way to be heard that doesn't require raising one's hand and speaking into the vast space of the classroom.

- Honor difference not as a problem or an obstacle to teaching but as something that can make our learning communities stronger than ever.

Cain also said the following:

> I . . . believe that introversion is my greatest strength. I have such a strong inner life that I'm never bored and only occasionally lonely. No matter what mayhem is happening around me, I know I can always turn inward. (quoted in Cook, 2012, p. 3)

Be sure you are calling attention not only to the child who is constantly raising his hand but also to the very quiet thinker, saying: "I am so pleased to see how deeply Rebekah is concentrating today."

The Highly Extroverted, Excitably Intense Student

At the other end of the spectrum is the student who is jumpy, can't sit still, and makes emotional demands on you by raising his hand or calling out constantly throughout the day. He needs to talk with you and be with you every minute. Here are some strategies to consider when addressing his needs:

- Use furniture to help students get centered: round, puffy cushions filled with air seem to help calm the excitable child, and standing desks help them focus more easily.

- Allow for numerous quick physical breaks. Have these students be your errand runners whenever possible; taking attendance slips to the office and other expeditions allow them to expend energy so that in just a few minutes they regain focus for classroom activities.

- Allow for plenty of movement in the room (the whole–small–whole model will help so that students are not sitting in one spot throughout the entire reading/writing time); also make transitions fun and active so that students are busy during them; for example, hold a "1-minute dance party" between classes.

- Model everything from lining up, to selecting a book, to taking an "eye break" during independent reading, to demonstrating how to get a crayon from the person across the aisle.

- Fill their buckets: First thing in the morning, during the backpack unpack, give the intense student some structured one-on-one time from the start so he can tell you everything he was storing up all evening to share with you. Taking just 2 minutes for this will get you and the child through the rest of the morning.

Affirm and Confirm Potential

The desire to please and to belong to a community is a fundamental and deep human longing. The most important thing we can do as educators and educational leaders is honor the child for what she brings to the community. This will make a bigger difference to the success of that child and the entire community than any measure of test preparation or reading worksheets. I understand that you may wonder what this has to do with academic achievement. It has everything to do with it! All the reading strategies in the world cannot compare to what you will accomplish by stoking the flames of a child's potential and her belief in herself.

Affirm the student when he does something well, even the smallest, smallest, smallest thing. These are your greatest teachable moments, and they include:

- Physical behavior (moving around the room efficiently, following basic safety rules, assuming a reflective and peaceful writing or reading position, managing longer periods of independent work, leaning in when someone is talking to show interest, creating a "quiet bubble" around oneself to maintain concentration)

- Emotional behavior (helping another child, smiling or exhibiting positive energy, remaining calm when things turn frenzied, using the "quiet bubble")

- Academic work (reading or writing for longer periods of time, adding on or otherwise engaging with another student's ideas, staying focused, working alone, reaching a new level in a task or skill)

Affirmations are simple gestures or acts that show your admiration for a student's work: private notes, emails, or texts, or hand signals or public statements of support that make it clear to the community that you value this learning and this learner. However, you must always affirm the learning and not the learner or you risk confusing the community. In other words, your language should mirror the sentence "I want to admire Patrick for the way he put his laptop away today because . . . " rather than "I want to admire Patrick." That way, we not only value the student, but also make it possible for others to envision themselves practicing that very same behavior.

Here are some of my favorite affirmations I have learned from teachers and students from around the world; they can be done quickly and frequently:

- Shooting stars: Kiss your palm and then spread your hand in the direction of the learner with a "whooshing" sound.

- Roller coaster: Move your palm up and down in a roller-coaster motion, saying, "Whoosh!"

- Choo-choo train (for younger students): Move both hands in a fist alongside your body like a train, saying, "Chooo chooo," and then point in the direction of the learner.

- Two hands: Flutter your fingers up in front of your face, saying, "Let's give two hands to Patrick for . . . "

Other ways to offer affirmations (especially for older students) include the following:

- Send a text message to the family to let them know the child had a good day.

- Have index cards handy with stickers on them and use them to write a quick note of praise to the student at the end of the day.

- Have a sticky note reading, "Glad today is going well!," handy to stick on the desk.

Work together to develop realistic instructional goals. For example, the student and teacher may identify a goal to work toward for a given type of skill, such as the ability to read an independent-level text aloud without errors. Once a goal is established, it is then important to monitor progress and use encouragement and positive feedback to motivate the student to voraciously attack the goal. In writing, you can say, "Let's decide together how much you are going to be able to write today." In reading, you can say, "Let's build your reading stamina. How many minutes do you think you could read today without getting too tired?"

Giving the child an active role promotes self-regulation, which is crucial for all learners regardless of their classification as a special needs learner. In the process of making goals and assessing whether they have achieved these goals, students are motivated to reflect on themselves as learners and to connect their actions and efforts to outcomes.

Helping the body work better helps the brain work better. Children learn better when they have time to move their bodies, get blood flowing, oxygenate their cells, and refresh their minds. This works for everybody, not just children. As a species, we are not meant to be sitting at desks for hours at a time. We need the stimulation of movement to be reinvigorated and allow the brain to work its mysterious magic by making connections, processing information, and generating new ideas while we are at play.

The extraordinary truth is that modifications to teaching geared toward reaching special needs learners are universally beneficial to the entire class. In fact, differentiated learning benefits *all* students regardless of any perceived learning disabilities. Therefore, delivering lessons rich in versatile approaches elevates the learning in your classroom as a whole.

The interplay between the key building blocks for developing our reading, writing, speaking, and listening lives is very often out of sync for the special needs child. The following are considerations for how to strengthen and synergize these building blocks for our most vulnerable students:

1. *Stamina.* Special needs students often have very low stamina for reading and writing and even for speaking and listening. Students with special needs may need more learning opportunities distributed over a longer time to make sufficient gains. Teachers can make decisions regarding the intensity and duration of instructional components by carefully monitoring progress and gauging a student's response to instruction (Blachman, Schatschneider, Fletcher, Francis, Clonan, Shaywitz, et al., 2004). Keep a close eye on your students' stamina. Their stamina levels are most successfully assessed via formative assessment tools over the course of weeks, as well as through anecdotal records. We can help build stamina in our special needs students by taking time to cheer them on for simply reading more minutes that day, or writing to the end of the screen or the end of a page. Setting a timer and inviting students to "read to 3 minutes today" is a great incentive, especially when you recognize that even a minute can be a lot for special needs children.

2. *Fluency.* This is another building block that is particularly challenging for many special needs students. The smoothness with which we read and write comes naturally

to some, but not so naturally to others. The choppy reading voice of a special needs student reading aloud or the length of time it takes him to finish a page of writing lets us know that fluency is not yet there. Reading aloud to the child so he can hear fluent reading modeled is important, as is giving him time to practice building fluency with lower-level texts. (Although some are interpreting the standards to say that children should never read below their levels, I very much disagree, especially in the case of special needs students, who may have a chance of meeting standards only if they are given the opportunity to read more and more smoothly over time.)

3. *Comprehension.* Students with special needs are particularly in need of guided practice and specific, explicit instruction that helps them transfer their skills to new problem-solving contexts and to situations that present new content but require previously taught skills (Baker, Gersten, & Scanlon, 2002; Fuchs, Fuchs, Prentice, Burch, Hamlett, Owen, et al., 2003a, 2003b).

We need to monitor our instructional language (both oral and written) to be sure we are meeting the needs of both the highest-level and the lowest-level readers. You may need to practice saying something two ways in every lesson. For example, if you are talking about character development, you can first say, "We are going to take a look at this character." Then, a few minutes later, you can also say, "We are going to examine this character." The higher-level reader will get a bump up in vocabulary while the lower-level reader will gain familiarity with new terms. But comprehension is often an ongoing challenge on far deeper levels for the special needs student. Stories and informational texts all contain minefields: time changing, characters with unusual names that confuse the reader, settings that also change—for the struggling reader, it's as if every single piece is a moving part, completely out of control. Again, the special needs student should practice higher-level skills in comprehension with lower-level texts. And then, when grade-level text is being introduced, the student will have had many opportunities to practice up to that time in ways that feel safer and more secure.

Special Needs Learners Can Build Critical Thinking Skills

We can help special needs students build critical thinking skills, but for this work, we may have to use lower-level texts. Even the most basic text can be a platform from which to help our students begin to think critically. If they are struggling deeply, I do not recommend asking students to decode difficult text and work on critical thinking at the same time. But we can do both separately. In small-group instruction, we can work with our special needs students to build their capacity for decoding texts, inviting their curiosity about vocabulary and new word strategy skills. To cultivate critical thinking

1. Let students read lower-level texts to practice higher-level thinking skills. The child who struggles needs permission to not struggle with every spinning plate. Make it possible for your most struggling readers to have book chats with friends about texts that are lower than their level of challenge.

2. Do not immediately break down critical thinking into separate parts. This may seem counterintuitive. For years, we have seen recommendations for teaching "inferring" and "connecting" strategies separately. But my perspective is that there's too much division of the cognition around reading. If we break things down too much, it doesn't even look like reading anymore, and our struggling readers are forced to do yet more juggling. They are spinning the inferring plate or the questioning plate, looking at each one separately. And this does them very little good because they are so busy looking at each plate that they have forgotten they are doing something much bigger—reading itself. I want to stop that. I want to take us forward to a more global approach to teaching reading to our struggling readers, one in which they are focused

on their own deepest thinking. The main questions should be "What are you thinking about?" and "What do you think the author is thinking about?"

There is one strategy that I believe to be the linchpin for why some readers can fall through the words into a story. This is the strategy of visualizing, of seeing the story as you read. The world is now driven by images. Entire social media campaigns are built around a single image. We have to work explicitly with our most struggling readers to help them "see" the story. Here are three ways to do this:

1. Read aloud. There is huge value in regular daily read-alouds. The more we do this, the more our students at all levels are going to start creating visual images in their minds to go along with the text. This happens for informational text as well as narrative fiction.

2. Model your own experience of becoming absorbed and falling through the words into the story. Give your students the gist of how that feels for you. For example, when I read *The Chronicles of Narnia*, I get a sensation when I enter Narnia. It's a sensation that comes from fashioning the world of the story in my mind. When I invited author Katherine Paterson to speak to some of my students, she told them she was worried about the film of her book *Bridge to Terabithia* because "Everyone has their own Terabithia." How would the film portray it? The problem I see most with struggling readers is that they cannot or never have fashioned their own Terabithias. Let us model how we do this. We can use the arts, music, and drama to help our students live out what it means to feel the world of the story.

3. Create "thinking equations." We can give struggling students a smooth way to experience our modeled reading through what I call thinking equations. In a thinking equation, the reader understands that X plus X equals understanding. For example, a strong reader will ask herself, "Why did the character just do that?" Then she imagines a logical answer based on what she knows and draws a conclusion, sometimes nearly instantaneously. So it's X plus X equals understanding. We can practice doing these thinking equations slowly or quickly with our students. Writer Malcolm Gladwell (2005) has said: "There can be as much value in the blink of an eye as in months of rational analysis" (p. 17).

We can walk our readers through a thinking equation. For an inference, a reader asks, "Why did the character just do that?" and then imagines a logical answer based on what he knows about the world and about what he has read. This practice with thinking equations is necessary for all students, but perhaps even more necessary for our most struggling readers. They rarely get to practice such critical thinking because they are so busy with the slow work of decoding the text and deciphering vocabulary.

Special Needs Learners Can Build Independence

This is actually both the easiest and the most challenging aspect for me to address. I know your inclination is to be right there alongside your most struggling students. I have worked closely with schools for the deaf my entire career, and I have seen some of the most tender teaching of my life in these schools. The teachers are well aware that many of their students have missed some fundamental nurturing they could not get at home because parents might not actually know their children's language (sign language). As a result, I have seen teachers do everything for their students, to the point where I call out in frustration, "I know Jonny can do that himself!" But I see where that instinct comes from—you are used to intensive nurturing, to filling the gaps that may not have been filled by other adults in that child's life to this point.

But we have got to give our struggling learners the opportunity to build independence. Choice is crucial here. The more a student struggles, the more we fill her time with activities designed in the hope that they will fill in her gaps—and the more we take away her ability to choose. I understand this instinct, but refrain from it. It might take her longer to finish a sentence, to turn a page, to express an idea—but give her every chance to get there. She

needs to know what independence feels like. Whether it is choosing what she reads, creating her own book basket, or choosing what to write about, making decisions will empower the special needs child in literacy, and be so crucial to her development. She needs the pleasure and the power of entering her own question into Google. She needs to feel the power of her capacity to grow and change.

Do not criticize the child for selecting a lower-level text to read on his own; celebrate a writing topic he has chosen many times before, and teach the entire class to become patient while he formulates an opinion of his own. Our instinct is to solve his problems and fix all the moments when struggle creeps in. Don't do it. We have all been and still are in some ways struggling learners, each in our own way. And those moments of independence became, for us, transcendence. They can be the same for all our students.

Special Needs Readers Must Have Time to Read

I hope I have convinced you that we can prepare all students to be productive, competent, and career and college ready at graduation. We know the average work environment is fast paced, with deadlines, group work, and ever-evolving technology, but make no mistake, we are preparing children to steadily climb the staircase of complexity with this reality in mind. We are building skills with careful thought for the child's mental readiness. We must not pressure them so severely that they are more likely to drop out when they reach the end of middle school or high school: "[T]he presence of an eighth grade promotion test requirement is strongly associated with an increased probability of dropping out prior to tenth grade" (Reardon & Galindo, 2002, p. 16). This must change now. Let us reimagine the classroom so it is a more hospitable place for special needs readers while at the same time moving them toward achievement of grade-level standards.

This will require some courage on our part not to do what we've done before—not to fall into the trap of worksheets and mindless activities to fill some gap we perceive in our students—but instead to ensure that they receive time each and every day for reading at their levels. We have to stop cringing when a student in eighth grade needs to read Dr. Seuss. Is that her reading level? Then she *must have time to read at that level.* Does this preclude us from inviting her to explore more challenging text with us? No. Does this preclude her from reading above her level? No. But still, she must have time to read at her level—with no shame and no embarrassment. Just determination.

It is crucial to make a distinction between high expectations and unreasonable pressure, because there has been alarming discourse in the education community insinuating that struggling learners should read only at grade level, regardless of their independent reading levels. This is absurd. Years of important research have shown that children who read at their independent reading levels for dedicated time each day learn more vocabulary and learn to read more effectively than those who do not.

We as educators are pressured by a society that expects fast results and immediate solutions. When we don't see immediate results, we get impatient and eagerly discuss adopting a new strategy. This may be the status quo in a boardroom; however, children are not machines processing information. They are not widgets. They are real people with real challenges and huge potential. Time to learn is crucial. The more students struggle, the more distractions and roadblocks we often put in their way. We are pushing, assigning tasks and assignments that pull strategies apart and break down reading into components that often only confuse students even more.

To learn to read, the struggling reader *must read.* This seems overly simplistic at first glance, but stop to think about it: When have you ever gotten better at something you never really got to do? Probably never. If you don't cook well, and all I did was explain to you about each ingredient and taught you in isolation how to mix, dice, and chop but never actually let you cook the dinner, you would never be able to put those pieces together. Working with the pieces is definitely important, but it's putting the pieces together that we've often forgotten to model. Let's do that too.

The struggling reader will struggle in math, in science, in history, in everything if he still cannot read. If the result of the Common Core State Standards is that we punish and systematically lock special needs students into texts they cannot read in the desperate hope that they will pass high-stakes tests, we are dooming them. This is not humane, and it's not sensible.

---

career ready **Physician**

Reading is central to the daily work of physicians. Most of the preparation of physicians, beyond the skills in scientific thought and reasoning, involves the exposure to large volumes of material. Perhaps more critical to survival later is your ability to synthesize the content and thought process behind articles, medical text chapters, and the like. This ability allows you to establish what material is critical and what is interesting but not relevant to your practice or research interests.

The medical world requires significant writing skills, even in an era of electronic health records that provide templates for the user. Writing scientific papers is different from writing medical charts, but both require clarity of expression, focus, and, interestingly, integrity. The French have a fitting expression: "Qui ne sait se borner, ne sut jamais écrire" ("One who cannot limit himself will never know how to write"). Medical records carry the burden of someone's health and personal information to be read by other physicians for decades, and in some cases by lawyers and judges whose only information comes from the physician's writings.

After all these years, I still derive great pleasure from reading some of my medical records, and even a cursory reading of an article with new knowledge is a thrill that is hard to compare!

But there is one way to get every student to meet the standards. Our most struggling readers must absorb as much print as possible, for as much time as possible, every day and every evening. In this way, they build stamina by adding volume to their reading lives. We must offer a balance of guided practice through challenging text and ample time for independent practice at each child's own reading level. Both can happen and both must happen. Too often we isolate struggling readers. But reading is a highly social act. There are plenty of new and easy ways to invite our most struggling readers into the reading community, such as online through great new publishing apps that create podcasts of choice-driven selections and encourage readers to share across reading levels with one another.

The same applies to writing. Stamina is key, and we build students' stamina when we care. Remember what I said in Chapter 7 about how many thousands of hours our students spend playing games online? We have to make writing feel more like that: driven by individual passion and interest, rewarding, full of big ideas and epic wins. Students should write in the widest variety of genres: science fiction, informational blogs, letters to friends across the world.

Have High Expectations, but Cherish the Small Steps

Do not be afraid to have high hopes for your special needs students. They can and will excel, if only we give them time to practice in ways that are joyful, individualized, and relatable to the lives they lead as readers, writers, thinkers, dreamers, and learners outside the classroom. But it is true that everyone marches to his or her own drummer. Let's model for families that we love their children as they are, with all their uniqueness and quirks, and that not everyone travels the same pathways. Your role as educator is to set the tone that it is not only OK but a blessing to have a child who is not like all the others in your community.

We cannot be afraid to truly delight in these students before us, sharing with us their gifts and their small steps forward, so exquisite and subtle no test can measure them.

chapter 12

Making Assessment Matter

"Data not only measures progress, it inspires it."
—Hillary Clinton

The standards era demands a highly rigorous approach to assessment. Rather than collect data for collection's sake, let's collect data to inspire us to teach and learn more fully and richly than ever before.

Assessment should help us with the following core questions:

1. What skills do my students have firmly in place?
2. What skills do my students need to better develop?
3. What does the data tell me, the educator, that I should do next?
4. What does the data tell my students they should do next?

The Common Core State Standards plan for development over time by identifying core skills and outcomes for every single grade level. We must do the same for our students, who are constantly growing and changing. Let's "measure what we treasure," as the old saying goes. A once-a-year standardized test will do something to help us understand our students and maybe even our instruction, but it is not nearly enough, and the results never come in time for us to use the results for the students we have right now.

Let us use assessment methods wisely and to the best possible benefit of our students—not overdoing the assessment protocols, but instead creating a strategic plan for assessment. We need to stop thinking of assessment as something we do periodically with standardized measures on a particular schedule and start thinking of it as an inherent part of our teaching practice.

Meaningful assessment leads to meaningful teaching. And meaningful, effective teaching leads to meaningful outcomes. Set up a strategic plan by asking the following:

1. How will we know our teaching has been successful? How will kids know they have learned successfully?
2. What tools will we use to help us know where our kids are?
3. How will we embed assessment into the daily flow of our teaching?
4. What will we do to understand the data we get? How can we collaborate with other educators to understand it?
5. When and how will we enact changes to our teaching based on what the assessments say?
6. How will we share assessment results and next steps with students and families?

Let us first discuss the different kinds of assessment. Later in this chapter, you will see a chart describing each. When you are creating your strategic plan, be sure to consider the interplay between the many assessment options available. The two principal types of assessment are *summative* and *formative*. Each type of assessment can take many different forms; the key difference lies in the intention behind the assessment and how the results are used—either to evaluate performance (summative) or to inform instruction (formative). However, certain modes of assessments lend themselves more or less to one of the two types. This chapter focuses mostly on *standardized tests* as a common form of summative assessment and *performance-based assessments* as a powerful form of formative assessment.

Summative Assessments

Summative assessments are critical to any comprehensive plan for assessment. In general, any time students are assessed for the purpose of providing a grade or score, and not to inform subsequent teaching and learning of the students in question, the assessment is summative. Summative assessments evaluate learning and teaching that is already done. Summative assessment can take many forms, including state assessments, district benchmarks, end-of-term exams, end-of-unit or chapter tests, or scores used for report card grades. Summative assessments typically occur after instruction and help to evaluate student proficiency in the specific skills that were taught. A summative assessment may occur at various intervals (yearly, monthly, weekly) but, in my opinion, educators need to shift away from frequent summative assessment (testing to evaluate), and move toward formative assessment, which is focused on helping kids grow. I discuss formative assessment in greater detail later in the chapter.

Thoughts about Standardized Tests

In school, our children will have to take standardized tests that reflect the state's perspective on what they should be learning. These tests will become more coordinated with the Common Core State Standards, so that when we measure the success of students from state to state, we will know we are comparing apples to apples at long last. Tests in their best form serve a purpose: to help determine whether public institutions are providing what is necessary to make a just and equitable society.

Standardized tests should protect and defend our most vulnerable children. We can begin to make demands on our systems to provide all children with equal access to books and technology, to quality teachers, to the kinds of supports that all children deserve. As of now, the correlation between low test scores and poverty is high. "Low-poverty schools are 22 times more likely to reach consistently high academic achievement compared with high-poverty schools. Schools serving student populations that are both low poverty and low minority are 89 times more likely to be consistently high performing compared with high-poverty, high-minority schools" (Harris, 2007, p. 367). This correlation should not overwhelm us; instead it should be a clarion call to action to equalize our schools—at least a step in the right direction toward combating poverty. Further, standardized testing shows us trends. We can look at gender disparities. For example, if we see that the girls in our school are less likely to answer non-fiction-related questions correctly, we can commit to focusing additional energy on being sure the girls are given enough time in class to develop this skill.

It is not possible to do a close read on a child's progress through the lens of a test score alone, but such a score can be a valuable addition to that child's portfolio and, more important, a valuable tool in analyzing the effectiveness of instruction.

The dark side of the standardization of assessment is that we begin to teach *only* what is on the test and not what is necessary for the child to learn in order to become college and career ready—basically, to succeed in life beyond the walls of the K–12 classroom. How do you know when you've gone over the tipping point in this regard? Here are some of the signs:

- You feel frustrated that you are "not really teaching anymore."

- Your students look or feel stressed and exhausted (or you do).

- You are referring to the test to decide what to teach each day.

- You are basing your teaching points on your anxiety that your students won't perform well.

- Your professional development is more about the test than it is about the children you teach.

If you are experiencing any or all of these, it is time to reevaluate your school's approach to assessment. No one, and I mean no one, looks back and says, "I remember Mrs. Smith, my favorite teacher, who did test prep all day." But assessments that are rigorous and challenging can be exciting and rewarding to practice for and to take. They really can be. We can achieve that perfect balance.

Prepare Wisely—Teach the Test Genre

When my daughter was in fourth grade, she came home and said, "You know, I think I did really well on that test. Because every time there's a question like the writing one on this test, I always answer it the same way." Fear struck me when she said this. What was she saying? When I probed, she explained, "In second grade, I wrote a research report on Amelia Earhart. And since then, whenever I take a test, if the question fits, I just fit what I know about Amelia Earhart to answer it. Like: Who do you admire? What character in history is like a character in literature? It always works!" I was so relieved. I recognized that she had mastered the art of the test. And how did she do it? She refined a way to answer multiple questions. She looked carefully at the question to see what the test maker really expected of her. She understood the *genre* of the test.

These days, test makers are changing the tests often; they haven't gotten it perfect yet either. So we are lucky—we do not have to guess or predict exactly what's going to be on every test. What we can do as educators is to help our students think and plan in advance with a strategy. There are some patterns, again and again, year in and year out.

Recently, my younger daughter took the SAT. On her way out the door, I called out to her. She turned back and smiled at me, her young face filled with the hope and also fear of the newness and seriousness of the moment. And I said, "Just remember the word *mitigate*." She said, "Mom! C'mon!" And I said, "That word is always on the test!" Later when she came home, pale and tired after that long test, she was smiling still. I asked, "How did it go?" She said, "Well, I don't know if you helped me or hurt me. . . . The word *mitigate* was on the test! So I spent one quick minute getting it right and then about 10 minutes just sitting there thinking: 'How did my mother know this word was going to be on the test?'"

If we are doing our jobs well—if our methodology is powerful and effective—and if the standardized test matches the standards we are asked to teach, our students will know the information on it when the time comes. They will know how to comprehend and analyze what they read. They will have a toolbox full of academic vocabulary to use. They will be able to identify the common structures of text. They will know if a sentence is crafted correctly. But we also need to make sure they know how to demonstrate they know that information, so we must teach these skills too—not in a frantic cram session, but in thoughtful and well-timed ways throughout the year. Test takers will need to know that multiple genres of text might appear on a test and how to identify them when they do. They will need to be able to detect, from specific words in a prompt, what genre they should write in. They will need to understand that the test reader is a unique audience unlike others that might read their work. They will need to work under timed conditions. Like the Common Core State Standards themselves, these are life skills that students will bring with them into their academic and professional lives beyond their K–12 careers. If we generally teach *above and beyond* the test, rather than *to* the test, and then teach the testing genre thoughtfully, our kids will excel.

Here are some questions students should be able to answer about standardized tests:

- What is the purpose of a standardized test?
- Who is the audience? Who will be reading my piece of writing and how can awareness of this help me write?
- What does "testing language" look like? Sound like?
- What are the conventions of standardized tests? How are they commonly organized?
- What are some strategies that might be helpful when reading this type of text?

Formative Assessments

Donald Graves (1994) once said, "The teacher is the chief learner of the classroom." And how true this is! But the learning is not just about the content of the material. What Graves was so good at was letting us know how important *our* learning about each *child* was to our teaching. Formative assessment plays a vital role in helping us understand both where our students are and what we must do to support them. It helps us to know how to group them for more intensive instruction and how to provide differentiated material for homework and for independent practice. Best of all, formative assessment is a lever to drive our ongoing understanding of what makes the child tick.

In the era of the Common Core State Standards, formative assessments are as important as ever because they enable us to adjust our teaching in a timely manner and to tailor instruction to better meet the needs of our individual students. True formative assessment is *not* a shorter, more frequent standardized test. Formal formative assessments such as reading inventories or writing prompts should be administered at least three times a year, but the informal formative assessments—the "kidwatching" Don Graves and Yetta and Ken Goodman have described—or the natural, quick observations the teacher does within lessons or while mentoring her apprentice readers and writers, should happen continuously, daily, in every moment of the lesson.

One important component of formative assessment is student involvement. Formative assessment is not fully effective when students are left out of the equation. Because student ownership increases their motivation to work and to learn, students must be involved in this process as both evaluators of their

own skill and valuable partners in the learning of their colleagues. You are an important component in this equation too; you and your students should act as critical partners in driving the learning process. You can help the students identify learning objectives, set up criteria for measuring those objectives, and design specific tools for measuring the criteria you outline. Most important, students must receive timely, thoughtful feedback on their performance, both what they did well as well as guidance about what to do next. This feedback can come from you, their peers, or their own self-reflective process, but it must come from somewhere. The feedback loop is what makes formative assessment useful (Heritage, 2011).

Margaret Heritage tells us, "There is no single way to collect formative evidence because formative assessment is not a specific kind of test" (2011, p. 18). Perhaps you gather data a few times a year using a reading inventory that identifies each student's sight word knowledge, fluency, comprehension, and individual reading level. Maybe you are asked to collect a writing sample and score it on a rubric. You may give "exit tickets" at the end of a lesson to see who grasped the day's objective and who didn't. Surely, you make countless observations about your students as you interact with them on a daily basis. There are many versions of formative assessments, but all of them are designed to tell you a little something about specific reading and writing skills. If they are not already, the tools you use will eventually be aligned with the Common Core State Standards so that you can map the progress of your students as they make progress up the staircase of learning.

Tailored to You and Your Class

Whereas summative data informs the powers that be about aggregate data for your class, school, district, or even entire state, the formative data helps inform *you* about the students in *your* class over the course of the year, and it provides your students specific information about their own learning. But this is possible only if you take the necessary steps to analyze the data—finding the trends and red flags and then using the information to inform your collective decisions. Don't fall into the trap of gathering data simply to send it away to the administration—a formative assessment is *not* a mini-summative assessment. Use this valuable information to help you do a close reading of each of your students so that you can design individualized instruction that best meets their unique needs. Use the following four questions to guide you as you analyze your formative data to do a close reading of one student. Whether you're looking at notes from daily reading conferences or results from formal assessments administered only a few times a year, these questions should help you and your students figure out what to do next.

What Does the Data Say?

Whether the assessment renders an essay-style narrative (as in an informal observation or interview) or an actual score (as in a developmental reading assessment, a sight word test, or a phonemic awareness assessment), what are this child's results? What are her results on each assessment? What are the patterns in your observation of this student? How does that score or result compare to the rest of the students in the class? To the grade level? To her previous performance? Did the student "ace" the assessment or did she struggle? Is she where she should be for this time of the year? Begin your close read of your student here—in the results of the formative assessments.

What Does the Data Mean?

Once you have collected your data from your formative assessments, it is time to analyze the information and compare it to the Common Core State Standards staircase. What do the results tell you about what this child is able to do and what this child needs? What do the results tell you about the child's position on the staircase in relation to the standards categories? What skills are firmly in place? What is this child still struggling to do? Is this student performing below, at, or above grade level in the skill tested? What are the trends? Is this child scoring well on visual tasks like phonics but struggling with auditory tasks like phonemic awareness? Is she acing decoding but still not comprehending what is being read? Is she summarizing but still not inferring meaning from text? If the formative assessments are comprehensive and aligned with the Common Core State Standards, they should give you a clear read on each of your students in all categories of the staircase. When done as part of your daily instructional practice, you can be sure that you are effectively tracking the progress of your student.

You also will have a lot of very specific information to discuss with parents, administration, and, most important, your students themselves during the year. By sharing your results and observations with your students, and by bringing them (no matter how young) into an awareness of their specific skills, you grant them ownership of the process of improving by first helping them see their abilities and deficits. You are taking the first step toward inviting students to be partners in their own improvement.

What Does the Data Suggest I Do?

Once you have determined the trends and areas of need in your formative data by analyzing it, use this information to make curricular decisions. Can you re-teach this concept in a one-on-one conference? Are there other students in need of the same skills reinforcement who might make up a small group that could work together? Is the entire class struggling with a specific concept, indicating that it should be brought back into your whole-group instruction? What strategies do you know that can help you teach these specific skills? Are there students who need advanced challenges beyond the grade-level work? What might those challenges be? These are the types of choices you can make only if you have closely read your students and all of the layers of skills they bring to the classroom. By closely reading your students using these assessment tools, you are better able to bring the curriculum *to* your students rather than simply teaching your grade-level standards.

What Does the Data Suggest My Students Do?

Inviting students into the assessment of their own learning requires providing them with useful feedback right away, as they learn. This supports the mentor–apprentice relationship described in Chapter 4. Ongoing, useful feedback is extraordinarily significant to the progress of any learner. Show your students what they are doing well, and then use that foundation to also discuss with them the steps they might take to improve upon those skills to move higher on the staircase of learning. Dignify your students by discussing with them the specific steps they need to take to increase their reading and writing skills. Invite them into the process of deciding the best route to improvement. Share your ideas with students and find out whether they have ideas of their own that might enhance particular skills. Again, by providing students with the opportunity to take ownership of their own learning, you are more likely to see results more quickly.

Performance-Based Assessments

I spend the remainder of this chapter discussing performance-based assessments because I find them the most exciting development of the standards era. Work that was done 20 years ago promoting project-based learning and portfolio collections is enjoying renewed interest and getting a 21st century makeover, largely because they can render aggregate summative data and also useful, timely formative results.

First of all, kids love performance-based assessments. I am definitely a fan of kids' opinions. They tolerate standardized tests reasonably well (if the school doesn't go wild with the preparation), and they tolerate formal formative assessments like reading inventories quite well, because for the most part they should feel like the authentic work of the classroom, only under a microscope and with the handy resources that can help move that work along efficiently. But performance-based assessments (PBAs) actually feel like fun!

Everyone loves to share if they feel good about what they did. We are living in a moment in time when it is now possible to share our writing, reading, and thinking with audiences all over the world. The world has become one big opportunity for performance. Our children will not be daunted, I promise. In fact, this generation knows only a public culture. The lure of an authentic audience is too great. We all enjoy feedback, and best of all, we all enjoy connectivity. That's what PBAs are all about, because they require a viewer, a listener, and a reader.

And while the summative standardized tests and intermittent formative assessments have their function in schools, PBAs generate even more propitious data because they are collected while the child is in the act of performing the skill in an authentic setting. For the kinds of data that will give us immediate and dramatic feedback, both for our own teaching and for our students' ongoing understanding of themselves and the relationship they have to outcomes of their work, performance-based assessments are a dynamic component of the rich work of a reading–writing–speaking–listening classroom. The PBA invites children to be part of their own assessment process in an active, engaged approach to appraisal and reflection.

Robert J. Tierney (2000) suggests that goals for evaluation and assessment should befit the following tenets:

- Evaluation is a social construct that is a continuous, recursive, and divergent process (raising more questions than answers).

- Evaluation is an emergent process that cannot be fully designed in advance.

- Evaluation is a process for sharing accountability rather than assigning it.

- Evaluation is a joint face-to-face process that requires, at a minimum, the clarification of competing constructions and that is an educative and empowering activity for all.

- Evaluation respects diversity more than standardization and verifiability, and possible interpretations over consistency or traditional notions of reliability or reverence for scores.

- Evaluation is intent on affording students opportunities for engaging with teachers, caregivers, and stakeholders in meaningful partnerships involving genuine decision making.

Performance-based assessment befits all of these tenets when done in deliberate ways. So what exactly is performance-based assessment?

Catch Them in the Act

My neighbor's son practiced baseball in our joint backyards for years. I would hear the thump of the ball in his mitt on early Saturday mornings and marvel at his commitment and dedication. But really, what I marveled at was how much he loved what he was doing. His mother said she couldn't keep him in the house on those Saturday mornings, and at night he was dreaming of baseball. She'd watch him sleep with his hands moving in a circular fashion, internalizing the moves of the game even through his unconscious thought. When he got to high school, he played in the big games. His team went to championships. We all went to watch him perform the clutch plays, never losing his cool. We watched the smooth and perfect cycle of his arm—a reminder of the little boy he used to be as he threw the perfect pitch. The big game was his performance-based assessment. It was his moment to show the world what he could do.

In the classroom, performance-based assessment works much the same way. It's the process of using student performance instead of tests or surveys to assess skills and knowledge. Students engage in authentic class activities, projects, tasks, negotiations, debates, or conversations while the teacher observes and measures behavior. Two common styles of project-based assessments are *student portfolios,* where students collect products that represent their work over time, and the *assessment center method,* in which students are placed in simulated real-life situations while their performance is judged by the teacher.

Performance-based assessment is both rigorous and standards based. It is an asset model for assessing rather than the deficit model so common in today's classrooms. It also satisfies all of Tierney's (2000) tenets for assessment in this millennium—a time of dynamic reading and writing. Most important, performance-based assessment enables us to measure higher-order thinking skills. We aren't seeking to measure content knowledge here as much as we are seeking to measure habits of mind of real readers and writers. "More than standardized tests of content knowledge, performance-based tasks are able to measure students' habits of mind. Performance-based assessment requires students to use high-level thinking to perform, create, or produce something with transferable real-world application" (Stanford School Redesign Network, 2008).

The Student's Role in Performance-Based Assessment

This method of assessment requires the student to be active and "all in." He creates products or performances that help him demonstrate his knowledge and skill, and these tasks just might be open-ended and flexible. This is a departure from traditional testing methods that require a student to select a single answer or fill in the blank. The student participating in performance-based assessment must understand that he is not expected simply to regurgitate information. He isn't there to spill out the facts and figures memorized for a test. He is instead tasked with demonstrating higher-order thinking skills outlined in the Common Core State Standards. The standards require students to deeply analyze, infer, craft, create, and compare. Through performance-based assessment activities designed to utilize these skills, students have the chance to show their teachers, classmates, and themselves that they are indeed capable of such thinking.

The Teacher's Role in Performance-Based Assessment

The teacher's goal is to create authentic tasks that are important and interesting for the students, tasks that offer perfect opportunities to perform outcomes that correspond to the Common Core State Standards. The tasks should be authentic and represent the kinds of skills and products readers and writers will need to demonstrate outside of the classroom. Tasks should enable the evaluation of both process and product and allow for real, timely feedback and coaching between teacher and student. Teachers should also design accompanying recording tools such as rubrics, checklists, or observational notes to record subjective impressions and communicate these judgments verbally or in writing. This way, students can demonstrate application of new skills in real ways, teachers can record observations of successes and challenges, and students can be a party to the results. The caring educator would rather understand how students perform when engaged in the work of real readers, writers, speakers, and listeners than simply how they perform as test takers.

Performance-Based Assessments Combine Summative and Formative Assessment Strategies

Authentic assessments require students to be effective performers with acquired knowledge. Traditional tests tend to reveal only whether the student can recognize, recall, or "plug in" what was learned, but this is out of context. Many formative assessments offer context but still limit students to correct answers and measure only specific skills without much wiggle room for demonstration of other skills. PBAs are all about context and flexibility. They achieve validity and reliability by pre-identifying criteria for scoring a variety of products through the use of rubrics or checklists, whereas traditional testing does so by standardizing test items and requiring correct responses. Critics of testing point out that many tests, particularly multiple-choice tests, do not provide sufficient opportunities for students to think through what they are doing or make them want to do their best. "Portfolios and other forms of performance-based assessment, on the other hand, invite the student to show his or her 'best' work" (Belanoff & Dickson, 1991, p. xvi). "Performance assessment is used for both formative and summative purposes. When students are provided with multiple opportunities to learn and apply the skills being measured and opportunities to revise their work, performance assessment can be used to build students' skills and also to inform teachers' instructional decisions" (Stanford School Redesign Network, 2008).

What Are the Advantages of Performance-Based Assessments?

The advantages of PBAs are vast. They remind us that learning can and should feel natural. When a child learns something new at home, she says, "Hey, watch me!" PBAs are the classroom version of this. Students get the opportunity to say, "Hey, world, watch me!" PBAs also allow students to assess their own progress and therefore be more responsible for their ascent up the staircase—they take more ownership of the work needed to advance. For teachers, performance-based assessments provide us with more information about the learning needs of our students and enable us to modify our methods to meet these needs. They also help us focus on the positive—what students *have* learned, not just how well they *can* learn. PBAs provides us with the best possible tool for linking our own classroom and school practices with the authentic and rigorous work of the Common Core State Standards. PBAs highlight our teaching too. They show the world what we have all done together. PBAs are an exciting way to meet all the goals of formative assessment: feedback for teachers, feedback for students, and student involvement in the process of assessment.

Schools that have committed to assessing students with performance-based measures outpace their traditional counterparts as well. "When compared with the restrictions of schools geared toward standardized testing, [PBA schools] are the institutions most in touch with meeting the academic, social, and psychological needs of their students, the burgeoning requirements for achievement in the 21st century, and the 'skills . . . crucial to students' success as college freshmen, professionals, and participants in a democracy'" (Tashlik, 2010, p. 57, quoting Schmoker, 2008). In traditional schools that rely mainly on standardized testing,

[t]est-prep activities—not authentic teaching and learning—were responsible for much of the increase in test scores. This explains why achievement gains on state tests are often at odds with stagnant performance on the National Assessment of Educational Progress (Cavanaugh, 2007). It explains why higher passing rates on standardized tests have had little effect on the high proportion of students who enroll in remedial college courses (Fitzhugh, 2007; Kollars, 2008). (Schmoker, 2008, pp. 70–74)

Performance-based assessments, by their very design, ensure that students are not just performing on a test, but are instead demonstrating real skill in real situations where that skill is needed. These assessments are replicable in the real world. They are an example of teaching not *to* the test but, as I said earlier, *above and beyond the test*.

Assessment Pillar	Type of Data	Use	Examples
Summative	Renders aggregate data on larger groups, with individual scores also available; **provides a final score or grade; evaluator of learning**	Helps guide instructional decisions at the state, district, school, and (minimally) classroom level by showing trends; informs students and families **how kids *did*,** but not what to do next	**State standardized tests;** district benchmark exams; weekly spelling tests or end-of-unit tests (that are not used to inform later lessons)
Formative	Renders school, class, and individual data in an **ongoing, timely way;** inherent part of strong instructional practice; ***enabler* of learning**	Helps students, teachers, and administrators **guide the instructional choices** to move students up the staircase of learning	**Performance-based assessments;** anecdotal notes during lessons; records of reading behaviors (formal or informal)

What Does a Performance-Based Assessment Look Like?

The following is a PBA designed for fifth grade. This task also clearly defines standards-aligned learning outcomes.

Grade 5 Reading Unit 6: Historical Fiction

Focus Standard

RL.5.9 Compare and contrast stories in the same genre on their approaches to similar themes and topics.

Secondary Standards

RL.5.1 Quote accurately from a text when explaining what that text says explicitly and when drawing inferences from the text.

RL.5.2 Determine the theme of a story, drama, or poem from details in the text, including how characters in a story or drama respond to challenges or how the speaker in a poem reflects upon a text.

RL.5.3 Compare and contrast two or more characters, settings, or events in a story or drama, drawing on specific details in the text.

Performance-Based Assessment Students will prepare an interview, take notes, and write a summary to show an overall understanding of two historical fiction texts, using exact quotes and thinking about themes from the books.

Part 1: Character Interviews: Students will be broken into pairs for this project. In each pair, one student will represent a character from Christopher Paul Curtis's story *Bud, Not Buddy* and the other will represent a character from Louise Erdrich's *The Birchbark House*. Thinking about his or her own character's experiences, and how they differ from his or her partner's, each student will prepare a set of interview questions as if his character were speaking to his partner's character. The students will then have a chance to interview each other in character.

- Interview questions will refer to specific instances from each story, using exact quotes from those parts.
- Interview questions and answers should all be asked and answered in character voice.

- Interview questions will focus on how each character experienced similar events in different ways.
- Students will take thorough notes of their partners' answers.

Part 2: Written Summary: After the interviews, students will use their partners' answers to write a brief summary. This summary will include the similarities and differences between the character's experiences, the assumed theme given these experiences, and accurate quotes from the text.

Success Criteria for Interview Projects

Standards content	• Student asks specific questions regarding the theme of each book.
	• Student accurately represents his or her character as the interviewer.
	• Student includes specific details from his or her own character's story in the interview.
	• Students includes specific details from his or her partner's story in the interview.
	• Student thoroughly compares and contrasts each character's experiences in the summary.
	• Student includes quotations from his or her own story and from his or her partner's answers in the summary.
Mechanics	• Student uses commas and quotation marks appropriately.
	• Student takes accurate notes.
	• Student uses paraphrased notes to write a clear summary with fifth-grade-level convention expectations.

Core Ready Performance-Based Assessment

The Core Ready program makes use of performance-based assessment measures. Performance tasks and measurement tools are provided intermittently throughout all of the lesson sets, which help teachers measure learning as it occurs in preparation for a summative assessment at the end of each unit. Core Ready teachers are encouraged to administer the Milestone Performance

Assessments at specified times within the lesson sets, which are associated with specific Common Core State Standards skills and which place students in authentic tasks where they demonstrate acquisition of those skills. While the lesson sets are designed to teach the standards, the milestone assessments provide teachers with the tools for measuring their students' progress along the way. Teachers can use the results of these assessments to make informed decisions about how to best mold the instruction to the unique needs of their students as they progress toward the overall summative assessment at the end.

In this example of a Core Ready Milestone Performance Assessment, students must demonstrate their achievement of the standards in a rich, comprehensive task that synthesizes skills built across the entire set of writing lessons.

Milestone Performance Assessment
Elements of Fantasy and Conventions

 Use this checklist to assess student work on their revised and edited fantasy story drafts.

Standards Alignment: W.5.3, W.5.4, W.5.5, SL.5.6, L.5.1, L.5.2, L.5.3, L.5.6

	Achieved	Notes
Composed an engaging lead		
Included a balance of real and imaginary elements		
Described the setting		
Developed outer and inner traits of the main character		

	Achieved	Notes
Main character faces a challenge		
Main character overcomes the challenge in a fantastic way		
Problem/solution relates to chosen universal plot		
Story conveys a lesson about life to the reader		
COPS Editing Check*		
Correct **c**apitalization		
Correct **o**rder of and usage of words		
Correct **p**unctuation		
Correct **s**pelling		

*We recommend that you focus your assessment lens in these areas. Select and assess a few skills you have previously taught or that have emerged as areas of need in your ongoing assessment of student writing.

In addition to Milestone Performance Assessments like this one, Core Ready also provides teachers with summative rubrics to be used at the end of each lesson set. Teachers can use these rubrics as a flexible tool to evaluate student performance on any or all goals of the lesson set. This way, a summary of the learning acquired within each study will not only be assessed in an authentic

career ready | Senior Product Strategist for Web and Mobile Development

I help create strategies for new website and mobile applications. It is imperative that I am constantly up to date on all technology news, which changes at a ceaseless rate, so my reading skills are key. I need to be able to process a tremendous amount of information and distill what is important for my clients.

Writing is my true product. I must present complex ideas in a simple way so that my clients get it and love it. Being able to write clearly and concisely is my most valuable skill set, and I work in technology!

format, but it will also be recorded clearly so that teachers can make use of this data to inform further curricular decisions. See the end of this chapter for two sample rubrics.

Performance-based assessments represent the best of all worlds. They provide opportunity for celebration. Children are afforded the time and space needed to show off their new skills, and teachers are given the chance to see the fruits of their labor in action. They are a necessary addition to the overall assessment package that needs to be done to accurately represent the whole of a child, a teacher, a classroom, a school—because while one kind of data gives us numbers and another kind of data quantifies behaviors, performance data gives us the spirit of the child.

> "Assessment is authentic when we directly examine student performance on worthy intellectual tasks."
>
> — Grant Wiggins

Core Ready Reading Rubric

Lesson Set Goal	Emerging	Approaching	Achieving	Exceeding	Standards Alignment
Recognize and explain that fantasy shares literary elements with other genres of fiction.	Student struggles to identify and explain the literary elements of fantasy. Student cannot explain the literary elements fantasy shares with other genres of fiction.	Student can recognize and explain some literary elements that fantasy shares with other genres of fiction.	Student is able to recognize and clearly explain many literary elements that fantasy shares with other genres of fiction.	Student recognizes and provides detailed explanations of multiple literary elements that fantasy shares with other fiction genres. Provides examples from texts to support claims.	RL.5.1 RL.5.5 RL.5.10 SL.5.1a–d L.5.1 L.5.6
Identify and compare the motifs common to fantasy texts.	Student cannot identify or compare the basic motifs common to fantasy texts.	Student attempts to identify or compare the motifs common to fantasy texts. Points may be unclear or may not provide evidence.	Student identifies and compares the motifs common to fantasy texts. Provides sufficient evidence to support comparison.	Student accurately identifies and compares the motifs common to fantasy texts. Provides strong evidence to support comparison.	RL.5.1 RL.5.2 RL.5.9 RL.5.10 SL.5.1a–d L.5.1 L.5.6
Recognize the human experiences and emotions characters face in fantasy worlds and uses that thinking to identify theme.	Student is unable to recognize the human experiences and emotions characters face in fantasy and cannot connect this information to identify theme.	Student sometimes recognizes human experiences and emotions characters face in fantasy worlds and makes some connection between these observations and overall theme.	Student consistently recognizes the human experiences and emotions characters face in fantasy and correctly applies this thinking to determine theme.	Student can recognize and make many, sometimes subtle, connections between human experiences and emotions characters face in fantasy worlds. Student uses this thinking to accurately identify theme.	RL.5.1 RL.5.2 RL.5.3 RL.5.9 RL.5.10
Explain how the sequence of chapters contributes to the overall plot structure.	Student is unable to explain how the sequence of chapters contributes to the overall theme of a poem.	Student has a limited understanding of how the sequence of chapters contributes to the overall plot structure. Explanations lack sufficient detail and clarity.	Student gives clear explanations and reasoning to explain how the sequence of chapters contributes to the overall plot structure.	Student accurately and effectively explains how the sequence of chapters contributes to the overall plot structure with consistency.	RL.5.1 RL.5.5 RL.5.10 SL.5.1a–d SL.5.4 L.5.1 L.5.6

Lesson Set Goal	Emerging	Approaching	Achieving	Exceeding	Standards Alignment
Collaborate with others to develop and share thinking about fantasy text.	Student makes little or no attempt to collaborate with others to develop and share thinking about fantasy texts. Student is reluctant to offer any ideas and may not pay close attention to what others are saying.	Student attempts to collaborate with others to develop and share thinking about fantasy texts. Student does not always contribute relevant information or stay on topic. May lose focus when others are speaking.	Student consistently collaborates with others to develop and share thinking about fantasy texts. May be better at either sharing or listening.	Student is highly effective when collaborating with others. Offers opinions and ideas freely and listens carefully to those of others and builds upon them when appropriate.	RL.5.1 W.5.1a–d W.5.4 W.5.9 W.5.10 SL.5.1a–d SL.5.2 SL.5.3 L.5.1 L.5.6
Quote accurately from a text when explaining what the text says explicitly and when drawing inferences.	Student shows little or no evidence of active, purposeful reading or searching the text for specific information and evidence. Student makes little or no attempt to provide details and examples when explaining what the text says explicitly and is unable to draw inferences from the text.	Student shows some evidence of active purposeful reading and searching the text for specific information and evidence. Student may provide some details and examples, with marginal accuracy, when explaining what the text says explicitly and when drawing inferences from the text.	Student shows solid evidence of active, purposeful reading and searching the text for specific information and evidence. Student usually provides appropriate details and examples when explaining what the text says explicitly and when drawing inferences from the text.	Student demonstrates exceptional evidence of active, purposeful reading and searching the text for specific information and evidence. Student provides accurate, explicit, and thoughtful details and examples when explaining what the text says explicitly and when drawing inferences from the text.	RL.5.1
Write a reflective opinion piece that includes a clear introduction, point of view, supporting reasons, linking words and phrases, and a concluding statement.	Student writes an opinion piece with little or no evidence of an introduction or concluding statement. Student does not articulate a clear point of view and supporting reasons are missing or insufficient. Omits linking words and phrases or uses inappropriately.	Student writes an opinion piece and attempts to include an introductory and concluding statement. Student attempts to identify a point of view but supporting reasons may be weak or irrelevant. May lack needed linking words and phrases.	Student writes an opinion piece with a solid introductory and concluding statement. Articulates a point of view and supports with relevant supporting reasons. Uses linking words and phrases when appropriate.	Student writes an effective opinion piece with a strong introductory and concluding statement. Point of view is apparent and supported with clear and relevant reasons. May use advanced linking words and phrases effectively.	W.5.1a–d

Lesson Set Goal	Emerging	Approaching	Achieving	Exceeding	Standards Alignment
Independently and proficiently read and comprehend a variety of literature at the high end of the grades 4–5 text complexity band by the end of the year.	Student shows little or no evidence of reading and comprehending texts appropriate for the grade 5 text complexity band.	Student shows inconsistent evidence of reading and comprehending texts appropriate for the grade 5 text complexity band with independence and proficiency.	Student shows solid evidence of independently and proficiently reading and comprehending texts appropriate for the grade 5 text complexity band.	Student shows solid evidence of reading and comprehending texts above the grade 5 text complexity band independently and proficiently.	RL.5.10
Write routinely over extended time frames (time for research, reflection, and revision) and shorter time frames (a single sitting or a day or two) for a range of discipline-specific tasks, purposes, and audiences.	Student shows little or no evidence of writing routinely for short or long time frames for a range of discipline-specific tasks, purposes, and audiences.	Student shows some evidence of writing routinely for short and long time frames for a range of discipline-specific tasks, purposes, and audiences.	Student shows solid evidence of writing routinely for short and long time frames for a range of discipline-specific tasks, purposes, and audiences.	Student shows exceptional evidence of consistently and accurately writing for short and long time frames for a range of discipline-specific tasks, purposes, and audiences.	W.5.10
In collaborative discussions, demonstrate evidence of preparation for collaborative discussion and exhibits responsibility to the rules and roles of conversation.	In collaborative discussions, student comes unprepared and often disregards the rules and roles of conversation.	In collaborative discussions, student's preparation may be evident but ineffective or inconsistent. May occasionally disregard the rules and roles of conversation.	In collaborative discussions, student prepares adequately and draws on the preparation and other information about the topic to explore ideas under discussion. Usually observes the rules and roles of conversation.	In collaborative discussions, student arrives extremely well prepared for discussions and draws on the preparation and other information about the topic to explore ideas under discussion. Always observes the rules and roles of conversation.	SL.5.1a SL.5.1b
In collaborative discussions, share and develop ideas in a manner that enhances understanding of topic and contribute and respond to the content of the conversation in a productive and focused manner.	Student shows little or no evidence of engaging in collaborative discussions and makes little or no attempt to ask and answer questions, stay on topic, link comments to the remarks of others, or to explain his or her own ideas and understanding in light of the discussion.	Student shows some evidence of engaging in collaborative discussions and, with marginal success, attempts to ask questions to check understanding of information presented, to stay on topic, link comments to the remarks of others, and explain his or her own ideas and understanding in light of the discussion.	Student engages in a range of collaborative discussions and asks questions to check understanding of information presented, stays on topic most of the time, and frequently links his or her own ideas and understanding in light of the discussion.	Student effectively and consistently engages in a range of collaborative discussions and asks high-level questions to check understanding of information presented, and always stays on topic. With great insight and attention to the comments of others, links his or her own ideas and understanding in light of the discussion.	SL.5.1c SL.5.1d

Core Ready Reading Rubric, Grade 5, *continued*

Lesson Set Goal	Emerging	Approaching	Achieving	Exceeding	Standards Alignment
Demonstrate knowledge of standard English and its conventions.	Student demonstrates little or no knowledge of standard English and its conventions.	Student demonstrates some evidence of knowledge of standard English and its conventions.	Student consistently demonstrates knowledge of standard English and its conventions.	Student demonstrates an exceptional understanding of standard English and its conventions. Use of conventions is sophisticated for grade level and accurate.	L.5.1 L.5.2 L.5.3
Acquire and accurately use grade-appropriate conversational, general academic, and domain-specific vocabulary and phrases.	Student shows little or no evidence of the acquisition and use of grade-appropriate conversational and academic language.	Student shows some evidence of the acquisition and use of grade-appropriate conversational and academic language.	Student shows solid evidence of the acquisition and use of grade-appropriate conversational and academic language.	Student shows a high level of sophistication and precision when using grade-appropriate conversational and academic language.	L.5.6

Core Ready Writing Rubric

Grade 5   Imagined Worlds, Human Themes: Reading and Writing Fantasy and Adventure

Lesson Set Goal	Emerging	Approaching	Achieving	Exceeding	Standards Alignment
Develop a sequence of events that unfolds naturally and use a variety of transitional words, phrases, and clauses to manage the sequence of events.	Student is unable to develop a sequence of events or develops a sequence of events that is unclear and disorganized. Does not include transitional words, phrases, and clauses to manage the sequence of events, or does so with many errors.	Student attempts to develop a sequence of events. The sequence has some organization but is choppy and may stray off course. Includes some transitional words, phrases, and clauses to manage the sequence of events.	Student develops a sequence of events that unfolds naturally, and consistently uses a variety of transitional words, phrases, and clauses to manage the sequence of events. Some elements may be more effective than others.	Student develops a clear and well-organized sequence of events that unfolds naturally. Includes many highly effective words, phrases, and clauses to manage the sequence of events.	W.5.3a W.5.3c W.5.4 W.5.5 W.5.10 L.5.1 L.5.3 L.5.6

Lesson Set Goal	Emerging	Approaching	Achieving	Exceeding	Standards Alignment
Use concrete words and phrases and sensory details to vividly describe the events.	Student uses few or no concrete words or sensory details to describe events.	Student uses some concrete words and sensory details to describe events. Misses opportunities to provide clarity.	Student frequently uses concrete words and sensory details to describe events.	Student uses concrete words and sensory details to describe events vividly with consistency and precision.	W.5.3d W.5.4 W.5.5 W.5.10 L.5.1 L.5.3 L.5.6
Create a balance between believable and unbelievable elements common to fantasy.	Student shows little or no evidence of creating a balance between believable and unbelievable elements common to fantasy.	Student attempts, with some success, to create a balance between believable and unbelievable elements common to fantasy. May be underdeveloped or unclear at times.	Student successfully creates a balance between believable and unbelievable elements common to fantasy. Basically clear and well developed.	Student creates a very clear and effective balance between believable and unbelievable elements common to fantasy.	W.5.3 W.5.4 W.5.5 W.5.10
Develop characters with a balance of heroic and human qualities as seen in descriptions and dialogue.	Student shows little or no evidence of a balance of qualities. Characters may be underdeveloped and writing lacks adequate descriptions or dialogue.	Student attempts to develop characters through a balance of heroic and human-like qualities, but may favor one end of the spectrum. Uses descriptions and dialogue but may be underdeveloped or unclear.	Student successfully develops characters through a balance of heroic and human-like qualities. Uses descriptions and dialogue effectively to give character depth.	Student shows an exceptional ability to develop characters through a balance of heroic and human-like qualities. Uses descriptions and dialogue skillfully to portray multidimensional characters.	W.5.3b W.5.4 W.5.10
Prepare and present their own fantasy stories using appropriate technology and resources.	Student presents fantasy stories with little or no evidence of preparation. Lacks most criteria. Struggles to use technology and resources appropriately for presentation.	Student presents fantasy stories to an audience with insufficient rehearsal or preparation. May lack some criteria. Student may incorporate some appropriate technology or resources at a very basic level.	Student successfully prepares and presents fantasy stories to an audience using appropriate technology or resources to enhance presentation. Meets all or nearly all criteria.	Student delivers a well-rehearsed, confident, and polished presentation of his or her fantasy stories. Uses appropriate technology thoughtfully and effectively to enhance presentation.	W.5.4 W.5.5 W.5.6 W.5.10 SL5.1b–d SL.5.2 SL.5.4 SL.5.5 SL.5.6 L.5.1 L.5.2 L.5.3 L.5.6

Core Ready Writing Rubric, Grade 5, *continued*

Lesson Set Goal	Emerging	Approaching	Achieving	Exceeding	Standards Alignment
With guidance and support from peers and adults, develop and strengthen writing as needed by planning, revising, editing, rewriting, or trying a new approach.	Student makes little or no attempt to develop and strengthen writing through planning, revising, and editing.	Student attempts to develop and strengthen writing as needed by planning, revising, and editing. Writing may still contain significant errors or lack clarity.	Student develops and strengthens writing as needed by planning, revising, and editing. Some areas of the planning, revision, and editing may be more developed than others.	Student extensively develops and strengthens writing by planning, revising, and editing as needed. Few or no errors or lapses of clarity are evident.	W.5.5
Write a reflective explanatory piece that includes a clear introduction of the topic, supporting details, linking words and phrases, and a concluding statement.	Student writes an opinion piece with little or no evidence of an introduction or concluding statement. Does not articulate a clear point of view and supporting reasons are missing or insufficient. Omits linking words and phrases or uses them inappropriately.	Student writes an opinion piece and attempts to include an introductory and concluding statement. Attempts to identify a point of view, but supporting reasons may be weak or irrelevant. May lack essential linking words and phrases.	Student writes an opinion piece with a solid introductory and concluding statement. Articulates a point of view and supports with relevant supporting reasons. Student uses linking words and phrases when appropriate.	Student writes an effective opinion piece with a strong introductory and concluding statement. Point of view is apparent and supported with clear and relevant reasons. May use advanced linking words and phrases effectively.	W.5.2
Write routinely over extended time frames (time for research, reflection, and revision) and shorter time frames (a single sitting or a day or two) for a range of discipline-specific tasks, purposes, and audiences.	Student shows little or no evidence of writing routinely for short or long time frames for a range of discipline-specific tasks, purposes, and audiences.	Student shows some evidence of writing routinely for short and long time frames for a range of discipline-specific tasks, purposes, and audiences.	Student shows solid evidence of writing routinely for short and long time frames for a range of discipline-specific tasks, purposes, and audiences.	Student shows exceptional evidence of consistently and accurately writing for short and long time frames for a range of discipline-specific tasks, purposes, and audiences.	W.5.10
Demonstrate evidence of preparation for collaborative discussion and exhibit responsibility to the rules and roles of conversation.	In collaborative discussions, student comes unprepared and often disregards the rules and roles of conversation.	In collaborative discussions, student's preparation may be evident but ineffective or inconsistent. May occasionally disregard the rules and roles of conversation.	In collaborative discussions, student prepares adequately and draws on the preparation and other information about the topic to explore ideas under discussion. Usually observes the rules and roles of conversation.	In collaborative discussions, student arrives extremely well prepared for discussions and draws on the preparation and other information about the topic to explore ideas under discussion. Always observes the rules and roles of conversation.	SL.5.1a SL.5.1b

Lesson Set Goal	Emerging	Approaching	Achieving	Exceeding	Standards Alignment
In collaborative discussions, share and develop ideas in a manner that enhances understanding of topic and contribute and respond to the content of the conversation in a productive and focused manner.	Student shows little or no evidence of engaging in collaborative discussions and makes little or no attempt to ask and answer questions, stay on topic, link comments to the remarks of others, or explain his or her own ideas and understanding in light of the discussion.	Student shows some evidence of engaging in collaborative discussions and, with marginal success, attempts to ask questions to check understanding of information presented, to stay on topic, link comments to the remarks of others, and explain his or her own ideas and understanding in light of the discussion.	Student engages in a range of collaborative discussions and asks questions to check understanding of information presented, stays on topic most of the time, and frequently links his or her own ideas and understanding in light of the discussion.	Student effectively and consistently engages in a range of collaborative discussions and asks high-level questions to check understanding of information presented, and always stays on topic. With great insight and attention to the comments of others, links his or her own ideas and understanding in light of the discussion.	SL.5.1c SL.5.1d
Demonstrate knowledge of standard English and its conventions.	Student demonstrates little or no knowledge of standard English and its conventions.	Student demonstrates some evidence of knowledge of standard English and its conventions.	Student consistently demonstrates knowledge of standard English and its conventions.	Student demonstrates an exceptional understanding of standard English and its conventions. Use of conventions is sophisticated for grade level and accurate.	L.5.1 L.5.2 L.5.3
Acquire and accurately use grade-appropriate conversational, general academic, and domain-specific vocabulary and phrases.	Student shows little or no evidence of the acquisition and use of grade-appropriate conversational and academic language.	Student shows some evidence of the acquisition and use of grade-appropriate conversational and academic language.	Student shows solid evidence of the acquisition and use of grade-appropriate conversational and academic language.	Student shows a high level of sophistication and precision when using grade-appropriate conversational and academic language.	L.5.6

chapter 13

Engaging Core Ready Families and Communities

"I really had a lot of dreams as a kid, and I think a great deal of that grew out of the fact that I had a chance to read a lot."

—Bill Gates

The Core Is the Family and the Community

The family and the community surrounding the child outside of the classroom environment are two of the most important supports to our students in reaching the goals set forth in the Common Core State Standards. Our job as educators is to enroll parents and the outside community in the process of creating literate learners, to break down the barriers impeding the active collaboration and participation of the family and the community, and to create a true partnership between the school and the child's world outside the classroom.

Researchers (e.g., Bandura, Barbaranelli, Caprara, & Pastorelli, 1996; Dearing, McCartney, Weiss, Kreider, & Simpkins, 2004; Frome & Eccles, 1998; Hoover-Dempsey et al., 2001) have noted the direct effects that family involvement in school has on children's literacy through reinforcement of the values of education and modeling, as well as indirectly through children's feelings, emotions, attitudes, and self-efficacy. Any activity that promotes storytelling, listening to stories, reading text, writing for purpose or fun,

developing Internet browsing and research skills, or simply talking with others in a purposeful way about stories, events, and interesting topics will lead to exponential growth in children's literacy ability, and reflects the goals of the Common Core State Standards. A vibrant literacy life at home and after school will make all aspects of the child's life more interesting; will substantially improve the fundamental skills needed to be an excellent reader, writer, and communicator; and will make teaching in the classroom easier and more effective. Community and family participation in promoting literacy can be the greatest untapped resource we have as educators.

Adults in many families may not have a real understanding of what they can do to help their children become great readers and writers, and they might be afraid to ask for help. A big stumbling block for families seems to be the child who does not want to read and the parent who insists that the child go to her room and read 50 pages of whatever book she has been assigned in school. This is a lose-lose-lose situation: for the teacher, for the parents, and especially for the child. This scenario frequently then devolves into questions about the child's impertinence to the parents, expressions of contempt for the child's "laziness," and an accelerated movement down a long pathway of difficulty in school, a discomfort and inability to read and write, and, in the worst case, a final flameout sometime during the high school years, with the child leaving school not just far from college and career ready, but in large part functionally illiterate.

I think we are worried too much about "getting parents into school" or we judge parent investment based on how many back to school nights they have attended as if that is the only way parents can demonstrate their commitment to a child's learning. The truth is most parents are working long hours and they are grateful to you for caring for their children during the school day. They may not be always able to come to school due to the hours they work or their own insecurity about being in a school setting. Yet in or out of school they can still be our best partners and should be treated as such: the best partners in raising lifelong readers and writers we could have. They need our committed help in feeling more comfortable about participating in this endeavor and we need to find every way we can to communicate really well with them. Here are my tips for gaining family and community involvement:

1. *Communicate about the CCSS regularly and positively.* Whether by text message or email newsletter or by phone, make sure you are in regular and open communication with your families, using the language of the Common Core State Standards as a way to create a great overall vision and set of goals together. Remember that families are busy, so couch the language of the standards in more concrete ways families can take action. For example, here are some tips including CCSS language you can insert into communications:

   a. **Challenge:** The Common Core State Standards promote balance in what your child reads! Solution: Read aloud to your child both informational texts and fiction books.

   b. **Challenge:** The Common Core State Standards plan for your child to read at higher and higher levels up the staircase of reading! Solution: Give your child lots of time to read at home in comfortable ways so as to build stamina. Make sure there is a reading spot for your child that is quiet and peaceful.

   c. **Challenge:** The Common Core State Standards champion writing as a key part of your child's education! Solution: Have your child keep a notebook at home to jot quick thoughts in every day. Even the smallest amounts of writing time will be helpful. Make it fun.

   d. **Challenge:** The Common Core State Standards celebrate critical thinking! Solution: Ask your child questions about what he is reading that you don't know the answers to! Have lively debates at home about the topics in his class. Don't worry about knowing the "right" answer on anything. Critical thinking means you are all learning together and discovering new ideas.

2. *Focus on ways families can support the speaking and listening components of the Common Core State Standards.* The most important thing families can do with children of all ages is to simply engage them in thoughtful conversation. Not with famous dead-end questions like "How was school today?," which will lead to a one-word response from all but the chattiest child, but instead through questions that generate some sort of real thinking on the part of the child: "What did you learn in science today?" "What did you do during recess?" "What was the best part of the day?" "What was the most interesting thing you talked about in English today?" The responses will more often than not lead to further conversation, and possibly lead to an opening about something that happened that either delighted or bothered the child, and real conversation can spring off of that. Through these conversations, the child learns the ebb and flow of dialogue, learns the nature of storytelling and listening, and comes to see the parent as an ally, a force of genuine concern for the child's well-being. These conversations then springboard onto other topics, galvanizing both parent and child to continue further down the learning journey. When teachers collect anecdotes on such conversations at home, they can be celebrated as Core Ready "actions" in the community, and families can be acknowledged for being part of the Core Ready campaign.

3. *Ask families and communities to contribute to the actual minutes the child is reading outside of school.* Let's create Core Ready communities by offering challenge opportunities to read millions of minutes together, or read one book together as a community, with the tag line "We are all Core Ready!"

   Help families out through more messages (and deliver those messages by phone if there is a question about the literacy skills of the family), again providing a positive message and including a simple task. For instance, you might discover a younger child is fascinated by volcanoes. Along with the two books on volcanoes the child is carrying home in her independent reading bag, include a note for the family telling them about this developing interest and asking them to ask their child about the books or to read the books together. If the family has a computer and Internet access, recommend that they search volcanoes together and see what they find. Encourage the family to understand that if the child chooses to read the same book again and again, that is great—she is building stamina and fluency. Eyes on text and intrafamily communication—those are two things families can do that will really help the kids. Have your PTA members or even older students in the community write thank-you notes to families who participate in any of the minutes contests for reading, saying you know how important reading is and how much the family is contributing to the Core Ready initiative by participating. And for you as a teacher or principal or superintendent to send text messages of thanks to families means so much to them.

Include religious institutions, community centers, and local businesses and chains as partners in Core Ready initiatives such as "Million Minutes for Core Ready." Invite them to take part by assigning someone at your school to be the community liaison to reach out to the organizations and businesses and keep them in the loop. Have them report their "minutes" and join in any culminating celebrations.

4. ***Reach out to the community to share what the Common Core State Standards are and why they are such a unique opportunity for us to all come together with a common objective.*** Reach out to religious institutions attended by your students and their families. Ask whether a message can go out from the pulpit encouraging parents to interact with their kids in some of the ways outlined here. Offer to speak on the subject of the Common Core State Standards, or nominate a teacher or colleague in your school as the Core Ready Ambassador to the Community. Reach out to doctors and health care providers—will they discuss literacy with the families who come to them seeking medical care? Little will have a more positive impact on the long-term health of a child than growing up literate. Will they put a varied selection of books in their waiting room? Can they speak to the importance of reading to one's child before bedtime? Will they be reading role models in the school so children see that doctors and nurses are also readers? All of this is what the Common Core State Standards are aiming for: common language, common community, common core. Use this chart to create a strategic plan for your school, families, and communities to work together.

Core Ready Community Engagement Table

District	• Enroll parents and the outside community in the process of creating literate learners; break down the barriers impeding the active collaboration and participation of the family and community, and create a true partnership between the school district and the child's world outside the classroom.
	• Help support the development of parents' understanding of the standards and how they can play a role.
	• Deconstruct the Common Core State Standards by grade level into widely accessible language that is available to parents and families in multiple languages.
	• Reach out to community organizations, churches, and civic leaders to share what the Common Core State Standards are and why we must come together to establish a community Core Ready compact.
Schools	• Seek out and campaign for professional development for colleagues at every level—whether one is a new or senior teacher, a principal, or a superintendent—to increase understanding of both the Common Core State Standards and how to support the development of parents' understanding.
	• Provide educators with collaborative planning time for the Core Ready program.
	• Enroll parents and the outside community in the process of creating literate learners; break down the barriers impeding the active collaboration and participation of the family and community, and create a true partnership between the school and the child's world outside the classroom.
	• Empower families with an understanding of concrete activities they can do at home to help their children become lifelong readers and writers.
	• Provide opportunities for parents and families to experience hands-on learning activities that build their knowledge of the standards.
	• Focus on ways families can support the speaking, listening, and language components of the Common Core State Standards.

The Core Is You

Being entrusted with the care of children is sacred work. Honor what you do. To call someone a teacher or an educational leader is to honor him or her with a title of great respect. If you teach me, I can improve myself, and I can work with others to improve the world. There are few people in our worlds whom we think of with more fondness and admiration and appreciation than those who were great teachers to us. A child's current and future academic and behavioral success rests heavily on the quality of the child's relationship with his teachers in the early grades (Howes, Hamilton, & Matheson, 1994; Hughes, Cavell, & Jackson, 1999; Meehan, Hughes, & Cavell, 2003; Pianta, Steinberg, & Rollins, 1995).

And yet the profession comes under relentless attack. Teachers are treated like laboratory specimens—a little salary incentive here, a little threat about test scores there. "Why, oh why," our society seems to relentlessly moan and groan, "can't the teachers do their job and fix our problems?" If only teachers would perform well, all would be right with the world.

Secretary of Education Arne Duncan has said, "We need to radically change society's views of teaching from the factory model of yesterday to the professional model of tomorrow, where teachers are revered as the thinkers, leaders, and nation-builders they truly are."

It is in some large measure a sign of the respect we hold for teachers that we believe they can almost single-handedly fix what ails us as a nation. Yet instead of turning to us for guidance, instead of asking us as teachers what we would recommend based on our experience and expertise and years of work in the schools, our society dictates to us. "Do this. Do that. Make this score go up. Do it now." And if you cannot succeed at this untenable task, operating under mandates and dictates imposed from above, you will be fired, or have

Teachers	• Seek out and campaign for professional development for colleagues at every level—whether one is a new or a senior teacher, a principal, or a superintendent—to increase understanding of both the Common Core State Standards and how to support the development of parents' understanding.
	• Communicate with parents and families about how Core Ready is being implemented in the classroom.
	• Create a supplemental reading list.
	• Regularly provide parents and families with supplemental activities and resources that they can do at home to reinforce the standards.
Parents	• Contribute to the actual minutes the child is reading and writing outside of school.
	• Encourage active speaking and listening among family members to foster strong language development.
	• Seek out and campaign for workshops for fellow parents and caretakers at every level to increase knowledge and understanding of the Common Core State Standards.
	• Work collectively to advocate for timely information, access to literature and resources, and opportunities to participate in literacy-based activities.
Community-based organizations	• Seek out and campaign for workshops for parents and caretakers and community members at every level to increase their collective knowledge and understanding of the Common Core State Standards.
	• Work with parents, teachers, and administrators to advocate for timely information, access to literature and resources, and opportunities to participate in Core Ready literacy-based activities.
	• Work with other organizations, school districts, and schools to provide community-based opportunities for stakeholders to come together and learn about the Common Core State Standards and participate in literacy-based Core Ready activities.

your "poor performance" broadcast in the media, or suffer the shame of being told that you are not good at what you do.

Who can function in such an environment of disrespect, distrust, and direct challenge? And so we are at a crossroads, where those who practice our most esteemed profession, the one most important in creating the future leaders of our society and our world, are often treated with extraordinary disdain and disrespect by that very society.

The good news is that the Common Core State Standards offer teachers a way to tell a new narrative. They are not a dictate from above; they are a vehicle for all teachers to reestablish the dignity and honor of teaching. The Common Core State Standards are your allies! Learn and embrace them, for they offer an amazing opportunity to re-energize our schools and to re-energize *us*. We are doing high-level, crucial work that requires high levels of training and development, with opportunity for innovation and support. Here are the ways the Common Core State Standards can help you advocate for what you truly need to illuminate your core:

1. Seek out and campaign for professional development for you and your colleagues at every level, whether you are a new or a senior teacher, a principal, or a superintendent. Professional development is something every professional gets on a regular basis; you should not be left to fend for yourself. Regular, sustained opportunities to further our learning as leaders is a must. The standards inspire it.

2. Advocate for better-than-adequate resources to access literature and all genres of reading and new media. Access to literature and new media is a key lever for our students in acquiring all the literacy skills of reading, writing, speaking, and listening. Technology also greatly aids in assessment, and the assessment plan can be fully strategic only if our schools are completely wired and connected, so you can connect to your families to monitor your students' development.

3. Create Core Ready study groups. Set goals, milestones, and deliverables for yourselves. Here is an example:

   Goal: Learn about close reading. Milestone: We read a chapter in Kylene Beers's book on close reading and the chapter on close reading in *Be*

Core Ready and met two times to discuss. Milestone: We created our own examples of a close reading text tree to share with our students by a given day. Deliverable: We created a collection of close readings for our grade level to post and share and save for the use of others.

Goal: Study assessment and how it can inform instruction. Milestone: We used the standards to outline the types of assessments we will need this year. We read the assessment chapter in *Be Core Ready* and met twice to discuss. Deliverable: We created a strategic plan for assessment, outlining when the assessments are administered and how we can reflect on how those assessments will impact our direct instruction.

The Core Is Your Student

Sam was a student in my class during one of my first years of teaching at a school for the deaf. He was 13 years old. Sam had no one to talk to at home who understood sign language, and school was the first place where he learned to communicate with others. He was a deeply communicative person—funny, charming, endlessly interesting, and interested in just about everything. But Sam had experienced obstacles to his ability to communicate. He was learning English as a second language without ever having heard it spoken, yet despite the added difficulty, Sam absolutely loved school. It was there that he could talk to everyone, there that he could tell his wonderful stories—and, as it turned out, the school day was not nearly long enough for Sam to fit in all his stories. He loved animals, so we got him lots of animal books. We purchased a tank and he raised tadpoles into frogs. He connected with his passions and connected with us.

I had always wondered what happened to Sam. Where did he go? What was he doing? Was he OK? As I do with so many of the students I have taught over the years, I worried about him navigating the big, wide world, where overwhelming amounts of information would be a constant and complex onslaught. I wondered if he were faring well and if he had someone with whom to share his stories. Then one day something wonderful happened. I got a Facebook message. It said: "Is this my beloved teacher?" My heart stopped. I knew his face the

minute I saw it, even years later. It was Sam. He is employed now, and Facebook is a treasured tool he uses to keep in touch with his friends from school—a tool I know is so crucial and inspiring for deaf people worldwide. A small slice of life, perhaps, and one you do not hear much about when people talk about the merits of Facebook, but for me it matters a lot. Sam's ability to write well has made it possible for him to escape isolation and be part of a much larger community. He has a young daughter, and he reads aloud to her the way I read aloud to him all those many years ago, through a combination of English and sign language. The world of children's literature and transformative literacy promised him a future not only for himself but also for the children he would have. People all over the world are hungry for meaningful work, for jobs that will not only pay the bills but also make them feel like they are contributing in some way, whether by building a road or writing a contract. The power of literacy is that it provides a child with a lifelong tool that can never be taken away from him. Sam could use his reading, writing, speaking, and listening skills to apply for a job and get it, have a baby, take care of his family, and read to his young daughter. Literacy is a versatile and life-changing tool!

But we can start even earlier now by enrolling our students in the vision of the Common Core State Standards. We can enroll them in the Core Ready initiative, and make them youth ambassadors for this vision.

What I have found in talking with young people around the country is how little they have ever actually known of the initiatives we are investing so much time in all around them. They never knew much about No Child Left Behind, balanced literacy, whole language, the strategy approach, phonics, kinesthetic and auditory programs, and on and on. That is not the language of childhood. It is not the language children would even understand or relate to.

This is our chance to tell a story about teaching and learning in a new way, and to include the most critical constituency group of all: the children themselves. Let us invite them to partake in the big ideas of the standards and also to play a part. A very wise person once said to me that the best initiatives are those in which everyone gets to be involved. That is what we need to do here with our most precious corps, the students.

1. *Have a Core Ready assembly.* Have a teacher ambassador for the Common Core State Standards explain them in kid-friendly terms. Here is a Top Ten list of key features of the CCSS that will most appeal to all age groups in language they will understand.

The Core Ready Commitments: We Will . . .

- Learn to read long, strong, and for the rest of our lives.
- Become the kind of writers who can write anything.
- Write and read well in all of our subject areas.
- Use technology to read, write, speak, and listen.
- Make friends all around the world because we can communicate with them.
- Figure out when something is or is not true because we will be critical thinkers.
- Ask great questions and search for answers.
- Read different kinds of things including information, fiction, and poetry.

- Learn all the skills we need to have to succeed in whatever we dream of doing.
- Use reading, writing, speaking, and listening skills to bring forth new ideas into the world.

2. *Appoint Core Ready youth ambassadors.* These young people can be any age. They can meet regularly and determine, based on the above Top Ten, how they want to make a Core Ready difference in their schools. Projects include:
   - A Core Ready assembly they plan themselves to celebrate reading or writing.
   - A display of their performance-based assessment work.
   - A community Core Ready reading marathon.
   - A schoolwide writing celebration.
   - A content area–related reading/writing event.
   - A Skype session with new friends across the world who have become pen pals.
   - A schoolwide blog to publish book reviews and other literary connections.

3. *Create a Core Ready newspaper or online magazine.* Use it to share the best work students have done and include comments from staff, community members, and families.

The Power Is in Coming Together

Some have worried that the Common Core State Standards will somehow constrain or confine us. I believe the opposite. Coming together like this is liberating, important, and game changing. The greatest creative changes in human history have happened when people collaborated (Johnson, 2010). For example, the writers of the Constitution worked on that seminal document together, not alone. Benjamin Franklin, Thomas Jefferson, and others crafted a vision of

democracy by working together. The Wright brothers took their risks in the air because they were able to test new ideas together. Martin Luther King, Jr., could not have walked those miles and achieved his objectives without Reverend Abernathy and many others, and they carried on his legacy after his life was tragically cut short. One of my favorite stories about Eleanor Roosevelt is how she and many others collaborated to create what would become the Universal Declaration of Human Rights, a seminal document whose profound impact still reverberates today in countries around the world. Steve Jobs may have been famous for being difficult to work with, but he worked very closely with his teams of brilliant designers and software technicians to create the groundbreaking Apple products. It is now a $500 billion company that has produced fewer than 30 products. Those 30 products were carefully constructed and innovated by a large number of people. In our democracy, we tend to idolize and idealize *individuals* as the source of all inspiration. And it is true that the individual is an essential contributor to the emergence of new ideas. But the best and most successful manifestations of great ideas are the ones that come from group collaboration, each idea building off of and being made possible by the idea that came before it.

career ready **Executive Assistant**

It is important to convey a message in a short, succinct way. Give me the abbreviated version. I believe this applies to both reading and writing. When preparing PowerPoint presentations, I must take what is submitted and boil it down to a few powerful, clear bullet points. This principle is also used in minute taking. In today's world, this is more important than ever. People tend to read the first two lines of an email or a memo and then skip to the end. If you don't say it simply and right away, the message is lost. I must use correct grammar and punctuation! Always! If it's sloppy, it's not taken seriously. I put myself in the place of my intended audience so that I can communicate effectively at the proper level.

Personal Steps to Finding Your Core

The great challenge of this era is to simultaneously cultivate your core and your spirit while providing the structure and vision the standards provide.

1. Write, read, speak, and listen *with* your students. Let them hear who you are, where you have come from, your history, your interests, your wonderings, your hopes and dreams. Be a co-learner. Do not be afraid to share what you do not know, to reveal yourself as authentic. Critical thinkers are questioners. People who take new and fresh paths toward careers are not followers. The more you can be yourself, the better off your students will be.

2. Fall in love with what you read. Let yourself feel your heart pounding over sports stories, choke back tears when the spider dies, get a catch in your throat when reading about the great fire, be stunned by the Whitman poem, be in fierce disagreement with an article.

3. Invite your colleagues to join you in active professional growth. Visit one another's classrooms. Engage with their students, and they with yours. Set up faculty meetings at which you do case studies on individual students who may or may not be yours. But there is always something to learn. Your teaching + their teaching = new learning.

4. Talk with colleagues about the work. Set up a blog with your colleagues near and far. Connect with teachers across the world. Let them know what you are doing. Get your teaching and learning voice going. (That means giving your students more time to talk too.)

5. Remember both your greatest teacher and all your precious students. Put a few of those names somewhere on your desktop or on a card in the corner of your desk where you can see the names and they can serve as beacons for you to be the best you can be. Let them inspire you to become a great learner and a great leader.

The Common Core State Standards do not tell you *what* you must teach or *how* you must teach. Instead they are guidelines meant to ensure equity while leaving some freedom for us to create and develop ideas for how we reach those goals. The Common Core State Standards and these times we live in give us all an extraordinary opportunity to come together for a common purpose: the right of every child to an excellent education. Having shared language across states means we can now collaborate not only with teachers in our immediate community, but also with teachers and leaders from many other schools across the country. We can work together with families and community-based organizations under the auspices of this common language to ensure common goals. The possibilities for connecting, sharing, supporting, and joining forces are deeply exhilarating.

Life is precious, and precarious, with the chance for very different outcomes in each child's life dependent to such a large degree on the education he or she receives. Give your students the gift of possibility and promise and hope. Level the playing field and raise the bar. If they want to be plumbers, doctors, software engineers, nurses, construction workers, executive bankers, or ballerinas, it is all possible. It can be real. College ready, career ready, life ready. Let us help them go do it all.

The Core Ready Experience Continues with Lesson Sets

Now you have studied text complexity, close reading, strategic use of technology and new media, persuasive writing, and seeking evidence to support claims. You are seeing the standards through the lens of English language learners and special needs learners. You have taken a rigorous look at classroom environments to be sure you have everything in place to teach and learn in standards-rich communities, including a balance of informational and literary texts and opportunities to collaborate effectively with colleagues. But this book is just the beginning.

Continue the Core Ready experience with the Core Ready program, organized for you into three sections: K–2, 3–5, and 6–8. Each grade-level band contains four books representing the Core Ready categories of The Journey to Meaning, The Shape of Story, The Road to Knowledge, and The Power to Persuade. I have created lessons and rubrics for every grade level, with increasing levels of complexity in both text and concepts as students move through the grades. As you know by now, I emphasize strategic use of technology. However, I am sensitive to the fact that you all may not have everything you need yet, so the lessons in the program include both high- and low-tech options. Each lesson set is written with deeply thought–out suggestions for English language learners and students with special needs. The lesson sets will meet the needs you have for Common Core State Standards alignment.

I leave you for now with this message: The power in education comes from our most authentic core—from the core within each of us, which carries the power of stories and words to truly change the world.

Core Ready Community Engagement Table

District	• Enroll parents and the outside community in the process of creating literate learners; break down the barriers impeding the active collaboration and participation of the family and community, and create a true partnership between the school district and the child's world outside the classroom. • Help support the development of parents' understanding of the standards and how they can play a role. • Deconstruct the Common Core State Standards by grade level into widely accessible language that is available to parents and families in multiple languages. • Reach out to community organizations, churches, and civic leaders to share what the Common Core State Standards are and why we must come together to establish a community Core Ready compact.
Schools	• Seek out and campaign for professional development for colleagues at every level—whether one is a new or senior teacher, a principal, or a superintendent—to increase understanding of both the Common Core State Standards and how to support the development of parents' understanding. • Provide educators with collaborative planning time for the Core Ready program. • Enroll parents and the outside community in the process of creating literate learners; break down the barriers impeding the active collaboration and participation of the family and community, and create a true partnership between the school and the child's world outside the classroom. • Empower families with an understanding of concrete activities they can do at home to help their children become lifelong readers and writers. • Provide opportunities for parents and families to experience hands-on learning activities that build their knowledge of the standards. • Focus on ways families can support the speaking, listening, and language components of the Common Core State Standards.
Teachers	• Seek out and campaign for professional development for colleagues at every level—whether one is a new or a senior teacher, a principal, or a superintendent—to increase understanding of both the Common Core State Standards and how to support the development of parents' understanding. • Communicate with parents and families about how Core Ready is being implemented in the classroom. • Create a supplemental reading list. • Regularly provide parents and families with supplemental activities and resources that they can do at home to reinforce the standards.
Parents	• Contribute to the actual minutes the child is reading and writing outside of school. • Encourage active speaking and listening among family members to foster strong language development. • Seek out and campaign for workshops for fellow parents and caretakers at every level to increase knowledge and understanding of the Common Core State Standards. • Work collectively to advocate for timely information, access to literature and resources, and opportunities to participate in literacy-based activities.
Community-based organizations	• Seek out and campaign for workshops for parents and caretakers and community members at every level to increase their collective knowledge and understanding of the Common Core State Standards. • Work with parents, teachers, and administrators to advocate for timely information, access to literature and resources, and opportunities to participate in Core Ready literacy-based activities. • Work with other organizations, school districts, and schools to provide community-based opportunities for stakeholders to come together and learn about the Common Core State Standards and participate in literacy-based Core Ready activities.

Bibliography

Abedi, J., & Liquanti, R. (2012, January). Issues and opportunities in strengthening large scale assessment systems for ELLs. Paper presented at the Understanding Language Conference Stanford University, Stanford, CA.

ACT. (2006). *Reading between the lines: What the ACT reveals about college readiness in reading.* Retrieved March 28, 2008, from http://act.org/research/policymakers/pdf/reading_summary.pdf

ACT. (2011a). *Affirming the goal: Is college and career readiness an internationally competitive standard?*

ACT. (2011b). *The condition of college & career readiness 2011.*

Akhavan, N. (2007). *Accelerated vocabulary instruction: Strategies for closing the achievement gap for all students.* New York, NY: Scholastic Teaching Resources.

Alliance for Excellent Education. (2006, August). *Paying double: Inadequate high schools and community college remediation.* Retrieved from www.all4ed.org/files/archive/publications/remediation.pdf

Allington, D. (2012). Private experience, textual analysis, and institutional authority: The discursive practice of critical interpretation and its enactment in literary training. *Language and Literature, 21*(2), (In Press).

Allington, R. L., & Gabriel, R. E. (2012). Every child, every day. *Educational Leadership, 69*(6), 10–15.

Allyn, P. (2009). *What to read when. The books and stories to read with your child-and all the best times to read them.* New York, NY: Avery Trade.

Allyn, P. (2011a). *Pam Allyn's best books for boys K–8: How to engage boys in reading in ways that will change their lives.* New York, NY: Scholastic Teaching Resources.

Allyn, P. (2011b). *Your child's writing life: How to inspire confidence, creativity, and skill at every age.* New York, NY: Avery Trade.

Allyn, P. (2012). Taming the wild text. *Educational Leadership, 69*(6), 16–21.

Anstrom, K., DiCerbo, P., Butler, F., Katz, A., Millet, J., & Rivera, C. (2010). *A review of the literature on academic English: Implications for K–12 English language learners.*

Arlington, VA: The George Washington University Center for Equity and Excellence in Education.

Asimov, I., & Clarke, A. C. (1997). *Roving mind.* Amherst, NY: Prometheus Books.

Bafile, C. (2005). *Guys read: Helping boys become better readers, better students, better guys.* Education World Weekly Wire Side Chat Series. Retrieved April 20, 2012, from www.educationworld.com/a_issues/chat/chat126.shtml

Bailey, A. L., & Heritage, M. (2008). *Formative assessment for literacy, grades K–6: Building reading and academic language skills across the curriculum.* Thousand Oaks, CA: Corwin/Sage Press.

Baker, S., Gersten, R., & Scanlon, D. (2002). Procedural facilitators and cognitive strategies: Tools for unraveling the mysteries of comprehension and the writing process, and for providing meaningful access to the general curriculum. *Learning Disabilities Research and Practice, 17,* 65–77.

Bandura, A., Barbaranelli, C., Caprara, G. V., & Pastorelli, C. (1996). Multifaceted impact of self-efficacy beliefs on academic functioning. *Child Development, 67,* 1206–1222.

Belanoff, P., & Dickson, M. (1991). *Portfolios: Process and product.* Portsmouth, NH: Heinemann.

Bhattacharjee, Y. (2012). Gray matter: Why bilinguals are smarter. Retrieved from www.nytimes.com/2012/03/18/opinion/sunday/the-benefits-of-bilingualism.html?_r=1&hp

Blachman, B. A., Schatschneider, C., Fletcher, J. M., Francis, D. J., Clonan, S. M., Shaywitz, B. A., et al. (2004). Effects of intensive reading remediation for second and third graders and a 1-year follow-up. *Journal of Educational Psychology, 96*(3), 444–461.

Cain, S. (2012). *Quiet: The power of introverts in a world that can't stop talking*[Kindle version]. New York, NY: Crown.

Cambourne, B. (1988). *The whole story: Natural learning and the acquisition of literacy in the classroom.* Auckland, New Zealand: Ashton Scholastic.

Cavanaugh, C. (2007). Effectiveness of K–12 online learning. In M. G. Moore (Ed.), *Handbook of distance education* (2nd ed., pp. 157–168). Mahwah, NJ: Lawrence Erlbaum.

Chamot, A. U., & O'Malley, J. M. (1994). *The CALLA handbook: Implementing the cognitive academic language learning approach.* Reading, MA: Addison-Wesley.

Ciletti, D. (2010). *Marketing yourself.* Mason, OH: South-Western Cengage Learning.

Cohen, L. M. (n.d.). *Meeting the needs of gifted and talented language minority students.* Educational Resource Information Center (U.S. Department of Education). Retrieved July 17, 2012, from www.education.com/reference/article/Ref_Meeting_Needs_Gifted

Coiro, J., Knobel, M., Lankshear, C., & Leu, D. (2008). Central issues in new literacies and new literacies research. In J. Coiro, M. Knobel, C. Lankshear, & D. Leu (Eds.), *Handbook of research on new literacies* (pp. 1–21). Mahwah, NJ: Lawrence Erlbaum.

Collins, A., Brown, J. S., & Newman, S. E. (1989). Cognitive apprenticeship: Teaching the crafts of reading, writing, and mathematics. In L. B. Resnick (Ed.), *Knowing, learning and instruction: Essays in honour of Robert Glaser* (pp. 453–494). Hillsdale, NJ: Lawrence Erlbaum.

Conley, D. (2007). *Redefining college readiness* (Vol. 3). Eugene, OR: Educational Policy Improvement Center.

Cook, G. (2012, January 24). The power of introverts: A manifesto for quiet brilliance. *Scientific American.* Retrieved from www.scientificamerican.com/article.cfm?id=the-power-of-introverts&page=3

Cummins, J. (2010). *Five principles for teaching content to English language learners.* New York, NY: Pearson.

Darcy Pattison, C. (2010). 15-part video series: Common Core State Standards. Retrieved from http://commoncorestandards.com/ela/15-part-video-series-ccss

Darling-Hammond, L. (2010). *The flat world and education: How America's commitment to equity will determine our future.* New York, NY: Teachers College Press.

Dearing, E., McCartney, K., Weiss, H. B., Kreider, H., & Simpkins, S. (2004). The promotive effects of family educational involvement for low-income children's literacy. *Journal of School Psychology, 42,* 445–460.

Duke, N. (2003). Reading to learn from the very beginning: Information books in early childhood. *Young Children, 58*(2), 14–20. Retrieved from http://journal.naeyc.org/btj/200303/informationBooks.pdf

Duke, N., & Pressley, M. (2002). Effective practices for developing reading comprehension. In A. J. Farstrup & S. J. Samuels (Eds.), *What research has to say about reading instruction* (pp. 205–242). Newark, DE: International Reading Association.

Durkin, D. (1988). *Teaching them to read* (5th ed.). Boston, MA: Allyn & Bacon.

Echevarría, J., Vogt, M., & Short, D. (2008). *Making content comprehensible for English learners: The SIOP model.* Boston, MA: Allyn & Bacon.

Ehri, L. C., Dreyer, L. G., Flugman, B., & Gross, A. (2007). Reading rescue: An effective tutoring intervention model for language-minority students who are struggling readers in first grade. *American Educational Research Journal, 44,* 414–448.

EngageNY. (2011). Retrieved from www.engageny.org

Fillmore, L. W., & Fillmore, C. J. (2012, January). *What does text complexity mean for English learners and language minority students?* Paper presented at the Understanding Language Conference Stanford University, Stanford, CA.

Fitzhugh, W. (2007, March 29). Edupundit myopia. Retrieved from www.ednews.org/articles/9510/1/Edupunditmyopia/page1.html

Frome, P. M., & Eccles, J. S. (1998). Parents' influence on children's achievement-related perceptions. *Journal of Personality and Social Psychology, 74,* 435–452.

Fuchs, L. S., Fuchs, D., Prentice, K., Burch, M., Hamlett, C. L., Owen, R., et al. (2003a). Explicitly teaching for transfer: Effects on third-grade students' mathematical problem solving. *Journal of Educational Psychology, 95,* 293–304.

Fuchs, L. S., Fuchs, D., Prentice, K., Burch, M., Hamlett, C. L., Owen, R., et al. (2003b). Enhancing third-grade students' mathematical problem solving with self-regulated learning strategies. *Journal of Educational Psychology, 95,* 306–315.

Gallagher, C., & Lee, A. (2008). *Teaching writing that matters: Tools and projects that motivate adolescent writers.* New York, NY: Scholastic Teaching Resources.

Gibbons, P. (1991). *Learning to learn in a second language.* Portsmouth, NH: Heinemann.

Gladwell, M. (2005). *Blink* (1st ed.). New York, NY: Little Brown and Company.

Graves, D. (1994). *A fresh look at writing.* Scarborough, ON: Irwin Publishing.

Hamayan, E. (2010). Retrieved from www.pearsonschool.com/index.cfm?locator=PSZoB1

Harris, D. N. (2007). High-flying schools, student disadvantage, and the logic of NCLB. *American Journal of Education 113*(3), 367–394.

Harvey, S., & Daniels, H. (2009). *Comprehension & collaboration: Inquiry circles in action.* Portsmouth, NH: Heinemann.

Haynes, J. (2007). *Getting started with English language learners.* Alexandria, VA: Association for Supervision and Curriculum Development.

Hepola, S. (2012). Gloria Steinem, a woman like no other. Retrieved from www.nytimes.com/2012/03/18/fashion/in-the-womans-movement-who-will-replace-gloria-steinem.html?ref=fashion

Heritage, M. (2011, Spring). Formative assessment: An enabler of learning. *Better: Evidence Based Instruction,* 18–19.

Hiebert, E. H., Pearson, P. D., & Taylor, B. M. (1998). *Every child a reader: Applying reading research in the classroom.* Ann Arbor: Center for the Improvement of Early Reading Achievement, University of Michigan.

Hoover-Dempsey, K. V., Battiato, A. C., Walker, J. M. T., Reed, R. P., DeJong, J. M., & Jones, K. P. (2001). Parental involvement in homework. *Educational Psychologist, 36,* 195–209.

Howes, C., Hamilton, C. E., & Matheson, C. C. (1994). Children's relationships with peers: Differential associations with aspects of the teacher–child relationship. *Child Development, 65,* 253–263.

Hughes, J. N., Cavell, T. A., & Jackson, T. (1999). Influence of teacher–student relationship on childhood aggression: A prospective study. *Journal of Clinical Child Psychology, 28,* 173–184.

Johnson, S. (2010). *Where good ideas come from: The natural history of innovation.* New York, NY: Penguin.

Jones, J. (2005). Priority male: If we want boys to love books, it's important to recognize what they want. *School Library Journal, 51*(3), 37.

Jones, P., & Fiorelli, D. (2003). Overcoming the obstacle course: Teenage boys and reading. *Teacher Librarian, 30*(3), 9–13.

Keller, T. A., & Just, M. A. (2009). Altering cortical activity: Remediation induced changes in the white matter of poor readers. *Neuron, 64*(5), 624–631.

Kist, W. (2009). *The socially networked classroom: Teaching in the new media age.* Thousand Oaks, CA: Corwin.

Kollars, D. (2008, May 12). Despite high school algebra focus, more students need remedial college math. *Sacramento Bee,* p. A1.

Krugman, P. (2012, January 10). America's unlevel field. *New York Times.*

Lane, B. (1999). *Reviser's toolbox.* Shoreham, VT: Discover Writing Press.

Lockett, M. (2010). Close reading: A synergistic approach to the (post)modern divide. *Changing English, 17*(4), 399–409.

Luke, A. (2007). The body literate: Discourse and inscription in early literacy. *Discourse Studies, IV,* 1–22.

McGonigal, J. (2010, February). Jane McGonigal: Gaming can make a better world [Video file]. Retrieved from www.ted.com/talks/jane_mcgonigal_gaming_can_make_a_better_world.html

Meehan, B. T., Hughes, J. N., & Cavell, T. A. (2003). Teacher–student relationships as compensatory resources for aggressive children. *Child Development, 74,* 1145–1157.

Migration Policy Institute with the National Center on Immigrant Integration Policy. (2010). ELL Information Center fact sheet series. Retrieved from www.migrationinformation.org/ellinfo/FactSheet_ELL1.pdf

Moffett, J., & Wagner, B. J. (1983). *Student-centered language arts and reading, K–13* (3rd ed.). Boston, MA: Houghton Mifflin.

Moje, E. B. (2008). The complex world of adolescent literacy: Myths, motivations, and mysteries. *Harvard Educational Review,* 107–154.

Moje, E. B. (2011). Developing disciplinary discourses, literacies, and identities: What's knowledge got to do with it? In G. Lopez-Bonilla & K. Englander (Eds.), *Discourse identities in contexts of educational change.* New York, NY: Peter Lang.

Moll, L. C., & Greenberg, J. B. (1990). Creating zones of possibilities: Combining social contexts for instruction. In L. C. Moll (Ed.), *Vygotsky and education: Instructional implications and applications of sociohistorical psychology* (pp. 319–348). New York, NY: Cambridge University Press.

Morrow, L. M., & Tracey, D. (1998). Motivating contexts for young children's literacy development. In J. L. Metsala & L. C. Ehri (Eds.), *Word recognition in beginning literacy* (pp. 341–356). Mahwah, NJ: Lawrence Erlbaum.

Moschkovich, J. N. (2012). How equity concerns lead to attention to mathematical discourse. In B. Herbel-Eisenmann, J. Choppin, D. Wagner, & D. Pimm (Eds.), *Equity in discourse for mathematics education: Theories, practices, and policies.* New York, NY: Springer.

Moss, G. (2000). Raising boys' attainment in reading: Some principles for intervention. *Reading, 34*(3), 101–106.

National Association for Media Literacy Education. (2012). Retrieved from http://namle.net

National Association for Media Literacy Education, Core Principles for Media Literacy Education. (2009). Retrieved from http://namle.net/wp-content/uploads/2009/09/NAMLE-CPMLE-w-questions2.pdf

National Center for Education Statistics. (2007). The NAEP reading achievement levels. Retrieved from http://nces.ed.gov/nationsreportcard/reading/achieve.asp

National Governors Association, the Council of Chief State School Officers, and Achieve, Inc. (2008, December). Benchmarking for success: Ensuring U.S. students receive a world-class education. Retrieved from www.achieve.org/files/BenchmarkingforSuccess.pdf

National Governors Association Center for Best Practices & Council of Chief State School Officers (2010). *Common Core State Standards for English Language Arts & Literacy in History/Social Studies, Science, and Technical Subjects.* Retrieved October 14, 2011, from www.corestandards.org

Newkirk, T. (2012). *The art of slow reading.* Portsmouth, NH: Heinemann.

Oakes, J., & Saunders, M. (2008). *Beyond tracing: Multiple pathways to college, career and civic participation.* Cambridge, MA: Harvard Education Press.

Olson, L. (2006). Skills for work, college readiness are found comparable. *Education Week, 25*(36), 1.

O'Mara, J., & Laidlaw, L. (2011). Living in the iworld: Two literacy researchers reflect on the changing texts and literacy practices of childhood. *English Teaching: Practice & Critique, 10*(4), 149–159.

Ovando, C. J., & Collier, V. P. (1985). *Bilingual and ESL classrooms: Teaching in multicultural contexts.* New York, NY: McGraw-Hill.

Partnership for 21st Century Skills. (2008). *21st century skills, education & competitiveness.* Retrieved from www.p21.org/storage/documents/21st_century_skills_education_and_competitiveness_guide.pdf

Pearson, P. D., & Gallagher, M. (1983). The instruction of reading comprehension. *Contemporary Educational Psychology, 8*(3), 317–344.

Peregoy, S. F., & Boyle, O. F. (2001). *Reading, writing and learning in ESL: A resource book for K–12 teachers.* White Plains, NY: Addison-Wesley.

Pianta, R. C., Steinberg, M. S., & Rollins, K. B. (1995). The first two years of school: Teacher–child relationships and deflections in children's classroom adjustment. *Development and Psychopathology, 7,* 295–312.

Prose, F. (2007). *Reading like a writer: A guide for people who love books and for those who want to write them.* New York, NY: HarperCollins.

Reardon, S. F., & Galindo, C. (2002). Do high-stakes tests affect students' decisions to drop out of school? Evidence from NELS. Working Paper.

Richards, J., & McKenna, M. (2003). *Integrating multiple literacies in the classroom.* Mahwah, NJ: Lawrence Erlbaum.

Robinson, R. D., & McKenna, M. C. (2007). Issues and trends in literacy education (4th ed.). Boston, MA: Allyn & Bacon.

Schleppegrell, M. J. (2004). *The language of schooling: A functional linguistics perspective.* Mahwah, NJ: Lawrence Erlbaum.

Scholastic & Yankelovich. (2008). *Kids & family reading report: Reading in the 21st century: Turning the page with technology.* New York, NY: Author.

Schmoker, M. (2008). Measuring what matters. *Educational Leadership, 66*(4), 70–74.

Scieszka, J. (2003). Guys and reading. *Teacher Librarian, 30*(3), 17–18.

Shanahan, T. (Ed.). (1990). *Reading and writing together: New perspectives for the classroom.* Norwood, MA: Christopher-Gordon.

Shanahan, T., Fisher, D., & Frey, N. (2012). The challenge of challenging text. *Educational Leadership, 69*(6), 58–62.

Stanford School Redesign Network. (2008). *What Is Perfomance Based Assessment?* Retrieved from http://edpolicy.stanford.edu/sites/default/files/events/materials/2011-06-linked-learning-performance-based-assessment.pdf

Strunk, W., & White, E. B. (1979). *The elements of style.* New York, NY: Macmillan.

Tashlik, P. (2010). Changing the national conversation on assessment. *Phi Delta Kappan 91*(6), 55–59.

Tatum, A. W. (2010). *Reading for their life: (Re)building the textual lineages of African American adolescent males.* New York, NY: Heinemann.

Taylor, D. L. (2004). "Not just boring stories": Reconsidering the gender gap for boys. *Journal of Adolescent and Adult Literacy, 48*(4), 290–298.

Thousand, J. S., Villa, R. A., & Nevin, A. I. (2008). *A guide to co-teaching: Practical tips for facilitating student learning.* Thousand Oaks, CA: Corwin Press.

Tierney, R. J. (2000). How will literacy be measured in the next millenium? *Reading Research Quarterly/International Reading Association, 35*(2), 244–250.

Trelease, J. (2001). *The read-aloud handbook* (5th ed.). New York, NY: Penguin.

Turner, J. (1995). The influence of classroom contexts on young children's motivation for literacy. *Reading Research Quarterly, 30*(3), 410–441.

Understanding Language. (2012, April). Challenges and opportunities for language learning in the context of Common Core State Standards and Next Generation Science Standards. Conference overview paper. Retrieved July 17, 2012, from http://ell.stanford.edu/papers

U.S. Department of Education, Institute of Education Sciences, National Center for Education Statistics, & National Assessment of Educational Progress. various years, 2005–2011 reading assessments.

van Lier, L., & Walqui, A. (2012, January). *Language and the Common Core State Standards.* Paper presented at the Understanding Language Conference. Stanford University, Stanford, CA.

Vasquez, V., Egawa, K, Harste, J. C., & Thompson R. (Eds.). (2004). *Literacy as social practice: Relocating your reading and language arts curriculum.* Urbana, IL: National Council of Teachers of English.

Vogt, M., Echevarria, J., & Short, D. (2011). *The SIOP model for teaching English language-arts to English learners.* Boston, MA: Pearson.

White, E. B. (1952). *Charlotte's web.* New York, NY: HarperCollins.

Williamson, G. L. (2008). A text readability continuum for postsecondary readiness. *Journal of Advanced Academics, 19*(4), 602–632.

Wills, G. (1992). *Lincoln at Gettysburg: The words that remade America.* New York, NY: Simon & Schuster.

Woolfolk, A. (2008). *Educational psychology: Active learning edition* (2nd ed.). Boston, MA: Allyn & Bacon.

Wu, Y., & Samuels, S. J. (2004, May). *How the amount of time spent on independent reading affects reading achievement: A response to the National Reading Panel.* Paper presented at the 49th annual convention of the International Reading Association, Lake Tahoe, NV. Retrieved from www.tc.umn.edu/~samue001/web%20pdf/time_spent_on_reading.pdf

Yaffe, D. (2007). *Other people's children: The battle for justice and equality in New Jersey's schools.* New Brunswick, NJ: Rutgers University Press.

Yates, J. R., & Ortiz, A. (1998). Issues of culture and diversity affecting educators with disabilities: A change in demography is reshaping America. In R. J. Anderson, C. E. Keller, & J. M. Karp (Eds.), *Enhancing diversity: Educators with disabilities in the education enterprise.* Washington, DC: Gallaudet University Press.

Index